The Music of Mzilikazi Khumalo

The Music of Mzilikazi Khumalo

Language, Culture, and Song in South Africa

Edited by Thomas M. Pooley, Naomi André,
Innocentia Mhlambi, and Donato Somma

BLOOMSBURY ACADEMIC
NEW YORK · LONDON · OXFORD · NEW DELHI · SYDNEY

BLOOMSBURY ACADEMIC

Bloomsbury Publishing Inc, 1359 Broadway, 12th Floor, New York, NY 10018, USA
Bloomsbury Publishing Plc, 50 Bedford Square, London, WC1B 3DP, UK
Bloomsbury Publishing Ireland, 29 Earlsfort Terrace, Dublin 2, D02 AY28, Ireland

BLOOMSBURY, BLOOMSBURY ACADEMIC and the Diana logo are trademarks
of Bloomsbury Publishing Plc

First published in the United States of America 2024
This paperback edition published 2026

Copyright © Thomas M. Pooley, Naomi André, Innocentia Mhlambi, and
Donato Somma, 2024

Each chapter copyright © by the contributor, 2024

For legal purposes the Acknowledgments on p. viii constitute an extension
of this copyright page.

Cover design: Louise Dugdale
Cover image: Opera Africa

All rights reserved. No part of this publication may be: i) reproduced or transmitted in any form, electronic or mechanical, including photocopying, recording or by means of any information storage or retrieval system without prior permission in writing from the publishers; or ii) used or reproduced in any way for the training, development or operation of artificial intelligence (AI) technologies, including generative AI technologies. The rights holders expressly reserve this publication from the text and data mining exception as per Article 4(3) of the Digital Single Market Directive (EU) 2019/790.

Bloomsbury Publishing Inc does not have any control over, or responsibility for, any third-party websites referred to or in this book. All internet addresses given in this book were correct at the time of going to press. The author and publisher regret any inconvenience caused if addresses have changed or sites have ceased to exist, but can accept no responsibility for any such changes.

Whilst every effort has been made to locate copyright holders the publishers would be grateful to hear from any person(s) not here acknowledged.

A catalog record for this book is available from the Library of Congress.

ISBN: HB: 979-8-7651-1326-4
PB: 979-8-7651-1330-1
ePDF: 979-8-7651-1328-8
eBook: 979-8-7651-1327-1

Typeset by Deanta Global Publishing Services, Chennai, India

For product safety related questions contact productsafety@bloomsbury.com.

To find out more about our authors and books visit www.bloomsbury.com
and sign up for our newsletters.

Contents

List of Figures	vi
Acknowledgments	viii

Introduction: The Music of J. S. Mzilikazi Khumalo *Thomas M. Pooley, Naomi André, Innocentia Mhlambi, and Donato Somma*		1
1	"UGqozi": A Biography of J. S. Mzilikazi Khumalo *Thomas M. Pooley*	17
2	An Interview with Diliza Khumalo *Thomas M. Pooley*	39
3	The National Anthem Committee *J. S. Mzilikazi Khumalo*	57
4	Nation Building Massed Choir Festival: Collaboration between Professor J. S. M. Khumalo and Maestro Richard Cock *Richard Cock*	63
5	The Use of Tonic Sol-fa Notation by Professor Mzilikazi Khumalo *Ludumo Magangane*	77
6	The Music for A Cappella Choir *David Smith*	87
7	The Evolution of *UShaka* as an African Epic *Robert Maxym*	99
8	*Sigiya Ngengoma*: Music Dancing History and Politics in *UShaka KaSenzangakhona* (1996) *Innocentia Mhlambi*	111
9	The Unique Collaboration Behind the Opera *Princess Magogo KaDinuzulu* *Sandra de Villiers*	135
10	The Music of *Princess Magogo KaDinuzulu* *Megan Quilliam*	145
11	"Walking in Thorns": Nested Contexts in the Creation of *Princess Magogo KaDinuzulu* *Donato Somma*	171
12	Representing Princess Magogo in the Opera *Princess Magogo KaDinuzulu* *Kholeka Shange*	189

Worklist of James Steven Mzilikazi Khumalo (1932–2021) *Thomas M. Pooley*	207
Score: "Ma Ngificwa Ukufa" (1959) by J. S. M. Khumalo	215
Score: "Izibongo ZikaShaka" (1981) by J. S. M. Khumalo	224

Editor and Contributor Bios	242
Notes	246
Bibliography	268
Discography	278
Index	279

Figures

1.1	"UGqozi" (Power of Inspiration)	25
1.2	"Inkondlo KaNandi" (Nandi's Love Song), bars 63–68	32
1.3	Sibongile Khumalo in the title role as Princess Magogo kaDinuzulu	38
5.1	"Xola Hleziphi" by J. S. M. Khumalo	83
6.1	Mzilikazi Khumalo, "Inkondlo KaMnkabayi," bars 26–33	90
6.2	Mzilikazi Khumalo, "Insizw'endala," bars 58–62	90
6.3	Mzilikazi Khumalo, "IZulu Elisha," bars 1–8	91
6.4	Mzilikazi Khumalo, "IZulu Elisha," bars 36–41	91
6.5	Mzilikazi Khumalo, "Woza, Mmeli Wami!", bars 33–39	95
6.6	Mzilikazi Khumalo, "Sizongena Laph'Emzini," bars 49–51	96
7.1	*UShaka*, Part 1, no. 3, "Imbizo Yezinyandezulu" (An assembly of the ancestral spirits). Khumalo, Msimang, James, and with orchestration and enhancement by Robert Maxym	105
7.2	*UShaka*, Part 1, No. 3, "Imbizo Yezinyandezulu" (An assembly of the ancestral spirits), Khumalo, Msimang, James, with piano-vocal score by Robert Maxym	106
8.1	"Ikloba Lothando" from *UShaka*	119
9.1	Professor Mzilikazi Khumalo and Prince Mangosuthu Buthelezi	138
10.1	Sibongile Khumalo (as Princess Magogo kaDinuzulu) with Ntsikelelo Mali	148
10.2	Transcribed excerpt from "Uyephi na?" by Princess Magogo kaDinuzulu (by Megan Quilliam from David Rycroft's original transcription)	152
10.3	Excerpt from "Uyephi na?" Prologue Scene 1, No. 2, bars 4–12	153
10.4	Excerpt from "Uyephi na?" Prologue Scene 1, No. 2, bars 1–7	154
10.5	Excerpt from "Sabulawa KwaZulu," Act 1, scene 5, no. 23, bars 1–14	156
10.6	Excerpt from "Woza S'ambe," Prologue scene 1, no. 3, bars 7–12	158
10.7	Excerpt from "Woza Mntanami! Woz'ekhaya," Prologue no. 4, bars 3–18	159
10.8	Excerpt from "Shayan' Ingungu MaZulu," Act 1, scene 1, no. 8, bars 35–48	161

10.9	Excerpt from "Wena Wendlovu, Bayede," Act 1, scene 1, no. 10, bars 10–16	163
10.10	Excerpt from "Siyakhuleka, AmaZulu," Act 2, scene 4, no. 12, bars 41–53	164
11.1	Sangomas and young Princess Magogo kaDinuzulu, Het Musiktheater, Amsterdam	173
12.1	Kelebogile Boikanyo, Thembisile Twala, and Zanele Gumede with Sibongile Khumalo in *Princess Magogo KaDinuzulu*	190

Acknowledgments

This collaboration began with conversations at an international conference cosponsored and hosted by the University of the Witwatersrand and the University of Michigan (UM) at the Cradle of Humankind in the Gauteng province of South Africa in 2017. While that conference ("Performance Arts and Political Action in Africa") resulted in another publication, the name James Steven Mzilikazi Khumalo kept coming up during those discussions and beyond.[1] As one of South Africa's most important composers, Professor Khumalo's activities as a scholar and artist were central to the work of many of the participants in the 2017 African Performance conference, and he was revered as a scholar, musician, linguist, mentor, and friend. It was there that ideas for a symposium in his honor germinated and took root.

These plans culminated in a two-day symposium, "The Intellectual Legacy of James Steven Mzilikazi Khumalo," that was hosted by the University of South Africa (Unisa) in Pretoria in August 2018. Right away, we realized that these papers and reflections on Professor Khumalo's life and works needed to be published. We think of this collection not as an end point, but as a beginning to move forward with future work. We are grateful to the UM for an "African Heritage Initiative Seed Grant" that enabled this project to get started and which funded important research opportunities. Our sincere thanks to our UM colleagues: Andries Coetzee, then director of the African Studies Center, who supported this work, and to Carl Abrego and Candace Middlebrook (both at the Residential College) who were very skillful and patient in administering the funds across multiple countries and foreign currencies. Many thanks also to Vivienne Pieters at Unisa who assisted us in organizing and documenting the event.

Professor Themba Msimang was the keynote speaker at the symposium. He shared his reflections on a decades-long artistic collaboration with Professor Khumalo and engaged us in many conversations that provided unique insight into the works.

The family of Professor Khumalo has been wonderfully generous and helpful since we first approached them in 2018. Thank you to Nomavenda Mathiane, Professor Khumalo's sister, who gave an address at the symposium, and to his children Busisiwe, Diliza, Themba, and Nonhlanhla all of whom attended. Their rousing and impromptu singing of a few numbers from *UShaka* at the dinner table was an unforgettable moment in this journey and a powerful testament to the importance of music that Professor Khumalo shared with his family. Special thanks to Diliza Khumalo who has been pivotal in facilitating our research and in sharing memories and documents that have enabled us to properly document Professor Khumalo's life and works.

The Southern African Music Rights Organization (SAMRO) holds important items in Professor Khumalo's archive. We are grateful to André le Roux, James French, Anriette Chorn, and especially Nandipha Mnyani who supported authors with queries about sources and scores.

Close friends and collaborators of Professor Khumalo have been generous with their time. Our thanks to his musical associates in South Africa and beyond: Ludumo Magangane, Themba Madlopha, Sidwell Mhlongo, Michael Dingane, Nomthandazo Solomon, Musa Xulu, and Richard Cock. We also record our gratitude to the late Prince Mangosuthu Buthelezi, who was interviewed by Thomas Pooley for this project.

Thomas Pooley's research is supported by a grant from the National Research Foundation of South Africa (Grant Number: 145699).

Thank you to our copy editors Leonie Viljoen and Ronel Gallie, as well as to Chesney Palmer for setting musical examples.

Thanks to Maestro Robert Maxym and Maxym Music, who kindly agreed to give permission to reproduce materials in the published piano-vocal score of *UShaka KaSenzangakhona*. We are also grateful to publishers Shuter & Shooter and the Khumalo family for granting permission to reproduce selected examples and songs by the late Professor Mzilikazi Khumalo.

Sandra and Hein de Villiers lent considerable support in realizing this project. In particular, Sandra shared the unpublished score and libretto of *Princess Magogo KaDinuzulu*, as well as a wealth of documentary information from her personal archive. Opera Africa also granted permission to reproduce extracts from the score of *Princess Magogo KaDinuzulu*, as well as valuable photographs.

Welz Kauffman shared his experience of programming both *Princess Magogo KaDinuzulu* and *UShaka KaSenzangakhona* for the Ravinia Festival, Chicago (in 2003 and 2004, respectively). Thank you to Christine Taylor Conda for assistance at the Ravinia archive.

Sincere thanks to Rachel Moore, our editor at Bloomsbury Press, who has supported this work and saw it through to publication. We are grateful for constructive comments from two anonymous reviewers for the press.

Finally, as editors, we thank our families and loved ones for supporting us in advancing this research during a particularly challenging period. Much of what we wrote was completed during the Covid-19 pandemic as it spread across the globe. Through many changes—in jobs and houses, a new marriage, and several children growing up—all three of us are grateful for the community formed by this collaboration and our continuing friendship.

Thomas M. Pooley, Naomi André, Innocentia Mhlambi,
and Donato Somma
October 2023

Introduction

The Music of J. S. Mzilikazi Khumalo

Thomas M. Pooley, Naomi André, Innocentia Mhlambi,
and Donato Somma

South Africa is a nation revered for its rich choral heritage with singing the lifeblood of diverse cultures that range from popular competition choirs to Christian congregational singing, and folk, art, and indigenous music. James Steven Mzilikazi Khumalo (1932–2021) was unique in contributing to this diverse array of musical genres while pursuing a successful career as a scholar of African languages and literature. He was one of the leading Black composers and directors of choral music to emerge from South Africa in the late twentieth century who achieved international recognition for a series of choral and operatic works performed to critical acclaim in Africa, Europe, and the United States. This volume offers a summation of his achievement and demonstrates for the first time his broader significance to the history of arts and culture in South Africa and beyond. Indeed, this volume demonstrates the full scope of his musical activities in all spheres of public life and also touches on his deep contributions to understanding structure and sound in southern African languages.

This book frames Khumalo's achievements in musical culture with chapters on his life and works by academics, colleagues, and peers. Two items of documentary interest are also included: a chapter by Khumalo himself on South Africa's postapartheid national anthem committee and a worklist documenting his own compositions and the many he arranged for various ensembles. This introductory chapter contextualizes these contributions by situating Khumalo scholarship within the broader field of art and choral music in South Africa, and recent developments in postcolonial and decolonial musicology. The chapters in this volume explore the complexities of Khumalo's music and its reception, weighing the political and social dimensions to works that span the transition from apartheid to democracy. Authors reflect on the challenges, contradictions, and complications that figure in Khumalo's manifold commitments. Nuanced readings of his music point to the ways in which he pioneered new forms and genres, breaking with the Western choral tradition in concert works, and creating a new identity for Black opera in postapartheid South Africa.

Through a succession of careers—ranging from high school teacher to language tutor, lecturer, professor, and administrator—Khumalo consistently pioneered the way for others to follow. His career as an academic culminated in his appointment as one of the first Black professors of African languages at Wits University, as well as the first Black head of department. Through his music, Khumalo brought together the traditions of choral and art music in South Africa, and in his late works achieved a distinctly indigenous idiom by blending features of art music composition and opera with the Zulu choral tradition. This first volume on his life and music draws together critical and biographical perspectives on these diverse achievements.

Perspectives on a Life

Khumalo's life spanned the rise and fall of apartheid and the first decades of the democratic era of contemporary South Africa. Born to Salvation Army officer parents, a strong faith shaped his thinking and musical commitments, as did an immersion in the history of the Zulu people. Near to his birthplace in the Vryheid district was the site of the 1879 battlefield of Hlobane. Further afield were the battlefields of Rourke's Drift and Isandlwana which were iconic of the Anglo-Zulu war. All of this would later provide a resonant cultural landscape for his appreciation for Zulu history and culture. While battles with the British Empire fired his imagination, and a Wesleyan-Methodist faith grounded his ethics, the strictures of increasing legislative oppression would influence Khumalo's young adulthood. Matriculating high school in 1950, just two years after the National Party (NP) came to power, Khumalo's middle life, his education and career, unfolded in the ever-narrowing spaces open for a Black intellectual and artist. The white, Afrikaner Christian nationalism that underpinned the National Party since its founding in the early twentieth century came to fruition in the laws instituted between 1948 and 1994. These laws took *apartheid* (the concept of separation of races) as their racial ideology, and a conservative, inward-looking ethnic nationalism as guiding principle.

The early years of Khumalo's teaching were marked by the implementation of the 1953 Bantu Education Act designed by the white minority government under the ministerial leadership of Hendrik Verwoerd.[1] Though schools were segregated by race in this new system, schools for nonwhites were accorded disproportionately lower subsidies than those for "Europeans" (the catchall phrase for white South Africans of European descent). Blacks were subjected to a substandard form of education designed to relegate their labor to menial tasks (an ideology of "education for servitude"),[2] in this way limiting their ability to compete with whites for jobs.[3] The effects on music education, though peripheral to the apartheid project, were pronounced. The closure of the private and mission schools that had until 1955 educated generations of Black South Africans would be of major consequence to those seeking formal instruction in music. Still, even at established mission schools, such as the Lovedale Missionary Institute (1841–1955), music was largely an extracurricular activity with advanced instruction in musical instruments and staff notation available only to a select few.[4]

Khumalo himself did not have the opportunity to study music in school or at university level. This shaped his choice of career. The policy of Bantu Education effected the removal of music education from the curriculum, and so it was through school choirs that most young Black South Africans learned music.[5] Khumalo's early years as a teacher enabled him to direct choirs and start making the arrangements for which he would later become famous. The extracurricular competitions and festivals organized by African teachers' associations were central to the development of his musicianship. But his exclusion from formal academia and opportunities for studying music were a grating reminder of apartheid's structural inequalities.

Khumalo began his career as a high school teacher in the late 1950s. Church and school choirs were important to the development of his musical identity, and he was highly competitive in this sphere until his move to academia in 1969. But he was also active in his religious community, and with adult choirs on the Witwatersrand. In the 1970s and 1980s, Khumalo toured Salvation Army choirs to the United States, Europe, and the Caribbean, building important cultural ties with the African diaspora at a time when South Africa was isolated from the rest of the world because of its policy of apartheid.[6] Competitions and festivals were central to the culture of Black choral music during apartheid and have remained so into the twenty-first century. Khumalo was an adjudicator for festivals and competitions.

When the editor of the *Sowetan*, Aggrey Klaaste, propounded his vision for reconciliation in 1980s South Africa, he turned to Khumalo as one of the musical directors tasked with bringing together Black and white South Africans on the same stage. Khumalo codirected the festival with conductor Richard Cock from its inception in 1989. This annual event was televised by the state broadcaster and attracted thousands of joyous participants and a huge television audience. Many young soloists established their reputations at the festival and went on to successful careers in music. Khumalo and Cock also pioneered the innovative system of dual notation that combines staff notation and tonic sol-fa (see Ludumo Magangane's chapter in this volume). This system was employed in the score books for the festival, as well as in a later series of three publications that Khumalo edited for the Southern African Music Rights Organisation (SAMRO), *South Africa Sings*. Later in his career, Khumalo's contributions to choral music were recognized in his appointment as the chair of the national anthem committee for South Africa, and in his being awarded the Order of the Star in 1999 by President Nelson Mandela.

Khumalo's appointment as a "tutor" in the Department of African languages at Wits was an important turning point. In the 1960s, Blacks were appointed to support positions rather than tenured lectureships. Khumalo worked in a department of whites-only lecturers whose focus was the instruction of second-language learners with limited proficiency and background in African languages. The idea of an African language department for Africans would come much later. While in service at Wits, Khumalo completed a series of postgraduate qualifications culminating in a PhD degree. His leadership of the department in the 1980s was a critical step in this direction. When Khumalo retired in 1997, he had borne witness to the entirety of apartheid from 1948 to 1994. The chapters in this volume show how he responded to this changing context, and how his efforts were directed in constructive ways to developing music in and for society. Following his retirement, Khumalo's activities continued along themes of transformation and reconciliation through music; indeed, these ideas are implicit in both of his major works (the African epic *UShaka KaSenzangakhona* (1996), and the opera *Princess Magogo KaDinuzulu* (2002)).

In later years Khumalo turned to administration and became a key figure at SAMRO where he served as Vice-Chairman of the Board of Directors. Throughout his career, Khumalo had sought recognition for the work of his predecessors and contemporaries in the Black choral tradition, and in his work at SAMRO, he documented the history of Black choral forms in South Africa. He encouraged the postapartheid generation to work toward new forms through a return to South Africa's rich heritage of indigenous musics. Khumalo's achievements in and out of academia, as musician, public intellectual, linguist, and administrator, are documented here in chapters by former colleagues, friends, scholars, and critics. This chapter and the next reflect on the historical background and reception of Khumalo's work, and in so doing provide a context for its interpretation. How did Khumalo respond to the profoundly divisive and demeaning character of apartheid, and what role did he play in negotiating the social and political complexities of the transition to a democratic South Africa? We pose these questions to invite scholarly inquiry since Khumalo studies are still taking root. Our project here is to open the conversation rather than foreclose debate on a rich set of histories.

Traditions of Choral Music in South Africa

When missionaries and colonials introduced European four-part singing to their congregations and schools in the eighteenth and nineteenth centuries, they connected with a powerful tradition of indigenous song in southern Africa. The resultant fusion of traditions evolved into a new choral music. Initially, this was a tradition co-opted by the Black elite who received instruction in music at the mission schools beginning in the early nineteenth century. David Coplan's *In Township Tonight!* (first edition, 1985)[7] records the careers of some of these first Black composers in the nineteenth and twentieth centuries. Reflecting on the role and consequences of rising African nationalism in the 1930s, Coplan points to the complexities and contradictions of an emerging elite Black culture that drew on Western and indigenous traditions set against "the political intransigence of whites" and the continuing acculturation that was a consequence of imposed norms in schools and churches.[8] Basic biographical details of Black composers and their works are recorded in Yvonne Huskisson's *The Bantu Composers of Southern Africa* (1969) and its supplement (1992),[9] works that reinforced their otherness from a Western art tradition steeped in European concert music.

In 1991, Veit Erlmann lamented the neglect of Black composers in writings on South African music, pointing to the likes of John Bhengu, Mameyiguda Zungu, Enoch Mzobe, and Edwin Mkhize whose music remained largely unknown outside of their immediate communities. Erlmann's chapter on Reuben Tholakele Caluza (1895–1969) documents an extraordinary career fashioned on both sides of the Atlantic, and a legacy of compositions and recordings.[10] His chapter on Ntsikana Gaba's "Great Hymn" argues that the work "epitomized black South Africans' conflicted relationship with modernity."[11] This was true of near contemporaries, such as Tiyo Soga (1829–1871), John Knox Bokwe (1855–1922), and Enoch Sontonga (1873–1905), all of whom studied at the Lovedale Missionary Institute.[12] Sontonga is the composer of "Nkosi Sikelel' iAfrika," a hymn that in various arrangements found its place as the national anthem to several nations, including South Africa. These composers were taught staff notation at the mission schools and helped forged this choral tradition.[13]

By the mid-twentieth century, due in large part to the success of the Christian missions in helping to establish an African elite, choral music had become popular across a broad cross-section of the African population. By this time, choral song had developed into its own distinctive tradition of "Black" choral music.[14] That this distinct branch of choral music was racialized in the South African context is unsurprising, given the systematic nature of segregation and apartheid imposed by successive governments prior to 1994. The Black choral tradition came to serve multiple functions in worship, entertainment, and art music. The secularization of choralism that took place in schools evolved into the competition complex distinctive of late twentieth- and early twenty-first-century Black choralism. During the apartheid era, it was a tradition distinct from the art music practiced by white South Africans in schools and universities, and in opera, ballet, and symphonic halls and concert venues. Khumalo was a leading proponent of the early choral tradition coming out of colonialism before serving as a conduit to the tradition that grew during apartheid, and the worlds that separated them.[15]

The hermeneutics of choral music in South Africa have changed radically over the past two decades in this postapartheid era. The rise of decolonial thought and the recent Black Lives Matter movement have placed further scrutiny on questions of racial inequality and injustice.[16] The interpretation of works and performances by Black composers in South Africa is receiving renewed scholarly attention after a long period of neglect. Studies of Black choralism by Ndwamato George Mugovhani, Innocentia Mhlambi, Veit Erlmann, Christine Lucia, Grant Olwage, Markus Detterbeck,[17] and others have shed light on its history while monographs by Naomi André and Hilde Roos take seriously the history of Black opera in South Africa.[18] Until the early 2000s, musicologists had focused principally on white composers and institutions of art music rather than on the Black choral tradition or on Black composers of art music. David Coplan's important history of Black music and theater in South Africa, *In Township Tonight!*, detailed a history of these traditions largely focusing on urban settings.[19]

The early history is also served by Veit Erlmann in two of his books: *African Stars* and *Music, Modernity and the Global Imagination*.²⁰ Both focus on the late nineteenth and early twentieth century and detail the careers of composers such as Reuben Tholak Caluza and Ntsikana Gaba. Work on late twentieth- and early twenty-first-century Black choral music is receiving renewed attention in critical editions.²¹ The history of the Black choral tradition has often been studied in isolation from the art music tradition that has long been its Other.

This book, guided by the life and works of J. S. Mzilikazi Khumalo, interrogates this binary and the very nature of its construction. It is our goal to critically reevaluate the idea of race as a normative category of being, and to reorient our understanding of its insidious features. We are treating race as a construction, since it has had important meanings over time, but has no justification as a biological category.²² Race is a site of contestation, and of change, moving up and against the forces of power that structure regulated social interactions in society.²³

Khumalo's early choral works (1959–80) fall squarely within the tradition of Black choralism while the post-1980 works increasingly press at the boundaries of Black choralism and the wider practice of Western art music. Khumalo is not the first Black composer to challenge the art/choral division, but the scale of his works and their impact complements and exceeds that of composers of the preceding generation, such as Michael Mosoeu Moerane (1904–80).²⁴ Khumalo's *UShaka KaSenzangakhona* and *Princess Magogo KaDinuzulu* sit outside of a reception history of white art music composers in South Africa, stubbornly so. Studies by George Mugovhani have covered important aspects of Khumalo's work, including analytical and hermeneutic essays on several key songs, a dissertation on his "African style," and an important interview.²⁵

Why has Khumalo's work been excluded from consideration within the broader art music canon? Lucia writes of "a substantial history and repertoire of written Black South African choral music [. . .] going back more than 125 years, with John Knox Bokwe (1855–1922) usually seen as colonial founding father."²⁶ A product of the mission school system, he presented the multitalented face of late Victorian Black South Africa as a journalist, minister, and hymnist, extending the story of Black choralism into the nineteenth century. The depth and breadth of the accomplishments of Black South African musicians have only recently received limited state support at home and recognition abroad. It is the legitimacy of this tradition as art music, as equal in value and substance, that has yet to be properly recognized and accepted. Khumalo positioned himself within the choral tradition in his capacity as editor-in-chief of SAMRO's three-volume *South Africa Sings*, a series of volumes that begins in Volume 1 with Bokwe's "Vuka, Vuka, Debora!" (Awake, Awake, Debora!) and ends in Volume 3 with Khumalo's own "Insizw'endala (The Youthful Aged Man)."[27]

Through his work Khumalo can also be placed within the tradition of Western art music stemming from Johann Sebastian Bach, George Frideric Handel, Josef Haydn, Wolfgang Amadeus Mozart, Ludwig van Beethoven, Franz Schubert, Felix Mendelssohn, Johannes Brahms, and other composers of common practice. His works show little evidence of engagement with twentieth-century art music. Perhaps this shows his distance from a field that was dominated by institutionalized composers in South Africa, including those at university music departments and the South African Broadcasting Association; these were spaces from which he was excluded. It is a tradition that finds its summation in Peter Klatzow's edited volume, *Composers in South Africa Today*, which focuses on composers Arnold van Wyk (1916–83), Hubert du Plessis (1922–2011), Stefans Grové (1922–2014), Graham Newcater (b. 1941), Carl van Wyk (b. 1942), and Klatzow (1945–2021) himself.[28] Many white South African composers studied in Europe and the United States. For instance, Grové was South Africa's first Fulbright scholar studying with Walter Piston at Harvard. Other examples include Kevin Volans (b. 1949) who was a student of Karlheinz Stockhausen and Mauricio Kagel in Cologne, while Klatzow studied at the Royal College of Music and with Nadia Boulanger.[29] Khumalo took a very different path as a largely self-taught musician and composer belonging to a tradition of Black choral musicians who were excluded from formal music education in South Africa.

These two traditions were racialized by the politics of white supremacy. The structure of their respective fields of production was shaped and, in many ways, defined by the tenets of apartheid policy and economy. It is for these reasons that the term "Black choral music" has been coined in reference to the tradition of Soga, Bokwe, and Caluza. The qualifier "white" has not been used for composers of art music, signaling the normative understanding that signs Western music as universal while confining Black creative expression to alterity. Lucia explains how Black choral music was set apart from the field of art music by the "ideology of separate development," enacted

> through the cultural power exercised by the South African Broadcasting Corporation (SABC) (see Walton 2004, pp. 70-71), the four provincial Performing Arts Councils, the White colonial public and private school system,

the Grade Examination system (see Lucia 2006, pp. 176-83), and university music departments. All these agents helped to establish orchestral culture as an overwhelmingly White prerogative. Most White composers did well within these parastatal organisations, as Peter Klatzow (1987) has demonstrated, but Black composers were prevented from obtaining the same degree of musical development from them, and to study music to degree level was virtually impossible.[30]

South African art music has been run through by this racial schism. To balance the powerful emphasis on white art music composition, a racialization that is inevitable in view of the lopsided structures of domination that shaped the artistic field,[31] means writing new histories with new methodologies that recognize new needs. These decolonial histories think anew the very basis for music history writing and its rationale. Whereas volumes such as *Composers in South Africa Today* (1987) served to establish an art music canon in South Africa—and in so doing to define the nature of the field itself—this chapter offers critical reflection on the ideology of canonic writing and its politics of exclusion. For too long, there has been a failure to recognize the contributions of so many Black South Africans to the development of music cultures largely outside of the Western concert hall. The prestige of elite art music has eclipsed in academic discourse the proper documentation of the choral tradition. In this context, it is also important to recognize the contributions of Black artists to jazz and popular music in South Africa. This book is part of the strong scholarly tradition committed to documenting the central contributions of Black musicians in a wide range of cultural traditions in South Africa, and the recognition of jazz as "serious" music offers a useful counternarrative to the emphasis on other art musics.[32]

The reception of Khumalo's music has focused principally on his major compositions on royal subjects: *UShaka KaSenzangakhona* and *Princess Magogo KaDinuzulu*. It is *critical* to reflect on the choice of royal subjects, and the symbolism that Khumalo and his collaborators constructed in these works honoring nonwhite heritage and what this reveals about South African culture (Shange, this volume).[33] But there is also a sizable repertoire of songs that are discussed by other contributors, including Khumalo's long-time choral collaborator, Ludumo Magangane. Khumalo's songs are a staple of the South African choral repertoire and featured as prescribed works from the very first National Choral Festival of the Africa Teachers Association of South Africa held in 1961. In fact, Khumalo was winning choral competitions with his compositions into the 1980s, and a special festival was held in his honor by Amazwi KaZulu Choir in 1983.³⁴ Ndwamato George Mugovhani's interviews with Khumalo offer vital biographical information directly from the composer, as well as close analysis of the indigenous African elements in his choral music.³⁵ In one of the few musicological articles on Khumalo's music, Mugovhani and Ayodamope Oluranti discuss the tonal elements situating his music within a choral tradition reaching back to Tiyo Soga, John Knox Bokwe, and Enoch Sontonga. But what marks Khumalo as distinct from the earlier generation, they argue, is the politics of Black nationalism that grew out of this choral music tradition from the 1950s onward. The indigenous elements come to the fore with *Izibongo ZikaShaka* (1981), which later became the basis for the much larger canvas of *UShaka KaSenzangakhona* (1996). The opera *Princess Magogo KaDinuzulu* is based on the life of Princess Constance Magogo, a musician herself and daughter in the Zulu royal family. Her father was Zulu King Dinuzulu kaCetshwayo and her mother was Queen Silomo. She was the sister of the late King Solomon kaDinizulu. Princess Magogo married Chief Mathole Buthelezi and was the mother of the late Inkatha Freedom Party leader Chief Mangosuthu Buthelezi, who served as minister of home affairs in the national government. Magogo made several recordings of *ugubhu* (Zulu bow) music, gave interviews, and became an authority on Zulu music through her performances and the publication of her ideas by David Rycroft.³⁶ The critical analysis and cultural critique of this central work is showcased in a section of this book that devotes several chapters to Khumalo's opera on Princess Magogo.

Decolonial Contexts

The scholarly context for this study is the decolonial turn that has shaped the humanities and social sciences over the past decade, and public discourse on academia in South Africa in particular. Decolonial thinking recenters our conceptual geographies by making local knowledge its sine qua non and breaking with the normative conditions of Western modernity. Mignolo explains, "Decolonial thinking and doing starts from the analytic of the levels and spheres in which it can be effective in the process of decolonization and liberation *from* the colonial matrix."³⁷ This matrix imposes hierarchies and a universalism that situates Western modernity at its center. The discourse of decoloniality in the humanities and social sciences, and what Jean and John

Comaroff describe as "theory from the south" (what we think of as the "global south"), enjoin us to refigure our conceptual imaginaries to voices long drowned out by the hegemony of colonial oppression.[38] It is only by recognizing anew the achievements, legacy, and power of African contributions to culture that African and African diasporic institutions will reclaim their heritage. There is urgency to projects documenting the contributions of generations of Black African intellectuals whose work is yet to be recognized, and whose presence is obscured or denied. Such work on the postcolony and the decolonial is being carried forward by Achille Mbembe, Sabelo Ndlovu-Gatsheni, and others.[39] Efforts to renew the curriculum with African indigenous knowledge systems, philosophies, and performance practices have yet to take root in postapartheid South Africa, despite powerful calls for change. Now is the time to conduct research on the role and contributions of Black South Africans to the cultural heritage of a nation long divided by racism and racialism. Projects in decoloniality serve to debunk the notion of a canon and the epistemologies that sustain it.

This project on J. S. Mzilikazi Khumalo is an intervention in postapartheid humanities that rethinks the theoretical and artistic domains of postapartheid South Africa from the inside out. By bringing together scholars, creators, performers, and critics from the United States and South Africa, we advance the conversations on decoloniality that have been taking place at the University of South Africa (Unisa) for many years in the Decoloniality Summer School and that are present also in the work of colleagues at Wits Institute for Social and Economic Research (WISER) at the University of the Witwatersrand, and the Humanities more broadly at Wits, as well as at the African Studies Center at the University of Michigan and several other places in South Africa and abroad. The emphasis on Khumalo enables us to take up a case study for this broader intellectual intervention. This book provides critical commentary on Khumalo's legacies in linguistics and music and aims to refigure the musical canon in South Africa by moving Black choralism, opera, and Black voices to the fore. The broad remit of Khumalo's interests and projects instantiates the "epistemic disobedience" that is a defining feature of the decolonial.[40] The chapters gathered here show him bringing linguistics to bear on his choral teaching and his musical ear to studies of phonetics and phonology in African linguistics. This interdisciplinarity was not coincidental but emerged from a perception of music and language as of a piece. This perspective disrupts Western academic disciplinary boundaries, and indeed skips over the traditional Western bias of musicology against the programmatic in music. In short, it constitutes an epistemic disruption.

Though his work prefigures the current move toward decolonizing curricula, it would be anachronistic to ascribe his own intellectual project as decolonial, even while his work fulfills many of the goals to include more Black composers on course syllabi and concert programs. Professor Khumalo's work unfolded within the systems of coloniality: academe, competitive choral music, and later, opera. His own projects aligned much more with the postcolonial establishment of Black intellectuals in academia, as it manifested in late and postapartheid eras. His struggle was for recognition within the disciplines that he practiced, and he received recognition for this, albeit belatedly. It was the depth of his engagement with his disciplines that pushed through their boundaries, moving from within the disciplines to across and beyond the disciplines. Underpinning all was an episteme that heard language and music together, an indigenous knowledge system that, through him, broke disciplinary boundaries. The study of his work creates a foundation from which a decolonized history may grow.

This book aims to foster connections between scholars and musicians working to document and reflect on Khumalo's contributions across many fields. Most of the book chapters began as papers presented at a symposium on Khumalo's intellectual legacy that took place at the University of South Africa, Pretoria, in 2018. The *Symposium on the Intellectual Legacy of Professor James Steven Mzilikazi Khumalo* (August 14–15) was the product of a collaboration between Thomas Pooley (Unisa), Naomi André (University of Michigan), Innocentia Mhlambi, and Donato Somma (both at Wits University). The event was an important first step in bringing together scholars, performers, composers, and public intellectuals with an interest in Khumalo's life and work. Professor Themba Msimang, also a linguist, and Khumalo's most important artistic collaborator, was the keynote speaker at that event which brought together the key stakeholders. This book builds on the insights and collaborations fostered at the symposium, and in so doing offers a set of texts for scholars and students to ponder and build on. The chapters that follow include essays on Khumalo's biography, his choral activities, musical works, as well as his contributions to African languages and linguistics. His many roles as teacher, academic, administrator, and musician are profiled, with each focusing on a particular theme or direction in his career.

Chapter Organization

This book is organized into five parts and brings together chapters on (I) Khumalo's biography and tributes from his family and close friends; (II) discussions of his choral writing and themes bridging linguistics with music (including special attention to the tonic sol-fa system); essays that closely analyze (III) *UShaka KaSenzangakhona* and (IV) the opera, *Princess Magogo KaDinuzulu*; and (V) a documentary section that provides a worklist of Khumalo's compositions and a Bibliography and Discography, as well as scores to two songs: "Uma Ngificwa Ukufa" and "Izibongo ZikaShaka." This introduction outlines the historical and cultural context and sets the scene for Khumalo studies in relation to a growing field of research on South African composers of art and choral music.

The first two chapters focus on Khumalo's biography and family history. Thomas Pooley's chapter is the first intellectual biography detailing the unfolding of Khumalo's education, and his successive careers as a teacher, linguist, musician, and administrator. Khumalo's innovations in choral music and opera are contextualized in relation to the two streams of "serious music" that he would refigure by combining art, choral, and indigenous music. The second chapter is an interview Thomas Pooley conducted with Mzilikazi Khumalo's eldest son, Diliza Khumalo, who trained as a musician and worked closely with his father as a singer and choral conductor. Diliza Khumalo details memories of his father that provide an intimate portrait of the person and his character, as well as key moments in his life. A third chapter is an essay in Mzilikazi Khumalo's own words outlining the work of the National Anthem Committee who were responsible for developing the new national anthem for a democratic South Africa. In this chapter, published posthumously and through the intervention of Ludumo Magangane, Khumalo describes the genesis of the anthem in its various forms drawing on his experiences as chair of the committee.

In Part II, the focus is on the construction of South African singing with chapters that explore the background to Khumalo's choral writing, his work with choirs, and the tonic sol-fa system. These chapters provide perspectives by Khumalo's contemporaries and collaborators. In Chapter 4, Richard Cock, a long-time artistic collaborator and friend, writes of his days working with Khumalo on the Sowetan Nation Building Massed Choir Festivals and describes the development of "dual" notation (tonic sol-fa and Western staff notation). This was a key moment in South African arts and politics during which race relations were negotiated through collaborations in music. The Nation Building Festival was an experiment in social engineering that succeeded beyond expectations and successfully enabled white and Black South Africans to perform together on stage and thereby to explore new repertories.

In Chapter 5, Ludumo Magangane explains Khumalo's innovations in tonic sol-fa notation, explaining how he incorporated the tonal features of African languages into the dual notation project. Magangane was also a music director and conductor in the Nation Building series, working with several important choirs, and an adviser on SAMRO's *South Africa Sings* project which Khumalo edited. In this chapter, he explains how dual notation works and how it was used by Khumalo in two important examples: "Ma Ngificwa Ukufa" (1959) and "Izibongo ZikaShaka" (1981). Magangane shows how Khumalo's music changed from a predominantly hymnal style interspersed with African rhythms to a style shaped by the distinctive rhythms and melodies of Zulu music. Magangane further explains Khumalo's use of glides to denote linguistic tones both in tonic sol-fa and staff notation. This is a useful introduction to later chapters in which these scores are discussed in detail. David Smith's chapter on "The Music for A Cappella Choir" rounds out Part II with music analytical perspectives on the songs and arrangements that were at the core of his compositional practice. Smith deftly shows how Khumalo's work emerged from the Western common practice tradition, as well as the distinctly indigenous choral idiom with roots in South Africa.

Part III consists of two chapters detailing Khumalo's epic work, *UShaka KaSenzangakhona* (1996). The genesis of a major work is always a collaborative process. Khumalo worked with numerous librettists, orchestrators, and arrangers. Opening the section on *UShaka*, Robert Maxym charts his experience as its final orchestrator. Maxym explains how his collaboration with Khumalo and Msimang developed, and how through orchestration and composition the work took shape from the earlier orchestration by Christopher James. The second chapter on *UShaka* ("*Sigiya Ngengoma*: Music Dancing History and Politics in *UShaka KaSenzangakhona* (1996)") was written by Innocentia Mhlambi, and she interprets the work as a site in which Zulu singing genres and performance cultures are wrought into art music. She explains how Khumalo's background in linguistics and African languages shapes the work's sonic-somatic repertoires and discusses themes of identity and history in her analysis of the work's grammars.

Part IV consists of four critical chapters on the opera *Princess Magogo KaDinuzulu*. As with the first chapter in the *UShaka* section, this opening chapter documents the origins and issues pertaining to the compositional genesis of the opera *Princess Magogo*. Sandra de Villiers discusses the commissioning of the work by Opera Africa as well as its reception history. The complex interplay of artistic personalities important to the development of the opera is crucial to understanding its creation. De Villiers explains how the artistic collaboration between Khumalo as composer, Msimang as librettist, Hankinson as orchestrator-composer, and Prince Buthelezi as custodian of his mother's legacy, came together. She also discusses the premiere of the work at the centenary of the Ravinia Festival in Chicago, 2004.

Megan Quilliam focuses on the music of the opera and the collaboration between Khumalo and Hankinson. Khumalo depended on others to write orchestrations and instrumental music for his compositions because he had no formal training in Western notation. Quilliam explains Hankinson's role as orchestrator and composer of incidental music through score analysis. She also discusses the importance of Magogo's own compositions in the work as a "third compositional voice." Quilliam, like Mhlambi in her chapter, frames the opera within the narrative of reconciliation that Desmond Tutu described as a "rainbow nation."

Donato Somma's chapter, "'Walking in Thorns': Nested Contexts in the Creation of *Princess Magogo KaDinuzulu*," is a critical reflection on the dialogue that exists between the fictionalized world of the staged work and that of the society from which it emerges. He provides an insightful context for how an opera about historical people and events, in the past, can say something about our present. Somma explains Khumalo's project in the opera as emerging from a postcolonial context in which opera operates from the periphery and argues that the confines of the genre both facilitated and frustrated the composer's efforts.

The final chapter in Part IV by Kholeka Shange considers representations of the princess through a critical reading of Magogo as Blackwoman, drawing on feminist and decolonial theory. Shange problematizes Magogo's relationship to the monarchy and the nature of her representation as mother, matriarch, and iconic culture-bearer. Together, these perspectives on Mntwan' Magogo offer the most detailed account to date of South Africa's first Black opera.

Part V provides documentary information which includes a worklist, two musical scores, a bibliography and discography. The worklist is a preliminary study of the available sources and details Khumalo's compositions and arrangements compiled by Thomas Pooley. The Bibliography and Discography contain the books, articles, and materials that were used to pull together the historical and cultural context surrounding Khumalo and South Africa during his lifetime. It also has the most complete listing of studies and recordings relevant to Khumalo and his music. The two scores reproduced by kind permission of Shuter & Shooter are his first published work, "Ma Ngificwa Ukufa" (1959) and "Izibongo ZikaShaka" (1981) which was the foundation stone for his epic, *UShaka KaSenzangakhona* (1996).

Altogether, this collection documents each of the major components in Khumalo's life as a composer, musician, academic, and administrator. It is inevitable that with the passage of time more details on Khumalo's life and legacy will come to light, and there will no doubt be further opportunity for reevaluation and critical appraisal. What we set out to accomplish is to present primary texts and fresh perspectives that document knowledge about Khumalo and his work by his contemporaries and critics in the context of early postapartheid South African politics and culture. As coeditors, we hope this volume can launch new studies, looking backwards and forwards, on Professor Khumalo's career, and the rich South African musical heritage to which he belongs.

*

Mzilikazi Khumalo passed away on June 22, 2021, at the age of eighty-nine. This book offers a series of critical reflections on his life and music. Its purpose is to document Khumalo's career and achievements through essays by scholars reflecting on his biography and music along with contemplative essays written by his contemporaries and collaborators. The inclusion of critical voices and those with firsthand experience of his life and times is designed to offer a balance of perspectives on his music and legacy.

This collection aims through a series of biographical and historical studies to lend context to the story of his life and major works. A broader purpose pursued by some of the contributors displays a reflexive engagement with contemporary discourses of decoloniality and themes of identity, indigeneity, coloniality, and race. This volume aims to broaden the critical discourse on the history and reception of Black choralism, opera, and the nexus of traditional and art musics that Khumalo described as "serious music." The idea of an indigenous choral practice in South Africa was given fullest expression in Khumalo's choral works, and his studies of African languages established new ways of thinking about this field in a postcolonial world. In sum, this body of work serves as an invitation to Khumalo studies for a new generation of scholars and musicians in the humanities and social sciences.

1

"UGqozi"

A Biography of J. S. Mzilikazi Khumalo

Thomas M. Pooley

Mzilikazi Khumalo was a bridge between worlds.[1] He brought disparate communities together at a time when South Africa's future as a democratic nation was in the balance. The themes of reconciliation and forgiveness that figure in his major musical works are testament to a principled conscience that found meaning in its commitment to achieving meaningful social change. Similarly, in his career as a teacher and linguist, Khumalo sought to advance African perspectives and persons in ways that would cement their place in the academy. To understand how Khumalo bridged worlds, we must take account of the complex web of cultures—both African and Western—that made him, and out of which he fashioned new ways of being in a postcolonial world. This chapter charts the contours of his career, focusing on his efforts to validate and integrate the works of Black composers into what had been a wholly Eurocentric canon and arts establishment. It also shows how Khumalo succeeded in establishing a new paradigm for serious music in postapartheid South Africa by elevating traditional music to the same plane as art music. Through a series of ambitious artistic experiments, Khumalo enabled dialogue while seeking transformation and justice. Yet, to the end, Khumalo remained true to his roots in rural Zululand, which is where his story begins.

Youth

James Steven Mzilikazi Khumalo was born on June 20, 1932, at KwaNgwelu (Mountain View), a Salvation Army mission farm. His parents, Senior Major Andreas Khumalo and Ntombizodwa Johanna, completed their training at this remote outpost in the Vryheid district of Natal. KwaNgwelu was equipped with its own hospital and school. The purpose of the mission was principally to evangelize the adjacent Zulu communities through cultural adaptation.[2] In this, the Salvationists were quite unlike the Anglican, American, and other missionary boards for whom evangelism was bound to education, industry, and "civilization." They sought instead to adapt to Zulu cultural norms, permitting ancestral belief and sacrifice, which most other denominations outlawed as heathen. The Khumalos were committed Christians rooted in their Zulu lifeways and language. The young James, or Jimmy as he was then known, grew up with an appreciation for the Western ways of the church while always retaining a belief system shaped by the values, history, and traditions of the Zulu people. These factors were decisive in forging the musician, linguist, and intellectual whom he would develop into in the eight decades to come.

His father, Major Andreas, was moved from post to post in the church throughout Khumalo's childhood. The family spent one important stint at Hlabisa, the ancestral home of both parents. It was here that Jimmy began to take an interest in music. Not only was he an enthusiastic member of the school's children's choir; he also began to experiment with brass instruments at church. These sounds were overlaid with the imprint of traditional cultures of song and dance. Wedding and other dance songs entered his imaginary, and in later years, these would influence his development as an arranger and composer of choral music. His father instilled a strict discipline, waking his sons in the early hours to prepare fires for the day. Jimmy remained resolutely disciplined in adult life, and this, together with his natural competitive streak, would prove a formidable combination. But Khumalo's steely determination was moderated by a mother's love. "It was my mother," he said, "who told us stories in the evenings, and most of these folktales were interspersed with folksongs. And these, she sang such that they remained memorable even up to my adult days."[3] Growing up as the third of nine children on a minister's salary meant there were numerous lean times for the family.[4] In times of need, his mother would sew him school trousers from her own skirts.[5] The two would remain inseparable well into Khumalo's late adult years.

The Khumalos moved to Vryheid in the late 1930s, where Mzilikazi attended primary school in the location. At the age of eight, his father taught him to play the euphonium and to read the fundamentals of staff notation. Most of the songs he learned here, and at subsequent schools, were in English. This was where he first heard Handel's *Messiah*, a work that would play a vital role in his development as a musician. The choirs sang using tonic sol-fa, and this soon became his preferred method of musical invention and performance.[6] The family moved again when Jimmy was in standard 5, this time to Vendaland. Khumalo spent his first year of high school there before enrolling as a boarder at Fred Clark Secondary School, a Salvation Army High School in Nancefield, Soweto. He participated in the senior choir which he would lead from time to time, training soloists. It was at this time that he participated in the first Johannesburg Bantu Music Festival established in 1946. This proved to be a key moment, as he later recalled in an interview:

> this is a very lovely memory for me because Anne, one of the girls I "trained" for a soprano solo, introduced me to my wife at the festival. Litlhare (Rose), my wife, then sang in the Sharpeville High School choir under Mr. Ngamone. It was love at first sight and we got married in 1958 after having trained together as teachers in Pretoria.[7]

Theirs was a powerful partnership founded on shared values, faith, and discipline; it would last until their last days.

Studies and Teaching

Khumalo graduated from high school in 1950, two years after the Afrikaner National Party won the 1948 general election promising to institute a policy of "apartheid." Africans did not have the franchise, and the opportunities for a young African high school graduate in the 1950s, already limited by segregation, were further constrained under the new apartheid laws. Fort Hare was the only university designated for Africans. It was possible to register at the University of the Witwatersrand (Wits), but permission was required from the minister, and fees were prohibitive for all but the elite. Khumalo spent a year working and saving before being awarded a bursary toward a three-year teaching diploma at the Pretoria Bantu Normal College. This was the only tertiary institution for African students in the Transvaal, but it did not confer degrees.

College life was rich in activities and friendships. Khumalo enjoyed playing football, tennis, and cricket, and he was the leader of a jazz quartet called the Gay Gaieties. One of the singers in this group was Abiah Mahlase, who became a lifelong friend. Later, they worked together as teachers at Wallmansthal Secondary School in Pretoria where they sang in the Four Larks with Solly Pelo and "Dougie" Kutumela. Other classmates included Desmond Tutu and Stanley

Mokgoba who went on to become leaders of the Anglican Church. Khumalo graduated in 1954 but continued his studies through distance education at the University of South Africa (Unisa), graduating in 1956 with a BA majoring in English and isiZulu. For Africans who could not afford to attend Fort Hare University in the Eastern Cape Province, Unisa was the only option for obtaining a degree by correspondence.

James and his wife Rose married on January 4, 1958, and had four children: Busisiwe, Diliza, Themba, and Nonhlanhla. All grew up singing and making music in Khumalo's choirs. Teaching was a career that offered musical opportunities through extracurricular activities. A strong African choral music fraternity had been established in the Transvaal, and competitive choir singing culminated in annual festivals. Khumalo enjoyed his choirs and won many competitions both as conductor and choral director. His first job was as a high school teacher of English, isiZulu, and Mathematics at Wallmansthal Secondary School in Pretoria from 1955 to 1960. This was followed by a year at Lady Selbourne High School, Pretoria (1961), and Mamelodi High School (1962–4). Later, he was appointed principal at Mamellong Nqabeni High School in Brakpan, serving from 1964 to 1968. Khumalo was a member of the Transvaal United Teachers' Association (TUATA), which awarded him a Certificate of Merit for distinguished service for the years 1955–69.

The African Teachers Association of South Africa (ATASA) was responsible for organizing an annual National Choral Festival from 1961. Khumalo's song, "Ma Ngificwa Ukufa" (1959), was prescribed at the inaugural event in Bloemfontein that year. Khumalo trained both school and adult choirs, winning first prizes in 1962, 1963, 1965, 1968, and 1970. "At the first national choir contest, Abiah won the high schools' section while I won the teachers' section. Later, I was to feature in many ATASA national contests, and was indeed fortunate not to have lost in any 'National' final in which I partook, both with the school and adult choirs."[8] Important friends and associates of Khumalo at this time included Elkin Sithole, who met Khumalo through the choir competitions, and who went on to become a professor at Northeastern Illinois University in the United States. Simon Ngubane, inspector of music in Zululand, was another friend, who would encourage his music activities.[9] From these friendships came inspiration and the occasional commission or festival invitation. Many of his works were commissioned and prescribed by music competitions, such as ATASA, Ford Choir Contests, Botswana National Eisteddfod, Swaziland National Eisteddfod, and Transkei National Eisteddfod.

The early songs were mostly based on poetic texts by B. W. Vilakazi and J. C. Dlamini. But this period of musical success and advancement ended with an abrupt change of career and a new focus. Apartheid under Verwoerd was proving tremendously taxing on Africans who had to navigate a complex web of government agencies, officialdom, and law.[10] Khumalo found a way through this to a better life for his family.

Academia and Soweto

In 1969, Khumalo accepted a post as tutor in the Department of African Languages at the University of the Witwatersrand, then one of the leading departments of its kind. At this time, there were no Africans employed as lecturers in the department. Clement M. Doke, formerly professor and head of the department at Wits, had proposed Benedict Wallet Vilakazi for a lectureship in African languages in the 1940s, but this was rejected by the parents of Wits students and by the state.[11] The situation had not improved by the 1960s and so Khumalo's position was limited to "tutoring" white students as second-language speakers. Mostly, this involved rudimentary literacy and speaking skills. Still, Wits did offer opportunities for further study and remained a place of political upheaval and resistance in the 1970s and 1980s. Khumalo was determined to excel in his new career and returned to academic studies at Unisa, enrolling for an honors degree in "Bantu studies." His honors article on plot and character in Vilakazi's novels was completed in 1972.[12] Interestingly, Vilakazi had preceded Khumalo as a language tutor in the Department of African Languages at Wits, also having gained his first degree from Unisa, as had the influential Pan-Africanist, Robert Sobukwe.

Khumalo's appointment at Wits would shape home life, too. In 1952, an Act of Parliament had been instituted requiring all Africans over the age of sixteen to be in possession of a "pass" book that detailed their place of origin and permissions for work in any given place.[13] This system was integrated with the legislation of the Group Areas Act (1950) that categorized persons by race and ethnicity and made it illegal to reside outside of designated areas prescribed in legislation. When local authorities discovered that he no longer worked as a teacher in Brakpan, they reviewed his pass. Since Khumalo was now a worker in Braamfontein, Johannesburg, the authorities ruled that he was not eligible to live in Brakpan. He was given three months to relocate to Soweto (Southwestern

Townships), what the government classed as a "location" some 25 kilometers from Johannesburg. Making hasty arrangements, he scrambled to find new accommodation. The first place was at a new township at Emdeni. This proved too basic, and so the family moved to Rockville a year later where they could occupy their own home.[14] The children attended school in Naledi.

Khumalo became a respected member of the community in Soweto and rejoined the Salvation Army for worship. This also drew him back to sacred choral music, an important influence on his development as a composer. He maintained his job at Wits while continuing to improve his qualifications. Once employed as a language tutor, he devoted himself to linguistics through a series of postgraduate degrees focusing on the phonology (sound structures) of isiZulu. His Masters on isiZulu tonology was awarded in 1980 and published almost immediately in two volumes of the journal *African Studies*.[15] This fascination with the sounds of language would shape his approach to choral music. Khumalo was among the first to realize the significance of speech tone in setting African languages to music. Singing was not simply about achieving the correct intonation, which was always a challenge with amateur choirs. It was also about achieving the appropriate pitch height and movement when singing in African languages. Finding a practical solution to representing these features in music notation would remain an important goal in his later years as a linguist and musician.

The 1980s were a period of political and social turmoil in South Africa. Internal and external pressures on the government forced a series of changes. Some of the segregationist laws were rescinded or relaxed, including the "pass" system, and Khumalo was finally appointed to a full lectureship in 1980 marking a new era at Wits. Soon, he was collaborating with colleagues in the department and abroad on studies of African languages and linguistics.[16] He enrolled for a doctoral thesis at Wits on isiZulu phonology applying the insights of autosegmental-metrical theory to the structures of isiZulu. Much of this work was completed while in the United States as a visiting scholar at the University of Illinois, Urbana-Champaign. This visit was made possible by his association with Charles (Chuck) Kisseberth, one of the leading generative linguists of his era, and an expert on African tone systems. Khumalo was awarded a Doctor of Philosophy in African Languages in 1988. Shortly thereafter, he was appointed associate professor and head of Department of African Languages, and then to a professorship in 1989. He continued to serve as professor until the end of 1997, before retiring as Professor Emeritus in

January 1998. His teaching at Wits incorporated segmental phonology and tonology, as well as language studies in isiZulu and Sesotho (he was also fluent in Tshivenda).[17] Fellow linguist and friend professor D. B. Z. Ntuli described his contributions to linguistics in the citation for a doctorate awarded honoris causa at Unisa:

> One of his main contributions was a new analysis of the morphological structure of Zulu and Southern Sotho which incorporates a paradigm of tense and aspect. This approach has helped tremendously in simplifying the teaching of the morphology of African languages. He was among the first South African phonologists to teach and read papers on the application of the theories of, among others, autosegmental phonology, CV-phonology, feature geometry, under specification, lexical phonology and optimal domains to African Languages. Numerous present-day scholars were his pupils. His melodic rendering of the beautiful Zulu language with its tonal variations endeared him to both students and colleagues alike.[18]

Khumalo published on all these topics in phonology, tonology, and morphology. He received the Via Afrika Prize for Linguistic Studies for his article "Leftward Ho! In Zulu Tonology" published in the *South African Journal of African Languages* (1990). Khumalo's work on tonology advanced that of his predecessors. An accessible summary of his views is printed in the Zulu-English Dictionary published by Wits University Press.[19] A most unusual feature of this dictionary is the inclusion of a system of tone marking first described by Clement Doke. This system showed that tone is used for multiple purposes, including semantics, grammar, and emotion—points that Khumalo emphasized in his phonology. Doke employed a system of tone marking that uses nine distinct pitch levels that he notated musically. Khumalo's contribution was to simplify this method to a dual-tone contrast between High and Low tone but incorporating Rising, Falling, and Rising–Falling tone. These tones are notated in the musical works he created from the 1980s onward, and it is this melding of tone and tune that reinforces the beautifully crafted sounds of his mature music.

At Wits, Khumalo was credited with transforming a department that in 1980 was staffed largely by white lecturers who taught the basics of second-language acquisition. There was also a shift from teaching grammar and translation to literature, as well as formal and socio-linguistics. Not only that, but the teaching was now "informed by the key issues and principles of modern linguistic theory." His colleague Mary Bill described Khumalo as "one of the giants in African Linguistics in Southern Africa, and in isiZulu linguistics in particular."[20] By the end of his career at Wits, he was being recognized nationally and internationally for his contributions to the transformation of linguistics in southern Africa.

Khumalo was also honored for his skills as a leader, mediator, and negotiator during the 1980s at the African Languages Association of Southern Africa. He opened doors for South African academics abroad through his contacts, especially in the United States, but also regionally. Professor D. B. Z. Ntuli remarked on this, too, saying:

> Before his time these languages were taught as academic subjects to students whose mother tongue was mostly English. Literature was taught in a prescriptive way. When he retired, cognizance had been taken of the fact that most of the students were mother tongue speakers of these languages. Literature teaching had shifted from rigid formalism to accommodate interrelationships between literature and society.[21]

The character of the man was famously formidable. He was direct, forthright, and would always argue his point to its logical conclusion. Yet, despite this uncompromising demeanor, he was respectful, and he expected the same of his colleagues and students. In all facets, then, Khumalo was a leader, a beloved and respected colleague who spoke his mind and maintained high standards that he expected others to keep.

Choir Master

"UGqozi" (Power of Inspiration) is an important early song that remains popular with choirs today. Khumalo's explanation is captured in an interview transcript: "I found inspiration in [a] dream in which I saw KwaDukuza [Stanger] ... shocked, I stood praying to forefathers when [a] voice commanded me not to sit on my hands, not born to do nothing, to go out and relate [the] Zulu past for future generations."[22] This crucial moment of inspiration would culminate in a lifelong creative quest to advance the understanding of Zulu culture rooted in historical narratives. Both the later *UShaka KaSenzangakhona* (1996) and the opera *Princess Magogo KaDinuzulu* (2002) may be interpreted throughn this lens. Still, *UGqozi* (Figure 1.1) retained the hymn-like harmonic features and tonal palette

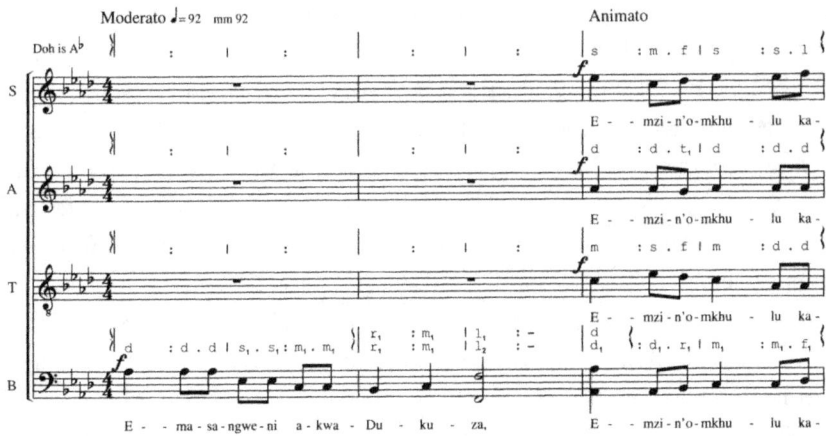

Figure 1.1 "UGqozi" (Power of Inspiration) by Mzilikazi Khumalo.

of his early works while elaborating on Vilakazi's message in a powerful delivery that ends with these lines:

"Vuka wena kaMancinza!
Kawuzalelwanga ukulal' ubuthongo.
Vuk' ubong' indaba yemikhonto!
Nank' umthwal' engakwethwesa wona."

"Arise, O you son of Manzina!
Your destiny bids you to waken
And sing to us legends of battle:
This charge, I command you, fulfil!"[23]

In the 1970s and 1980s, Khumalo worked with amateur and church choirs and continued to play a role as an adjudicator at the ATASA National Eisteddfod, Ford Choir Festival, and Roodepoort International Eisteddfod of South Africa, among others. His own choirs were the Soweto Songsters and the Central Division Songsters of the Salvation Army. With them, he embarked on tours to Germany, England, Scotland, Norway, the United States, and Jamaica, performing at festivals and by invitation. The Soweto Songsters became a vehicle for Khumalo's musical arrangements and compositions. With them, he created intricate arrangements of African folk music which became central to the choral repertoire in South Africa. The Soweto Songsters had the honor of representing the entire African continent during the 100th Year Congress of the Salvation Army in London, 1982.[24]

Khumalo's standing as a figure of national importance was reinforced by his appointment with Richard Cock to direct the Sowetan Nation Building Massed Choir Festival launched in 1989.[25] There were several iterations of this festival, including regional and national events. There was also the Caltex Massed Choir Festival (Cape Town) and the Sowetan/Caltex/SABC1 Massed Choir Festival (Durban) broadcast on national television. Khumalo insisted on the inclusion of African traditional music on the programs and created most of these arrangements himself. The blend of African and Western choral music performed from notation and with orchestra gave the Black choral community standing as "serious music," a position that had been denied to Black musicians during apartheid. Cock and Khumalo became a formidable team, and their scores in dual notation established a repertory that was widely disseminated (see Cock, this volume).

"I think the Good Lord wanted me to be a musician," remarked Khumalo in retrospect. "I became an academic because I had to live. During my time I couldn't live on music."[26] There was no career path in music available to him, and it was only when he retired that he could devote himself to it full time. But this left him with many frustrations because he lacked formal music education.[27] Music was not taught as a school subject in Black schools in the 1940s, and there was no option for a university education in music. While most children did learn the basics of four-part singing and the ability to harmonize (Soprano-Alto-Tenor-Bass), there was no established culture of singing from staff notation or learning music theory. To improve himself, Khumalo took private lessons while a student in Pretoria. Charles Norburn taught him the basics of harmony, counterpoint, form, and composition. Much later, he embarked on voice lessons with his close friend Khabi Mngoma, a man who was an elemental force in music development for Black South Africans in Soweto and Johannesburg.[28] Mngoma was later commissioned to establish the music department at the University of Zululand, and Khumalo remained in close contact with him. His compositions were performed at the university's Ongoye campus, and Mngoma's passion for documenting and arranging indigenous musics rubbed off. Mngoma would later play a crucial role in the development of Khumalo's compositions in the 1990s.

Mngoma's influence on Khumalo's son, Diliza, who studied music with Mngoma at the University of Zululand, resulted in a turning point in his musical development.[29] Diliza's critique of the "Western" sound of Khumalo's choral music forced a rethink. For a time, he stopped composing altogether and dedicated himself to the study of African music, taking instruction from Andrew Tracey at the International Library of African Music, and gaining further insights from the linguist and ethnomusicologist David Rycroft at the School of Oriental and African Studies, University of London (a frequent visitor to South Africa). The songs Khumalo wrote prior to 1980 mostly contain sections in what he called "traditional style." But Diliza suggested he make them *altogether* traditional by including not only indigenous rhythms, but melodies, scales, and harmonies, too. Experiments with this new style were conducted with the aid of the Black Orpheus Folk Singers.[30] Khumalo recalled:

> I collected and arranged folk songs of all the South African ethnic groups and we sang these at our performances. This, to my knowledge, was the first attempt at placing traditional African choral music on par with folk music of the rest of the world. It gave me the opportunity to study folk music. It was during this time that I again re-learned the different modes (e.g., the "Soh" mode, the "Lah" mode, etc.) of the pentatonic and hexatonic scales of traditional African music. From a study of the scales, I also got into the study of harmonies employed. In this endeavour, I used mostly my mother and my very musical cousin, Zebulon Nkosi, then Bandmaster at Peart Memorial Corps.[31]

Jabulani Mazibuko was a good friend and the conductor of the Soweto Teachers Choir, one of the foremost ensembles of that generation. Khumalo described this choir as "the testing ground" for his new compositions.[32] Other important choirs who collaborated on *UShaka KaSenzangakhona* were Abiah Mahlase's Daveyton Adult Choir, Themba Madlopha's Cenestra Male Choir, and Ludumo Magangane's Bonisudumo Adult Choir. This web of connections between choirs shows Khumalo was at the center of a strong choral practice in the 1980s. This was essential to Aggrey Klaaste's decision to invite him to join Richard Cock as the inaugural music directors of the Nation Building Massed Choir Festival in 1989.

The new direction in Khumalo's music was also influenced by his work on isiZulu tonology. The careful notation of speech and dance rhythms shows a marked sensitivity to the sounds and tonal contours of speech. The contrast between works of this period and his earlier choral works can be seen through comparison of the songs "Ma Ngificwa Ukufa" (1959) and "Izibongo ZikaShaka" (1981). The hymn-like choral setting of the first of these is characteristic of the choral tradition to emerge from the mission-educated composers of previous generations, including Moerane, Sontonga, and Bokwe. The scales are mostly diatonic with traditional part-writing the norm. In the later "UGqozi," there are hints of an emerging indigenous practice. With "Izibongo ZikaShaka" Khumalo takes this further by adopting a pentatonic system that is characteristic of several Zulu music traditions, such as the classic tradition of *ugubhu* songs performed by uMntwana Magogo kaDinuzulu.[33] The rhythmic vitality that had formerly characterized the middle section of his songs now pervade entire works.

UShaka KaSenzangakhona

In his call to arms, *Decolonizing the Mind: The Politics of Language in African Literature*, Ngũgĩ wa Thiong'o wrote: "Language as culture is the collective memory bank of a people's experience in history. Culture is almost indistinguishable from the language that makes possible its genesis, growth, banking, articulation and indeed its transmission from one generation to the next."[34] Mzilikazi Khumalo, perhaps more than any other African composer, took seriously the spirit of Ngũgĩ's rallying cry when in 1981 he composed *Izibongo ZikaShaka*, which would later become the third part of the African epic he completed in all its parts in 1985, and which he dedicated to his mother.

> I think I have been under Shaka's spell from the time, on my mother's knee, I first listened to her narrations of Zulu history, and then to the time when, as a small boy, I learned at school to recite the traditional praises of the Zulu kings, right up to the time when I then read R.R.R. Dhlomo's "UShaka"—the authoritative text on this revered founder of the Zulu nation.[35]

Themba Msimang, then a lecturer in the Department of African Languages at Unisa, was the librettist for this epic work.[36] It was Khumalo's youngest child, Nonhlanhla, who recommended the author to her father.

I read his play "Izulu Eladum'eSandlwana" and I knew that this was the man I had been looking for. I contacted him and asked him to provide me with lyrics for "Siyashweleza Nodumehlezi." And that was the beginning of a fruitful partnership that has produced compositions like "Inkondlo kaMkabayi"; "Isibaya Esikhulu se-Afrika" (African Bank song); "Xola Hleziphi"; "Intonga Yosindiso" (composed for the ordination of Archbishop Desmond Tutu); and the whole epic entitled *UShaka KaSenzangakhona* (an ambitious work which tells the story of King Shaka in music and praise poetry).[37]

The figure of UShaka kaSenzangakhona is central to the Zulu imaginary. Khumalo had studied literature on Shaka for much of his life, and the idea of writing an epic was a decades-long project. He began work on *Izibongo ZikaShaka* in 1979 and finished this first part of the work in tonic sol-fa notation in 1981. The revised tonic sol-fa score to the epic was completed in March 1985, but Khumalo pursued a series of collaborations in an effort to get the work orchestrated. Not having studied orchestration himself, he was in no position to set the work. This would prove to be a long and difficult process with the first complete orchestration completed in 1996, although further revisions were made up until 1999.

The concept for this African epic is underpinned by the need for forgiveness. Khumalo explained this in his interview with Ndwamato George Mugovhani in 2008. Reflecting on the initial encounter with Msimang, he explained the development of the work as follows:

> Then I wrote another song [following "Izibongo ZikaShaka"], which is also about King Shaka Zulu, "Siyashweleza Nodum'ehlezi" (We beg for your pardon). "Nodum'ehlezi" is Shaka. He had got killed very terribly and before he died he cursed the Zulu people saying, "so you think you will run this place? You won't rule this place." We know that the Zulus started suffering after Shaka's murder. I felt that we must say sorry and also beg for his pardon, and this is what this song did. This song came from "iZulu eladum' eSandlwana" by Msimang. I used the first words in that book that my daughter had brought.[38]

The first two pieces were expanded into a four-part dramatic work for the stage. Msimang's epic text was too expansive to be sung in a single performance and so parts of it are declaimed as praise poetry. This lends continuity between sections and animates live performances with an otherwise static choir, soloists, and orchestra. At the early performances, it was Msimang who took up the role of *imbongi* (orator, or praise poet). Khumalo tested out his new creation on his choirs, and several challenges were soon evident. There was a need to connect the different parts of the drama with instrumental music so that the movements join seamlessly rather than as independent numbers. Pianist-composer Mokale Koapeng worked with Khumalo on early efforts to harmonize an accompaniment and transitions. The next step was to orchestrate the piece. Khumalo approached colleagues in the music department at Wits, including the conductor Walter Mony and composer Carl van Wyk. But Mony's first orchestration was never completed. Khumalo then approached composer Christopher James of Unisa, this time with the backing of a SAMRO commission. At the time, James was working on his own African-inspired works for orchestra and was already experimenting with ways to create distinctively African textures and timbres with the orchestra. The James score has a distinctly transparent texture which foregrounds the voices and reinforces the dance rhythms with percussion. There was no prelude or overture to his initial effort. Instead, the emphasis was on supporting the voices. The James score does not solve two musical problems: the first is providing satisfying musical connections between the sections, and the second is the coordination of the orchestral players with the singers. At the first rehearsals with the Transvaal Symphony Orchestra, these challenges came to the fore. Most of the orchestral players were white and were steeped in the Western concert tradition. They had no knowledge of isiZulu or tonic sol-fa. On the other hand, the singers did not read staff notation. This presented insuperable challenges for the conductor since there were no cues coordinating the two scores. Coordination between the orchestra, conductor and soloists depended on a conductor who could read both staff notation and tonic sol-fa. Khabi Mngoma had been conducting these early efforts but ultimately ceded the task to a visiting American conductor, Maestro Robert Maxym. James, meanwhile, withdrew from the project due to ill health. This proved to be the turning point.

Khumalo formally appointed Maxym to revise and enhance the orchestration after the performance, and this was settled by a commission from SAMRO in 1995. The work was completed over nearly two years of close collaboration between Khumalo and Maxym (see Maxym, this volume). Maxym expanded the orchestral forces to give the work more power and drew out thematic material to thicken the texture. He added an overture derived from the work's main themes. This new version was premiered in the Johannesburg City Hall in 1996 with Maxym at the podium. Richard Cock made the National Symphony Orchestra available for a studio recording that was released by Sony Classical in 1997. The soloists were Sibongile Khumalo (mezzo-soprano), Sibongile Mngoma (soprano), Themba Mkhwani (tenor), and Peter Mcebi (baritone). Themba

Msimang performed the praise poetry. Four choirs massed together for the premiere performance and recording sessions. They were carefully prepared by their respective conductors and under Khumalo's supervision.[39] The combined forces of orchestra, soloists, and choristers numbered over 300 musicians for the recording at the SABC's M1A studio in Auckland Park.[40] This was the first major work for singers and choir by a Black South African composer recorded in the twentieth century.[41] In fact, *UShaka KaSenzangakhona* occupies a genre all its own. Khumalo and Msimang have given it the appellation "epic," thus moving the work into a literary-musical genre. Musicologists have suggested the terms oratorio, cantata, music drama, and the like, but all of these are restrictive in prescribing conventions the bounds of which are exceeded by *UShaka*. The fusion of music and language is perhaps its distinctive feature. This fusion could only have been achieved by two linguists working together, and by a composer with an ear acutely tuned for tone. Khumalo enjoyed a close working relationship with his librettist, Themba Msimang, who recorded audio tapes of the lyrics so that Khumalo could ensure the correct tonal rendering of the words to music. This was also important in Khumalo's collaboration with Robert Maxym, who incorporated the tonal features of the vocal melody into the orchestration, thus setting up a dialogue between orchestra and singers that emphasizes features of the rhythms and melodies of speech.[42]

Khumalo used various styles of performance in *UShaka*: in *Haya* style, the pitch features of spoken Zulu are retained. That is, the patterning of speech tones, glides, and intonation is faithfully represented. "These notes represent inflections of the spoken word which carry great semantic meaning."[43] In the *UShaka* edition published by Maxym Music, the glossary describes two main features of tonology, including a symbol linking two notes of the same duration to indicate a glide from one pitch to the next. The second set of symbols / and \ indicate up- and down-glides, respectively. These are "unrestricted" glides in the sense that the initial or final pitch is not determined.[44] Examples of these glides may be found throughout *UShaka*, but the examples from "Inkondlo kaNandi" are indicative (Figure 1.2).

UShaka KaSenzangakhona is Khumalo's best-known work, and it has been performed on numerous occasions in South Africa, the United States, and Europe. *UShaka* was chosen as the featured work for performances by the KwaZulu-Natal Philharmonic Orchestra in celebration of ten years of democracy in South Africa that took place locally and abroad. It was also featured at the Ravinia Festival, Chicago, in 2006.

Figure 1.2 "Inkondlo KaNandi" (Nandi's Love Song), bars 63–68,© Maxym Music.

SAMRO and Retirement

When Khumalo retired as Wits Professor Emeritus in 1998, he immediately sought new ventures in music. This included an appointment as vice-chairperson of SAMRO where he also served on the board of the SAMRO Endowment for the National Arts. There he played a critical role in the development of "serious" music in South Africa by advancing scholarships, bursaries, and commissions for promising young artists as well as established composers. Khumalo's vision for serious music was expansive and new, breaking with its emphasis on Western art music as the zenith of artistic achievement. His vision is detailed in an essay he wrote in 2003 in which he describes the relevance of "classic" forms to the African context:

> The genre in question falls, in the African context, into two distinct classes (I believe), namely traditional music and composed music. Another common name for serious music is "classic" or "classical" music [. . .], which applies it

mainly to the established repertoire of Western art music. The *Shorter Oxford Dictionary* defines "classic" and "classical" in that sense as "standard." The word "classical" in such context can thus also apply to African "art" music, as opposed to "popular" music.

Another definition for "classical" in the Shorter Oxford Dictionary alludes to the antiquity or historicity of the music or literature so described, and under that heading I should like to suggest that we subsume also African traditional music, subject to the qualification that, for our purposes here, the word be applied to music which appeals to a discriminating appreciation of the established body of the musical repertoire, whether traditional or composed. It thus also describes music that has been handed down or composed with the intention of preserving of amplifying the historically established body of the repertoire, or "canon" as it is often called.[45]

This approach to serious music in the African context was a paradigm shift for composers in South Africa. In the 1980s, there had been a move toward Africanist art music with composers finding various ways to engage with indigenous musics whether through paraphrase, quotation, exoticism, or borrowing. These efforts were largely by white South African composers who sought new ways to adapt to a changing cultural milieu.[46] In twentieth-century South Africa, traditional music had been relegated to the status of an inferior folk art denigrated by its classification according to ethnic or race-based terminologies that excluded it from serious study and performance. Mngoma had taken important steps to reevaluating African folk and art music traditions through his teaching and research at the University of Zululand, just as Hugh Tracey and Andrew Tracey had done through the International Library of African Music. Khumalo now asserted that both art and traditional musics occupied the same plane. This opened a new dialogue between practitioners in both fields that was to flourish in the early 2000s with the renewal of art music through the New Music Indaba.[47] Khumalo spearheaded this new way with his arrangement of songs by Princess Magogo kaDinuzulu, first in a song cycle with orchestration and piano arrangements by Peter Klatzow, and then in an opera. This validation of traditional music as serious music foregrounded the African in spaces that had long been reserved for European voices and instruments alone. The idea of traditional music as art music—being recognized as having equal status—was made concrete through these new efforts, and this two decades after Kevin Volans had pioneered the idea with his *African Paraphrases*.[48]

Khumalo continued to advance the careers of choral composers while at SAMRO. He was appointed chairman of the committee working to publish African songs in dual notation. This resulted in the compilation of three volumes of *South Africa Sings*.[49] The first volume appeared in 1998 and the last in 2012. Khumalo served as the general editor on the SAMRO Endowment's "Dual Notation" Committee that included Michael Masote, Dan Lefoka, Ludumo Magangane, and Nehemiah Ramasia. The purpose of this series was

> to make indigenous choral music accessible to the music-loving public in a definitive version. Another was to make such music available in both tonic sol-fa and staff-notations at the same time. Many, if not most, of South Africa's choirs learn their music from scores notated in tonic sol-fa, and it was felt desirable for choristers to familiarize themselves with standard staff notation as well, since this would enlarge the choral repertoire available to them.[50]

The importance of this project was threefold: first, it sought to establish important works by African composers in definitive published form. Second, it sought to standardize and make accessible notations for these works that were sensitive to the idiosyncrasies of the originals. Key to this was the use of notations for African tone languages, including the introduction of grace notes to indicate up- and down-glides. Third, the volumes sought to address the "obsolete orthography" of the original compositions to ensure that singers from different language groups would have proper instruction in the phonetics of the language concerned. Khumalo was of course the ideal candidate to facilitate this knowledge transfer, and he spent considerable time conducting research on these composers and searching for manuscripts of the original scores. A biographical entry precedes each score, as well as the lyrics and translation. Khumalo's role as a curator of South African song had developed over many years, beginning with his work as a music director and adjudicator in schools and taking on a much wider role when he took the reins at the Nation Building Massed Choir festivals. He took all that he had learned from those earlier experiences and curated what amounts to a canonic set of texts of Black choral music in South Africa.

Africanizing Opera

Khumalo may have retired from Wits in 1998 but he continued with many projects in addition to his work at SAMRO. There is a noticeable uptick in music composition activities in the mid-to-late 1990s that begins with the revision of *UShaka* and its orchestral premiere in 1996. During his first years of retirement, he created two new works based on the life and music of uMntwana Constance Magogo kaDinuzulu (1900–1984). Princess Magogo had played a central role in narrating the history of Zulu music and nation in an extraordinary career that is well documented by David Rycroft and others (Shange, Chapter 12).[51] The setting of her bow songs to Western common practice notation and tonic sol-fa canonized her work and was commissioned by SAMRO. Khumalo's role as transcriber and arranger required ingenuity because the original songs were sung to the accompaniment of the *ugubhu* bow. Many of these songs had been recorded and were regularly broadcast on Bantu Radio, and later Ukhozi FM.[52] David Rycroft's studies of Princess Magogo's music served as preparation, but the dialogue Khumalo had with her son, Prince Mangosuthu Buthelezi, was essential to the development of this song cycle, and more importantly, to the opera that followed.[53] Khumalo's respect and veneration of uMntwana Magogo's music—which he described as a form of classical or art music—stems at least in part from his reverence for the way she set isiZulu texts to music. The fascination with Zulu royalty that began with *UShaka* was extended in Khumalo's transcription and arrangement of the eight bow songs. The cycle was conceived for mezzo-soprano Sibongile Khumalo, with whom he had worked for many years on *UShaka*, and who premiered the work with Jill Richards at the piano. The world premiere took place on August 26, 2000, at the Linder Auditorium, Johannesburg. Peter Klatzow wrote the piano and orchestral arrangements. The orchestral version was premiered by the KwaZulu-Natal Philharmonic Orchestra in 2001 and is a remarkably successful arrangement of bow music for the concert stage. Klatzow's lucid piano accompaniment and orchestration provide the necessary color without invoking trite exoticisms, and the orchestral score sensitively supports the singer. Klatzow's imaginative harmonies extract intervallic features of the single-string bow music but must of necessity extend these to create a compelling tonal language.[54] This was an inspired project that demonstrated Khumalo's commitment to traditional music as serious music, showing beyond doubt how African and Western traditions could forge a compelling new art music.

It was at this time that Khumalo was invited to partner in a major new project that would further enshrine the musical legacy of Mntwan' Magogo. This project would also elaborate his philosophy of serious music and elevate its standing through recognition on the world stage. The opera *Princess Magogo KaDinuzulu* was commissioned by Opera Africa and premiered in 2002. Khumalo is credited as its composer with Themba Msimang the librettist. Khumalo's role in this work is multidimensional because of the highly collaborative nature of the opera's genesis (de Villiers, chapter 9). The scenario for the opera was workshopped between Khumalo, Sandra and Hein de Villiers, Khabi Mngoma, Themba Msimang, and Prince Mangosuthu Buthelezi, and with input from theater director Themi Venturas and conductor Gerhard Geist. The costume and set designs were created by the artist Andrew Verster. The music melds the original compositions of uMntwan' Magogo with original music by Khumalo, traditional Zulu songs arranged by Khumalo (including several workshopped with traditional leaders from KwaZulu-Natal), and the instrumental music of orchestrator Michael Hankinson (Quilliam, chapter 10). The work also includes Shembe religious musical instruments, songs, and iconography. It is rooted in the history of the Zulu monarchy and focuses on Magogo's life and times. The close collaboration with her son, Prince Buthelezi, was essential to the development of the libretto. Msimang's involvement as a historian and linguist was again indispensable to Khumalo who was at pains to ensure the proper setting of the songs in isiZulu. Similar artistic challenges to those experienced with the settings of *UShaka* arose in binding the various elements of the opera together. The Opera Africa conglomerate had decided on a number opera. This meant that Hankinson would have to compose incidental music to transition between numbers in the opera. The musical challenge is similar to that expounded by Klatzow in his comments on the orchestration of the song cycle. Khumalo once again made do with the imposition of a harmonic language onto his sinuous song settings but with limited agency as the opera's composer. With the *UShaka* setting, the consultations were lengthy, and he worked closely with Maxym at the piano. But with the song cycle and opera his relationship with the orchestrators did not benefit from close collaboration over time. For one thing, all parties were under considerable time pressure to complete the work in time for the rehearsals and premiere. The duration of the opera was nearly twice that of *UShaka*, a work that he had composed and revised over two decades. By the time the scenario had been worked out for *Princess Magogo KaDinuzulu*, he had just over a year to complete it. It is unsurprising, then, that the musical visions of Hankinson and Khumalo do not align with the same purpose that we find in *UShaka*, or even in the song cycle. The success of the orchestrations and instrumental interludes is dependent on Hankinson's minimal approach with its spare scoring and transparent use of contrapuntal, melodic and harmonic resources. Hankinson's background in music theater rather than opera (Maxym) or the symphonic tradition (Klatzow) is evident in this emphasis on an accessible musical palette. The mixed reaction from critics is notable in a review by Anthony Tommasini in the *New York Times*, who remarked on Hankinson's sensitivity to Khumalo's careful setting of Zulu vocal lines to music. But he was critical of the orchestration, a problem that vexed Khumalo to the end. Tommasini wrote:

> Mr. Hankinson essentially harmonized Mr. Khumalo's vocal lines, rightly discerning that the melodic notes tend to outline modal harmonies. But by making these implicit harmonies explicit, and by supporting the plaintive vocal lines with lush and warm sustained orchestra chords, Mr. Hankinson sweetened music that should sound tart. At times you thought that you had stumbled into Rimsky-Korsakov's lost African opera.[55]

Tommasini's final words are critical: "[Khumalo] doesn't have to add palatable Western-style orchestral harmonies to his music to call a score an opera." Khumalo was acutely aware of the problems of orchestration and the imposition of Western diatonicism, but he was powerless to address the need for suitable instrumental accompaniment and transition by his own hand. Ironically, his journey as a composer had taken an opposite course, moving from the Western-style choral imaginary of his youth to a new conception of African "serious music" created through the intense study of his own traditional culture. In retrospect, the artistic contradictions were inevitable and are indicative of the sociopolitical transition from which they emerged.

Princess Magogo KaDinuzulu is a bold statement in opera (Figure 1.3). The complex amalgam of Zulu cultural, linguistic, and historical elements may not have been evident to some critics, but they speak to the complexity of the early postapartheid period and striving for an authentic language for African voices in art music. Khumalo and Msimang's achievement is rooted in their vision for a composition constructed from the very fibers of African arts. The deep knowledge of Zulu history that is articulated in the full work has majesty that is communicated through singing, dancing, and oratory of unmatched power and vitality. In this it offers an archetype for the definition of "serious music" that Khumalo imagined for the next generation of composers. Christopher Ballantine described it as a "quantum leap" in the history of South African music.[56] *Princess Magogo* is the first opera by a Black South African composer in an indigenous African language. The work curates and rejuvenates Zulu cultural heritage through an epic story of love and loss. Its strengths and weaknesses inspired and challenged a new generation of African composers in search of opera.[57]

Figure 1.3 Sibongile Khumalo in the title role as Princess Magogo kaDinuzulu. Photo Credit: Opera Africa.

Last Years

Khumalo continued his work at SAMRO in the 2010s, where he retained an office long after he completed his work as vice-chairperson. But failing health eventually curtailed his ability to travel, so most of his time was spent at home in Kagiso on the outskirts of Johannesburg, where he resided close to his children. His wife, Rose, passed away on June 20, 2021, and he died just two days later, aged eighty-nine. This brought down the curtain on a formidable career in teaching, linguistics, music, church, and community life. Khumalo was a leader who fashioned a new South Africa by advancing reconciliation, Africanization, and transformation. He was fervently committed to the preservation and celebration of music by Black composers, which he sought not only to document but to advance through new methods of notation. His innovations as a composer and choral conductor have opened new horizons for generations of African composers, and his expansive vision for serious music incorporating traditional and art musics established a new and inclusive paradigm that celebrates African creative arts on their own terms.

2

An Interview with Diliza Khumalo

Thomas M. Pooley

Introduction

Diliza Khumalo is the son of Mzilikazi Khumalo and his wife, Rose Litlhare. Diliza studied music and African languages at the University of Zululand under his father's close friend, Professor Khabi Mngoma, and later assisted his father in training church and other choirs involved in the Nation Building Massed Choir Festivals. Diliza is responsible for his father's estate and has worked closely with the interviewer on compiling the worklist, biographical documentation, and other matters crucial to this volume. This Zoom interview took place on June 25, 2020, during the Covid-19 pandemic and at a time when South Africa was in lockdown. It was prior to the passing of Diliza's parents in June 2021.

Interview

Thomas Pooley (TP): The purpose of this interview is to discuss your recollections of your father, Professor Mzilikazi Khumalo, his life, his music, and to reflect on your unique perspectives as his son. We've discussed this before informally and I've read the essay you presented at the 2018 symposium which I really enjoyed. Getting a sense of his personality will, I think, be interesting for readers of the book. So, let's begin at the beginning: what do you remember of your grandparents?

Diliza Khumalo (DK): They were Salvation Army officers. My grandfather died, I was probably about ten years old. He was twenty years older than my grandmother; much, much older. He was a huge man, very strong, and even at that time I remember he used to walk us to the bus stop. When he died he was ninety-five!

TP: Was he living in Soweto?

DK: No, he was living at the time in KwaHlabisa in Zululand. So when I got to know him he was quite an old man, and what I got to know is that he was very strict. He wasn't just strict, he was very strict. There are quite a lot of stories about his strictness. He would be in church, and he taught his children how to play brass instruments and how to read music. And so, they say he would be at the pulpit there and somebody makes a mistake; and he would walk slowly down there, hit him or her on their head and say, "you're singing wrong!" "uyabimba!" And then he'd walk back to the pulpit and he used to do that right in church. So, he was a disciplinarian. And one of the things about him, my Dad's first composition was actually about his father. His very, very first composition as a boy because the grandfather used to wake up very early, and while they were sleeping he would shout at them and say, "bafana, balalelukwenza ngizomphoqoza amakhanda!" (Boys, why are you sleeping at this time, I am going to hit your heads!) That's the type of thing he used to say. "Ba-fan', ba-fan' balalelukwenza ngizomphoqoza amakhanda!" Hahaha.

So, that's basically the part that I remember of the old man. I remember that he was very protective of us as kids. When we'd been up to our tricks and Mom had given us a little bit. Yo, my Mum would get into very serious trouble because nobody was allowed to touch us in his place, not even in his presence, in his place. We were very safe. But my sister Busisiwe knew him more because she stayed a couple of years with them, she grew up actually with Grandad and Grandma. And then Grandma I know a lot about. She was a very streetwise old lady. Very smart. And she was a singer, too, and she seems to be, my Dad usually said he took his singing talent from her. She was a soprano. She was also a Salvation Army officer. She was so smart she ended up going to England with them, and to Israel. She raised most of us, and that's a lot of us. Because she had nine kids of her own. I think it was three boys and six girls. And the last two were twins. One of the things that my Dad used to speak about—he loved his Mum so dearly—he said that the priests in the Salvation Army were very poor. They were not really given a fair salary or something like that. It was a life of poverty and at one time my Dad did not have pants for school. And she took her skirt and cut it up and sew it up as pants for him to go to school. He always spoke about that, he never forgot what his Mum had done for him.

TP: It must have been very tough with nine children and little salary.

DK: Basically Salvation Army was very small salary for officers.

TP: What did they do in the Salvation Army?

DK: The priests supplemented with whatever you got from the congregation. It was so little that even I at some point was considering the idea of being a priest. I thought about this, and I said no ways. I love God, but I don't love poverty! So, it was quite difficult. The other thing is that they moved. Every year the priests don't know where they're going to be. They are told this year you go there. Sometimes they stay three years, sometimes five years, sometimes one year and then you're moved again. And so he moved a lot. And so one of the things about my Dad is that he spoke quite a lot of languages. You know he speaks Zulu very fluently, he speaks Sotho very fluently, and he speaks Venda very fluently. What happened is that at the time when he was doing standards five and six, I think, they were posted in Venda and he went with his Dad there. And he did his standard six in Venda because we used to, at the time, you studied in your mother tongue. And he did it in Venda, and I think he got a first class, if I'm not exaggerating. I think that's what he told me. So ya, he moved around a lot, he spent quite some time at Western township. There was a time when they were at Western. There was a Salvation Army congregation there. In fact, he even took us to see the buildings. We were still boys and the buildings were still there. I doubt if they are still there now.

TP: So Hlabisa was later?

DK: Yes, Hlabisa was his last post. My grandfather's last post. What he did then is he asked for land from the chief. And he was given some land and he established his home there. That's where we go. When we are taking our trip back home we travel to Hlabisa because that's where he died, and Grandma also was there. Right now, we have my uncle's children are living there in that province now. But that's where we consider that we come from. Our family, when we think of going home, we think of going to Hlabisa.

At first, we went by train and bus. We got onto a train here at Park station and it took us to Glencoe station around 12ish at night, and we had to wait for 4 o'clock for a train that would take us from Glencoe to Vryheid. And then we had to wait for a bus from Vryheid to Nongoma. And then we get off that bus and we get onto another bus to Hlabisa. And then when he started working at Wits he got his first car. And from then on we drove to Hlabisa. But it was a pilgrimage. Every Christmas we used to spend a week or two there. We learnt the language, that's the first thing, because the language is deeper that side. We also learnt ukulusa, herding cattle.

I remember that there was nowhere we went that my Dad didn't have his briefcase. I knew if we were going somewhere I was the one who was supposed to collect it from the dining room, you know. Because he used the dining room table to work. And I'd pick it up and take it to the car. We would visit.

Even when we were going to Everton where my maternal grandmother used to live he would sit and talk and chat for about an hour and then he would say, "Diliza, bring my bag." And I'd fetch his bag and he'd find a corner somewhere and work for about two hours. And then he'd come back and join the family. But it was guaranteed that everywhere we went, and I'm remembering in Zululand, right, in Zululand, we'd be there for about a week, and he would be having his briefcase; and from time to time he gets into a corner and he does his studies.

TP: So was this his linguistics work?

DK: Yes, that was his linguistics work, most of it.

TP: Would he not take his music compositions with him?

DK: You know the music compositions were more when we were much older. Originally, with music he composed when he was much younger, like "Kwadendani," "UGqozi," the first batch of compositions we were very young when he composed them. But when he got involved with linguistics, and particularly when he was studying his masters and his doctorate he was really concentrating on that.

And then, I think we were in Rockville when, because we were not actually attending church before 1972. Somewhere around 1973 he went back to church because we were now near to the White City Salvation Army Church. And that's when his music career changed direction and he now became the songster leader of Piet Memorial Church. And now it took shape. And most of what he did during that time was arrangements. He would arrange hymns, he would arrange traditional songs, and it gave him the opportunity to go to England for the first time. So the Salvation Army headquarters in England invited the choir, and so he took the choir, and some of the arrangements were made at that time in preparation for that trip. You know, that's one of the things that sort of pushed him to make more arrangements.

When I was in second year university, I did the analysis of his music. And when I came back I told him, "hey, I'm doing the analysis of your music," and bla bla bla, and he said, "ok, and what did you find out?" And I was very callous in the way that I spoke, and I said, "well my final decision is that yes, this piece is African music, because of this ostinato there, you've got the rhythms more than anything, but the rest of it the white man could write it." And I don't think that sat very well with him. So then he said, "what is it that is not African?" And I said, "well, the harmonies, the melodies, they are all diatonic, and therefore that's the major thing." And then he went and taught himself about African melodies and harmonies. I started hearing him. He went to his university, and there was this professor of African music [Andrew Tracey from Rhodes].

But he went and had a chat with that guy and he agreed that he would teach him about the African scales. So, he started going into the pentatonic scale more than any of the others. And he would come back to me and say, you know, in the Zulus, yes, they use the pentatonic scale in this way and that way, and you know he really got into pentatonic melodies. And so his shift was in making sure that the melodies become African. And that's where he started having that shift. And that was followed by the first song that came out of that which was "Izibongo ZikaShaka." So the song came out first on its own. And then after he had conceived that song and it was full, then he had the idea of the whole picture. So, you see in *UShaka KaSenzangakhona* he just used "Izibongo ZikaShaka," the praise songs of Shaka, which are available. *UShaka* we basically know them, we learnt them at school when we were growing up.

[Later], he was reading and there's a book by Professor Msimang that had been given to him by Nonhlanhla, his last born: *IZulu Eladuma Esandlawana*. It's the history of what happened at iSandlawana. So he read that book, he loved it, and then he contacted Professor Msimang. He looked for him until he found him. And that's when they got into this deal: "you write praise songs for me, the lyrics for me, and I will then set them to music." And that's the coordination the two of them started working from that time.

TP: How did Khabi Mngoma influence your Dad? He must have taught you at UniZulu?

DK: He taught me music, period. From childhood. They were friends. I don't really know exactly how they met. But I guess they met because Khabi Mngoma used to have the Ionian Orchestra and the Ionian Choir. And my Dad used to be a conductor of teachers' choirs. It was a standard thing that every area had a teachers' choir. And so there were competitions in between the areas, the different areas. And they were called TUATA: Transvaal United African Teachers' Association.

I actually remember the first time I saw Khabi Mngoma I was very young. Funny, I do remember. Probably was about six or seven because we had a very small house in Brakpan. It was actually a three-roomed house that he extended with corrugated iron. There was a system that they used to put in corrugated iron and line the inner side with ceiling boards and what not. And then you'd have extra rooms because of that. And I was sleeping in the room that was next to the lounge, dining-room. It was one thing. And that's where the piano was. And at that time he was still drinking. And so I have a very clear memory of myself waking up at night, in the middle of the night, and hearing music. There was a piano, there was a violin, and there were other people singing. So, I got quietly out of my room and sat next to the door, and just said absolutely nothing, and for about an hour they didn't realize I was there. [*Laughing.*] And I sat and listened. And what were they doing? They had a score on the piano and there was a colored guy. I've forgotten what his real name was, in fact I've never really known. But because of the Group Areas Act he was not actually allowed to be in the townships. So, he had an assumed name. They used to call him Dlamini, I think. They gave him an African name, but he was colored. [*Laughing.*] And he traveled with them wherever they went. So Khabi Mngoma was on the piano, and Dlamini was playing the violin, and the other guys were singing. I don't remember the actual music, but it was something that they were reading from the score. All of them. And I loved it.

And then this relationship between him, and me and my Dad grew because then he bought a hifi system. Do you remember the hifi where you could stack LPs? And then one would fall and then the other one would fall? So he bought that hifi system and I sort of learnt how to operate it and I was still very young. I couldn't read very well, but he would just say to me, look for an album it's got this picture on it. And it's this name. I knew words like Beethoven, Mozart, you know, a few of them. But he would give me instruction, he would say look for this particular one it's like this. At that time my Dad was buying LPs every month. There was this deal that you buy three, and each time when you buy you get a slip. And when you take three then you get one extra. And so he had quite a collection, you know. We used to listen to a lot of classical music at my home. When I grew up I got interested in the violin. I started playing violin. So I was listening to people like Jascha Heifetz, and I've listened to quite a lot of these maestros. So, part of our relationship it sort of grew because I now became his DJ of the time. [*Laughing.*] And it got to the point where he was would just say, just put in anything that you would like to put.

TP: And which composers did he enjoy most?

DK: Handel, Mozart, Bach.

TP: Your father went to Wits in 1969. How did that come about? From being a teacher how did he end up at the university?

DK: He was not employed as a lecturer at first. He was employed as what did they call it?

TP: I think it was as a tutor or language assistant. The universities weren't supposed to employ Blacks as lecturers.

DK: I've never heard him tell the story of how he moved from one to the other, but he was school principal at Mamelong Nqabeni Secondary School in Brakpan old location when he got the appointment at Wits.

TP: Because he was very successful as a teacher and principal. So he must have realized that this was an important opportunity.

DK: Yes. So, it actually caused us a lot of problems his shift to Wits. Because in 1970 he was summoned to the council offices. The superintendent said to him, "Mr Khumalo, I hear you have a promotion now, you're no longer working here in Brakpan, you're now working at the university in Johannesburg." He said, "ya, no, that's true." He said, "Congratulations Mr Khumalo. Where's your permit?" He had to have a permit. And so he takes it out and they tore it up. And they said to him, "Mr Khumalo, you'll have to find a place in Johannesburg because now you work in Johannesburg. You can't stay here." And I think he was given three months and he scrambled for us to get a house in Emndeni, Soweto. That's the first house we got in Soweto. I was nine years old. That must have been 1970. It was a new location at the time. We stayed there for a year. And he scrambled again and found a house in Rockville where he could buy sectional something something. And it was slightly bigger houses and they had electricity.

TP: How did he get to work, then?

DK: He was driving by then. He used the train at first, when we were in Brakpan, because he didn't have a car at the time. He used the train to Wits. And then, after a couple of months, then he bought his first car. But that reminds me that actually we didn't start music in Soweto, we actually started music while we were still living in Brakpan. Because he introduced us, he took us to Dorkay House to learn piano because we had a piano at home. That's where we first met Khabi Mngoma. He was called Chief because he looked like Chief Mangosuthu Buthelezi, and they were close friends. But somehow because we were very young, they didn't give a lot of attention to us. But we got to know a few things about piano and played a few songs and that type of thing. We used to travel the three of us: Busisiwe, myself and Themba. We'd get onto the train on our own and get off at Park Station and walk down Eloff street all the way to Dorkay House, and spend the whole day there, and walk back to the station, get onto a train, get off at Brakpan station, get into a bus, go home. Now we did that for quite a while. That's the introduction to music that I had.

TP: Did your Dad play the piano?

DK: Ya, he could play the piano. But he learnt enough for him to understand chords, melodies, and harmonies. He used it mostly for harmonies. So when he's writing he will play whatever sound that he is thinking. I've never really heard him play a full song, but most of the time it was just he would use it to develop his songs.

TP: The 1970s was politically a very tough time in South Africa. What was it like at Wits as a Black member of staff?

DK: No, I was still very young and so I didn't get to really know what was going on, or even the sense. We were just happy that he was working in a multi-story building and he had his own office. [*Laughing.*] And so, each time when we went to his office we knew we would get fast food. Wow, that was perfect! Haha [*Chuckling.*]

TP: When he did his honors at Unisa it was on Vilakazi, that was in 1972, 1973.

DK: I remember that he had to apply to be accepted as a student at Wits.

TP: As a Black student?

DK: Yes, he couldn't be accepted just like that. He had to apply for permission. At the time you applied from the Minister [of Bantu Affairs] to get permission to be a student at Wits. So, it was quite ironic because what he was talking about was that "I work at Wits but I have to apply from the Minister in order to be able to study at Wits."

TP: The contradictions of apartheid. He said in one of his interviews that he wanted to study at university but the only university was Fort Hare and it was too expensive, so he ended up going first to the Bantu Normal College, as it was called, in Pretoria, and then transferred to Unisa. Because Unisa was at that time a distance learning institution and you could still enroll as a Black student. But with the residential universities it was virtually impossible, especially if you didn't have money.

DK: But you see quite a lot of that stuff happened when we were still very, very young. And quite a lot of the time I couldn't distinguish between his studying and his work because he's the type of person who worked at home almost every day. He is the person who woke up at 4 in the morning almost every day to work, and when he shifted, and stopped working at Wits, then he went to music and would wake up at 4 and start composing his music. He used to say that the ancestors speak to him at that time and they give him melodies at that time. [*Chuckling.*]

TP: So, it was when he retired from Wits that he started focusing on composition?

DK: Yes. He's always been a 4 o'clock person. Half past three, 4.

TP: Now tell me, you were talking about sacrifice earlier. When he talks about the ancestors, what role does that play in his life?

DK: OK, my grandfather is original, original Black. From the rural villages. With the wars and all that they eventually had to go and work. What he did is, he went and he worked in Joburg or Transvaal area and then I think his sister got seriously ill and was about to die. And my grandfather said to the priest, or whoever, he said. "If God can save my sister, then I will follow." And somehow the sister got saved and that's how he became a priest. Now, his belief system prior to that was the African belief system of ancestors, of following tradition, culture and all that. So now he picked up Jesus Christ as his savior. But he did not drop the ancestors. So, he was priest in church but when he was home he made sacrifices, he slaughtered cattle. He followed the tradition of speaking to ancestors and he used African herbs and the like. So, when I got to hear from my father he would always say to us, "I believe in Jesus Christ, and I believe that my ancestors still are there for *me* and I can communicate with them." That's what I picked up from my father. That's what he used to say. So, coming from my grandfather there was this dual practice of spirituality: Christianity and African tradition. It also made sure that he became part of the people in Zululand, because that's what was practiced in the culture of the area. And so he became part of it in that way. So my Dad picked up the two. And he also is Christian, but he never let go of believing that ancestors are connected with him, and that he didn't do it to the extent that it was done by his father and other people. But we did slaughter sheep and goats, and that type of thing. And particularly when we were in Zululand he honored the practices that were done there.

TP: He didn't become Shembe. He remained within his own denomination while still practicing those rituals.

DK: Yes, he didn't go and step into Shembe and the likes. It's like he used to say, "I'm a Christian but I know my origins." I know where I come from.

TP: If I could just go back to *UShaka*. It is said that Msimang and your father wanted this work to be a form of reconciliation for Zulu people with what happened to Shaka. Is that the vision he had?

DK: I agree with that notion because if you remember, the last words of *UShaka* were: "Angeke nilibuse," which means, "You will never reign, it will be taken over by the swallows." It is understood that he was referring to white people, and that they would come and take over the country. And so, he believed strongly that that's the curse on the Black man that really resulted in us not getting our freedom. And he felt that in order for us to be free there is a need to appease uShaka and the other ancestors. And in a big way he really was pleading with uShaka to change that. I've heard him refer to that. The person that really hooked up to that idea is Sibongile Khumalo. I've also heard her talk about it. . . . My father used to talk a lot about the anger of the ancestors. He used to say they are very, very wrathful, and when they are angry they will mess things up for you. And so [*Laughing.*] it was a way for the ancestors to say please, forgive us as a nation so that we can move forward.

TP: So that's an understanding of Zulu history, then. So as a Zulu nation how do we come to terms with this?

DK: Yes, how do we move forward from this. Because we are carrying this burden which was left by an angry king who actually started the Zulu nation. Because there were tribes and Shaka put them together into a nation.

TP: It's interesting that the opera *Princess Magogo* also has a royal theme. So, I take it that he thought of the royal line as a legitimate and important aspect of Zulu identity?

DK: Yes, he had great respect for royalty. He had gone to Chief Buthelezi's place and they gave him a sheep. So they give you a live sheep and you decide if they slaughter it for you, or you take it live with you. And that whole package he related it with such awe, reverence. He loved I think the traditional way of people, of the Zulu people. He really loved that.

TP: Back to *Princess Magogo*: what I've noticed from my own experience is that some of the songs are familiar to me from my fieldwork in KwaZulu-Natal, especially *amahubo* [anthems], and so I think that your father must have drawn a lot on his experiences at Hlabisa, or songs that he learnt in childhood. What do you think about that?

DK: I think he got them much later in life. I think he used recordings to write *amahubo* and such things. You see, he never really lived in Hlabisa because he was already working in Joburg, in the Transvaal. And when they lived in Vryheid he was still very young. So it was Vryheid, then Venda, then from Venda he was this side. So his teenage years, and young adult years were all here in the Transvaal. So, I think he researched them and got recordings, and he worked from there. And that's how he came up with it.

TP: So, he had LP records of some of these songs?

DK: Yes, like Princess Magogo's songs, quite a lot of it you'd get at SABC music archives.

TP: Yes, and the International Library of African Music. [. . .] Now, in later years he worked at SAMRO. That was after he became emeritus professor in the late 1990s. Do you recall what he did there?

DK: The one thing that I always found him working on was the bursaries. That was a big one. He would spend hours sitting on selecting who gets, who doesn't, type of thing. So I think he was a chairperson of one of the committees that did that. The second thing that he did was they were compiling books for his music.

TP: This one? [*Holds up* South Africa Sings, Volume 1, *published by SAMRO*].

DK: [*Nods.*] And then, he was, what position was he occupying. Was it not deputy chair? So he chaired meetings when the chairperson was not around. He had an office at SAMRO once he'd got out of Wits. So it's like he'd wake up every morning and go to this office. And interestingly, even after they retired him he still had an office.

TP: When did he start with the SAMRO scores? I think it actually started a long time before this with the Nation Building Massed Choir Festivals.

DK: Yes, because it's got something to do with Nation Building. Because with Nation Building he made a lot of his traditional arrangements because when they were selecting music for the year he would then find some traditional song and then arrange it specifically for the national choir festival. So quite a lot of those traditional arrangements were done specifically for that. And I think that's how they started getting into the SAMRO Collection.

TP: Because I think with the choir festival they had their own scores that they used to sing from. Were you involved in that at all?

DK: All the way! [*Laughing.*] You see, I was the reluctant assistant of my Dad in the church choir. And this is a story. My problem was drinking, ok, and so that kept me away from church. And so one time he comes to me and he says [in high-pitched voice, imitating his father], "you know Diliza I have a problem. I have a problem, you know my basses are not coming to practice, but it's because they know how to learn music quickly, and the ladies struggle because then they don't know how the basses are singing." And we were doing what, er, a Handel song, I don't remember what the song was. But it had a lot of melisma. And so there was a need for the other parts to hear the bass line so that they can connect with the others. So he said, "please man, come and join me, until the ladies are able to get it." "Er, ok, I'll do that." And so I started going to practice. And it's very interesting when you're working with him. You're the only bass and you've got the ladies, and maybe one or two tenors. And if you make a mistake, he says, "Basses, what's going on with the basses?" And you are alone! [*Laughing.*] And so, I learnt the song but there were several songs to be learnt. I learnt the songs. And like he had said, a few weeks before the performance the basses came and within a few sessions they had the music because they were playing in the band. Because they all could read and they could read very quickly, but because of the entries and all that they struggled. And so I became the key person to help them with that.

And so, once we had done that whole thing and the basses knew the music, so my expectation was the job is done, I'd helped him with what he'd asked me to do. And so, two days before the performance he calls me to his bedroom. So, I go over there and on the bed is a Salvation Army uniform. He says, "Why don't you try that, I think that will suit you." I said, "Wo wo wo, for what now?" He says to me, "Well those basses don't know it enough to do all the entries. You have to be there to lead them." [*Laughing.*] So, reluctantly I got into it and it was an exact fit. It was his old one. And it was an exact fit. And so that's how I did the first performance. And from then on I was expected to be there. And it was difficult to avoid going to practice because I lived with him at the time. [*Laughing.*] And so that's how I got in. And later on, when he was not able to go to practice on that particular day he would then ask me, can you take them through this and it's this area that I want you to do. Because basically there wasn't anybody who could help with the complex music that we chose. But I knew how to read music, I knew how to take the choir with me and teach them. And in fact one time he says to me, "You know, the choir says you actually teach them better than I do!" [*Laughing.*]

TP: Well, you have a degree in music. You had an advantage, I suppose!

DK: Ya, so that's basically how I got into the choir. So, I ended up assisting him from time to time. But each time when he spoke about me taking the official position of being assistant songster leader, then I said no we are not going there at all. And so I became unofficial assistant. [*Laughing.*] So, when the choir festivals started I was in the choir, I was unofficial assistant at that time. And so, I started working.... He would get the music early for us and he would say, we need to know the music so that we lead the other choirs. So we would learn all the music and know all the music. And when we know all the music, and it was quite a lot of complex music like Mendelssohn, and Mozart, and then what he would do is we would then call regional rehearsals. Like the Soweto rehearsal, and the Daveyton rehearsal. Different areas, like Pretoria rehearsal. And he would call all the other choirs to come in. Because most of them were quite good at their own music, and their traditional music, but they struggled with the music which was prescribed for the festival. And so now I started going around with him so that I would just go into the rehearsals and I could lead them. And so like I tell you, I was there for the first ten years of the festival, every performance, even though, at that time like I say, I would work very hard.

I was part of that whole process and I was working with my Dad, training the Soweto Songsters, and then the Songsters would then join the other choirs at the other festivals and help them, and I would be at the performances too. And I also got to know, in later years, I got to know Aggrey Klaaste, too. And I really got to know him quite close.

TP: Was it his idea to start with?

DK: Yes, it was him and his friend (see Richard Cock, Chapter 4). There was another journalist friend of his. They were the two who came up with this idea. And I do know that quite a lot of his other friends were totally against this. Because everybody said, the world, the country is burning and you are calling people to come and sing. Ya, so they were totally against that. What's interesting is that later on, I heard them say, he was a visionary because we couldn't see what he could see.

TP: And what did the community think of this when it first started? Was it entirely pro, or did people have mixed feelings.

DK: You see, there was something very wise, I believe, in establishing the choir festival and it was in putting together a *massed* choir. You see the *massed* choir, the goal eventually was it must be more than a 1,000 voices. So already the concert has 1,000 people. OK, and each choir has got a following. And so, if you've got 1,000 people guaranteed you've got people who will come because each person who comes is coming for their own choir. And the culture of choral music was very, very strong during that time. And I think it was strong because it was one of the few things we were allowed to do. There wasn't much interference. That is the first thing. The second thing is that a lot of people were involved in choral music, not only in singing but in listening to it because it's there in the churches. You know, we've got church choir competitions. It's there in the schools, it's there even for the teachers. It's something that involves a lot of people directly. And so, I also noticed that quite a lot of people that would come and listen are choral members of choirs that are not part of it. So they would come and listen. And I had people who would even come to me and say, can't you talk to your Dad and see that they include us into the festival. So that was a very wise strategy, just having those 1,000 voices made sure that there would be a following.

The first year it wasn't that big. But from the second year it really started picking up. And by the tenth year it was really mature. It was a matured performance. It had come into the calendar of choral music of South Africa. And quite a lot of people knew about it. And the other very important thing is that they put together seasoned soloists with up and coming soloists. So, we had people that we knew and we would listen to those; Nomthandazo Solomon and Sibongile Khumalo, we had those people, but then we also had new guys all the time. They would audition new soloists. I remember in one year we had one guy who was a tenor who came from P.E. [Port Elizabeth]. He got onto a plane in order for him to be auditioned. That's how seriously he took this thing. And he got it. And he came there and he wowed the whole hall. When he finished everybody was standing up on their feet. And the following year, or the year after, he actually died. But he had his "wow."

And then there was also another very important thing. The traditional music, that really played a very big part of the show. Because what they would do, and my Dad was the one who conducted the traditional songs, so he would do it with the choir arrangements and everything. But as you know, we Blacks, we know most of our own music, that's one, and if we don't know it we learn it in a very few minutes. And so there would be, "Thina lapha emzini. Thina lapha emzili." The choir would do the arrangement and sing it, and when it comes to the end he wouldn't stop the song. Then he would turn to the audience, and then the audience would then stand up and they would sing. Can you imagine about 6,000 voices, and with the African music we don't sing unison, we harmonize. Everybody knows their own part. It was amazing! You know it would make my hair stand! You know being part of that and listening to that. You know we would do that and sing and sing and sing, and he would come back and wrap it up with the orchestra and the choir. And when the show was finished there would be one traditional song which would be picked up by everybody, and it would be the song that we used to walk out of the show. So it gave you goosebumps. It was amazing.

TP: And was this at the Standard Bank arena?

DK: It was always at the Standard Bank arena.

TP: And did most choirs at that time read tonic sol-fa?

DK: Yes, I guess even now most choirs read tonic sol-fa. But what they would do was they would take the music and they would write it into two ways of writing. They would use staff notation and tonic sol-fa. And I remember, there are many songs that I actually wrote into tonic sol-fa from staff notation. There's quite a lot that I did personally just to help out.

TP: To transcribe.

DK: To transcribe into tonic sol-fa. I did quite a lot for the nation building. I should say, not for nation building—I did it for my Dad. [*Laughing.*]

TP: How did your Dad and Richard Cock divide their duties? Did they both decide on the music together? And with the conducting was Richard doing the orchestra mostly?

DK: You see what they did was this. In fact, it was not only the two of them. Magangane became part of it. Who else? You see what they did was they took the senior conductors from the different areas, a few of them. Magangane was one of them. I think there were two others. And what they did was, the bulk of European music would be conducted by Richard Cock. The bulk of the African music would be conducted by my Dad, and then they would give these other conductors maybe one song each. But that's basically how they divided it.

TP: And what about the Gauteng Choristers?

DK: OK, Gauteng Choristers was very close to my Dad. This young man, Sidwell Mhlongo. Sidwell, I actually knew Sidwell when he was a young boy. I was actually teaching and living in Kagiso because he comes from Kagiso. And he used to continue to help his teacher at the Mosupatsela High School. So he was like my Dad, the singer-conductor. So, he worked with his teacher and at some point they invited me to come and help them with one of Baba's songs and I taught them how he conducted the music. And it was Khosa who adjudicated on that particular day and he was horrified at how they sang the particular song. The African way. And they lost, and they were quite upset with me. [*Laughing at length.*]

TP: Was it SJ Khosa?

DK: Yes, the composer. Because SJ Khosa was the [adjudicator] [*singing, high pitched*, by way of illustration], "da ti di da da de." Because my Dad introduced these sliding tones, ja. So I was teaching them to use that. And so, he was horrified [to hear this].... "But you taught us this!" But that's how the composer sings the song. You know I had to explain that some people don't understand what he is doing, and that's what happened. But then that's my introduction to Sidwell. And then at some point I remember I wanted to organize that Sidwell meet with my Dad, and I discovered that they were already working together. [*Laughing.*]

I'm not sure how they really got going together. But what I know is that at some point Sidwell's choir became the main choir that was now performing my Dad's music, and so he would go to give them tips on how he wanted the music done, and all that.

TP: But your Dad seems to be the only composer who uses these slides, these glides?

DK: Yes. You see, he started introducing the glides when he got into the new scales, the old scales I should say, pentatonic, ya. He said, "True Zulu music has glides." And basically that's how we sing. And he said, if you remove those glides then it becomes European music. His attempt was at being as authentic as possible.

TP: Themba Msimang told me how your Dad tried to get him [Msimang] to record himself speaking or declaiming the words so that he could get the glides correct.

DK: Yes, that's also the influence of him studying tonology. You know, after he had studied tonology he was horrified if you set your music to an opposite tone to the one when we speak. If the tone is ye—bo [*glide up then down*], then the music is supposed to move dai-da [*imitating tone*], and if you take it down and say, "Where does he come from? People don't speak like that." And my Dad can be quite rigid. When he believes in something, that's it. There is no gray. It's either black or white. And so he was very, very strict on that one.

TP: When you think of your Dad's compositions do you think that the bulk of the work is *UShaka* and *Princess Magogo*. Or do you think that there are other songs that are as important? Where does the emphasis lie?

DK: I think it's in three phases. Phase 1 is his earlier music which was influenced a lot by hymns. The combination of hymns and traditional music because he would have these hymnal sections and then the traditional. [*Singing: bass voice*] "Siyagi-ya, siya giya, esiqethu, giya," you know that kind of thing. So it was divided into two so you could distinctly see this is European music, and then on the other side you see the African, [*high pitched falsetto*] "Akukhom' lungu, akukhom' basi—zi la da da." That's pure European. But then "ziya giya, gi-ya," that's, so you know, his first music, "UGqozi," "Lala Nokuthula," "Emasangeni," you know, again, you see the two parts being brought together. That I believe is phase 1. Then in the middle you have the bulk of his arrangements. There's a lot of his African arrangements. And he also has, you know the choral arrangements were for church. He also did that. If he was going to do a hymn for church he would change words, change harmonies and do that. So, there's that music too. So there's a phase when he made a lot of arrangements. So the third phase would be when he started with *UShaka* where his tones, tonality changed, you had the glides, you have the very strong emphasis on following traditional music. And that forms the third part of his compositions. And in that you find *UShaka KaSenzangakhona* and you also find *Princess Magogo*.

TP: And after he finished *Princess Magogo* did he continue composing? Because he finished it in about 2002.

DK: Mostly it was arrangements, I think. I don't remember any major work after that.

TP: Ya, because I think it was a very intense process as well.

DK: Ya, and also there was a lot traveling. So he was now involved in taking *Princess Magogo* around the world. And after *Princess Magogo* he traveled with *UShaka KaSenzangakhona*.

TP: And do you remember when he was involved with the National Anthem committee?

DK: A little bit. Everything I was sort of involved. [*Laughing*.] Because they would go and have their discussions and he would come back, do some writing, and then we would have to sing it. In fact, I remember one time, I think it's the last version of the national anthem, putting the two together. I believe it must be the last version. He came with it at home, and he said, I want to hear what this is sounding like, and Busi pitched up, and I pitched up, they were here in Kagiso already by that time. And so it was myself, bass, Busi soprano, Mum alto, and my Dad sang tenor. In fact, if I'm not mistaken he recorded it on the tapes. And so we had our copies and we were singing, "Nkosi Sikelel' iAfrika," and blab bla bla, and as we were going on, the cat, we had a cat, kitty, jumped onto the table and also, "meawu, meauw," and we also just burst out laughing and stopped singing! [*Laughing*.]

TP: That's a musical family! [*Laughing*.] So your Mom used to go to a lot of his choirs, is that correct?

DK: My Mum was in *every* choir of his except the male choirs. Ya. She once said when he was being honored at the festival, the Nation Building Festival, I can't remember how old he was, but they sort of did it in his honor that year, and my Mum was given a chance to speak. And she said, when she got up there, "well, there are certain things I had to understand about this man. The first thing I had to understand was music is his first love, and I am his second love. [*Laughing.*] And so, if I want to stay with this man the easiest thing is just to love music too." So, she was in every choir.

TP: Thank you, Diliza, for sharing these stories. This has been incredibly helpful and illuminating.

DK: I'm always willing to help.

Interviewer's Note

Diliza Khumalo has been indispensable to the ongoing project of documenting his father's life and works. This interview touches on many important topics of biographical interest that would otherwise have remained within the restricted realms of family history. I am sincerely grateful to Diliza and his family for their collaboration and support.

3

The National Anthem Committee

J. S. Mzilikazi Khumalo

The multiparty negotiating process that commenced in April 1993 produced South Africa's Interim Constitution. Professor Elize Botha was appointed chairman of the Commission on National Symbols by the Multi-Party Negotiating Council. This council invited the public to submit compositions for a new national anthem. Professors Musa Xulu and Mzilikazi Khumalo were part of the subcommittee appointed to oversee the submission process. They received more than 200 proposed anthems, none of which were considered suitable. The main reason was that these submissions would be easy for choirs to sing but not for the general public.

The subcommittee then suggested that "Die Stem van Suid Afrika" and "Nkosi Sikelel' iAfrika" be sung together as one national anthem. The Negotiating Council accepted this proposal, and from 1994, the combined compositions became the new national anthem. This was done under the provisions of the proclamation by the then president on April 20, 1994, in Section 248 (1) together with Section 2 of the Constitution of the Republic of South Africa, 1993 (Act 200 of 1993).

The new anthem was too long. Dr. Ben Ngubane, the then Minister of Arts, Culture, Science and Technology, was subsequently mandated by cabinet to convene a committee which would shorten the combined anthem.

Members of this committee were Ms. Anna Bender, Professor Elize Botha, Mr. Richard Cock, Professor Mzilikazi Khumalo (chairman), Professor Mazisi Kunene, Professor John Lenake, Professor Fatima Meer, Professor Khabi Mngoma, Dr. Wally Serote, Professor Johan de Villiers, and Dr. Jeanne Zaidel-Rudolph. The secretary of this committee—the Anthem Committee—was Mr. Dolph Havemann from the Directorate of Arts and Culture.

The Anthem Committee started on its task on February 10, 1995. Dr. Ngubane welcomed the committee with the following words: "We must take the precious heritage of our people and use this as a cornerstone to build our common future and destiny."

The committee first had to attend to the length of the combined anthems. After studying twenty-seven national anthems, the committee realized that the average duration of each anthem was 1 minute 47 seconds. The Swiss anthem was the longest in this group—2 minutes 40 seconds. The combined South African anthem was 5 minutes 4 seconds.

To start the shortening process, the committee first removed all repetitions. A further suggestion was that sections whose lyrics would not be accepted by certain sections of the community should also be left out.

The first section to be cut was "Makube njalo," an ending of certain hymns in African churches, because it was neither part of "Nkosi Sikelel' iAfrika" nor "Morena Boloka Setjhaba Sa Heso."

"Woza Moya" bore reference to the Holy Spirit in the Christian religion and was therefore removed. The Council of Muslim Theologians felt that by singing it they would be violating their Creed (Kalema). This would be in defiance of monotheism, which is the oneness of Allah.

Repetitions in "Nkosi Sikelel' iAfrika" and "Morena Boloka Setjhaba Sa Heso" were removed—as indicated above. This was the resultant new "Nkosi Sikelel' iAfrika":

Nkosi Sikelel' iAfrika	Lord bless Africa
Maluphakanyisw'uphondo lwayo	Let its horn be raised
Yizwa imithandazo yethu	Hear our prayers
Nkosi sikelela thina lusapho lwayo	Lord bless us her offspring
Morena boloka setjhaba sa heso	Lord bless our nation
Ofedise dintwa le matshwenyeho	Let there be no strife and hardships
O seboloke	Preserve it,
O seboloke setjhaba sa heso	Preserve it, our nation
Setjhaba sa South Africa	The South African nation

The last line of the Southern Sotho section used to have "sa heso" or "sa Africa." The committee removed these words and replaced them with "sa South Africa" to dilute the Pan-African flavor of "Nkosi Sikelel' iAfrika." "Sa South Africa" would have a direct reference to the South African nation as opposed to "setjhaba sa heso" (our nation) or "setjhaba sa Afrika" (the African nation).

The lyrics of "Die Stem van Suid Afrika" had twelve lines:

Uit die blou van onse hemel
Uit die diepte van ons see
Oor ons ewige gebergtes
Waar die kranse antwoord gee,
Oor ons ver-verlate vlaktes
Met die kreun van ossewa
Ruis die stem van ons geliefde,
Van ons land Suid Afrika.
Ons sal antwoord op jou roepstem,
Ons sal offer wat jy vra
Ons sal lewe, ons sal sterwe
Ons vir jou Suid Afrika.

Because some sections in "Nkosi Sikelel' iAfrika" and "Morena Boloka Setjhaba Sa Heso" had been left out, the same had to be done in "Die Stem van Suid Afrika." The lyrics that bore reference to the Great Trek (Met die kreun van ossewa) had to be omitted. So, the four lines starting with "Oor ons ver-verlate vlaktes" were left out because they represented only one section of the community. To be inclusive of the English speakers in the community, the committee suggested that lines 9, 10, 11, and 12 should be in English. A member of the committee—Dr. Jeanne Zaidel-Rudolph—was asked to compose new English words in the place of the last four lines of "Die Stem van Suid Afrika." The following are the words that she proposed:

We can hear the land rejoicing,
With a voice not heard before
Let the people of our country
Live in peace forever more.

The Anthem Committee then had to decide on which should come first—"Die Stem van Suid Afrika" or "Nkosi Sikelel' iAfrika." The committee decided on starting with "Nkosi Sikelel' iAfrika" followed by "Die Stem van Suid Afrika." The reason was purely musical—the committee felt that "Die Stem van Suid Afrika" had a climactic ending.

The key for the original hymn "Nkosi Sikelel' iAfrika" was in B flat major but it was always sung in G major. "Die Stem van Suid Afrika" was composed in E flat major but was generally sung in D major. The committee felt that B flat major and E flat major were a bit high for communal singing and decided on G major and D major instead. This then required a musical "bridge" between the two keys. This was made possible by adding a bar where each syllable of "South Africa" would be sung to the note A, which is a supertonic in G major and a dominant in D major.

Doctor (now professor) Jeanne Zaidel-Rudolph was requested to provide the orchestration for the new anthem.

Submissions by the Anthem Committee

On April 4, 1995, the chairman and secretary of the Anthem Committee submitted the shortened choral version of the anthem to the cabinet. The cabinet was pleased with the result but requested more work on the English words. They wanted the words to encourage people to work toward nation-building, instead of merely capturing the prevailing joyous mood in the country at the time.

The shortened anthem with the initial English words was premiered on May 7, 1995, at the Cape Town Massed Choir Festival.

The committee reconvened on May 9, 1995. They agreed on the following English words:

> Sounds the call to come together,
> And united we shall stand.
> Let us live and strive for freedom,
> In South Africa, our land.

The revised version of the shortened anthem became:

> Nkosi Sikelel' iAfrika,
> Maluphakanyisw' uphondo lwayo,
> Yizwa imithandazo yethu,
> Nkosi sikelela,
> Thina lusapho lwayo.
>
> Morena boloka setjhaba sa heso
> Ofedise dintwa le matshwenyeho.
> O se boloke, O se boloke,
> Setjhaba sa heso,
> Setjhaba sa South Africa – South Africa.

Uit die blou van onse hemel,
Uit die diepte van ons see,
Oor ons ewige gebergtes
Waar die kranse antwoord gee,
Sounds the call to come together,
And united we shall stand.
Let us live and strive for freedom
In South Africa our land.

Ms. E. M. Hoeksma was tasked with adding tonic sol-fa notation to this choral version of the completed anthem.

The cabinet requested the Anthem Committee to look at other options as well for English words. The committee did as they were asked, even though they all preferred the first four lines of "Die Stem van Suid Afrika" to be in Afrikaans instead of the last four lines. The committee considered the English translation of the first four lines of "Die Stem" by Mr. H. D. Shaper from Cape Town. This version had the following words:

From our blue eternal heavens,
From the depths of our deepest sea.
From our everlasting mountains,
Comes the vow we make to thee!

Ons sal antwoord op jou roepstem,
Ons sal offer wat jy vra.
Ons sal lewe ons sal sterwe,
Ons vir jou Suid Afrika.

While the committee submitted both versions to the public, they recommended that the first version be adopted. At the submission on May 17, 1995, the cabinet accepted the first version.

A parliamentary group called the Theme Committee One held a public hearing on "Seats of Government, Languages, and Names and Symbols" at the Old Assembly Chamber of Parliament on June 10, 1995. The chairman of the Anthem Committee, Professor Mzilikazi Khumalo, was invited to make a submission on the national anthem. The Theme Committee One and members of the public who were in attendance were satisfied with the Anthem Committee's shortened national anthem.

4

Nation Building Massed Choir Festival

Collaboration between Professor J. S. M. Khumalo and Maestro Richard Cock

Richard Cock

Nation-Building means picking up the pieces and rebuilding all structures that have collapsed in our communities. It means striving for the best in all that we do for ourselves and our people. It is the search for the acquisition and control of structures of power required for the survival of a nation. It is creating an efficient leadership and increasing the value and quality of life among all inhabitants of our country.

We have a vision of a future society we want to create for ourselves and our people. Let us therefore set ourselves goals and design objectives and a programme of action that will set the wheels of Nation-Building in motion. Nation-Building is our hope for the future.

These are powerful words by Aggrey Klaaste which appeared in the first program of the Massed Choir Festival, the purpose of which is encapsulated in this statement. The concept was realized in 1989, but of course it had its origins earlier than that.

In 1988, in collaboration with Ludumo Magangane and George Mxadana, I presented a concert titled Partners in Harmony, sponsored by IBM, which featured three choirs: Imilonji kaNtu, Bonisudumo Choristers, and the SABC Choir (as it was then). Circumstance had dictated that Black choirs and white choirs had not previously often sung together in the same space, but in this concert, a white choir joined two Black choirs for a grand concert with an orchestra, and the conducting was shared between the three choirmasters. It was held in the City Hall in Johannesburg and was accompanied by the

Transvaal Chamber Orchestra. One important factor was that this was not a competition because many choir gatherings, even to this day, are competitive. I was never very much in favor of competitions, partly because they engendered such strong feelings of animosity for the "losers" and did not promote sharing. The joy of this concert was that we all went away as "winners," united by our love for music.

At the end of 1988, I had just finished our annual Christmas concert at the City Hall with my choir and the National Orchestra when, after the concert, the General Manager of the Sowetan newspaper, Rory Wilson, approached me. He wanted to talk about a concept which was being developed by the editor of the newspaper, Aggrey Klaaste, called "Nation Building."

Early in 1989, we had a meeting convened by the PR company Sussens Mann. Present at the meeting were Aggrey, Rory, Aubrey Sussens, Peter Mann, and I. Aggrey described his vision of Nation Building, which is summed up in the quote at the beginning of this chapter, stating that he wanted to start a Nation Building Massed Choir Festival. Also at that meeting, he told me that many of the staff of the Sowetan thought he was crazy. The period 1988/89 was a time of unrest in South Africa. Many people were being murdered for their political views. There were frequent strikes in the country, and the staff of the newspaper were opposed to the idea of a choir festival when there were much larger political problems to deal with. Segregation, at its height in the 1960s and 1970s, was by the late 1980s starting to crumble, along with the general fabric of society. Lawlessness was becoming endemic. However, Aggrey was convinced that music would be a great unifier and a way of bringing people together in a neutral context. He had a vision of numerous choirs coming together and singing together with orchestra. Aggrey himself came from a choral music background as his father had been a choir conductor. He understood that South Africa needed to repair the damage which apartheid had wrought on society at large, both white and Black. In fact, Aggrey had a much grander scheme up his sleeve, involving not only music but many other aspects of community work, including teaching, agriculture, health, and community building in general. He told me to talk to "Jimmy" Khumalo, as he then was known. I knew him as Professor James Khumalo. Soon, this became Professor Mzilikazi Khumalo, or Mtungwa, which was his clan name, or Mzilikazi kaMashobane in honor of his illustrious ancestor.

I had met Professor Khumalo, a lecturer in African Languages at Wits University, in the context of a fundraising concert on behalf of his choir, The

Soweto Songsters, who were traveling to Canada. We did this fundraising concert together at the Soweto Teacher Training College in 1987. Our coming together again under the auspices of the Sowetan newspaper was the beginning of a long and fruitful working relationship, which also developed into a deep friendship and mutual admiration.

Sussens Mann appointed Di Sutherland from an events company to develop the concept of the massed choir festival along with "Prof.," as he affectionately became known, and myself. In September 1989, the first iteration of the Sowetan Nation Building Massed Choir Festival was held in the Standard Bank Arena at Ellis Park. Both Prof. and I saw the possibilities of this Massed Choir Festival as starting to bring people together, to unify people, and to recreate those structures that Aggrey was talking about, and which had been destroyed by the apartheid system. From then on, the festival happened annually in spring, which was appropriate because, in many ways, Aggrey's Nation Building signaled the birth of a different type of activism in South Africa.

Indeed, both Prof. and I accepted Aggrey's challenge because both of us knew deep down that what we were doing was important and right.

After much planning, the first festival took place and was an enormous success. We had nineteen Black choirs and one white choir. The orchestra was the Transvaal Chamber Orchestra, which was filling the gap left by the removal of the SABC orchestra to Pretoria to join the PACT orchestra as the National Orchestra. The choirs filled one side of the Standard Bank Arena, and the audience, friends, and families of the choristers filled the other.

I well remember when my Chanticleer Singers, who were 20 strong in a massed choir of 1,000 voices, sang their solo item "Ingoma KaNtsikana" and how the crowd started roaring in appreciation even before we finished the song.

That song was our contribution to the first half of the program, which consisted of twenty items. Each choir had to sing a traditional South African number because preserving a heritage of traditional songs which were being lost in the wake of urbanization was one of our aims. The cultural convention of oral transfer among African choirs, as opposed to written music, meant that the songs were dying with the people who knew them. We hoped to reinvigorate and nurture the knowledge of traditional songs.

The second half of the concert consisted of items sung by the massed choir. There were arrangements of traditional songs, composed South African songs, and pieces from the Western oeuvre. All 1,000 choristers sang together, conducted by both Prof. and me. This was something extraordinary! I remember Prof. telling me of the feeling of power that came from conducting 1,000 singers and the sound that was created. Once we realized that the concept worked, we could then develop an agenda to take us forward.

Sponsors

For the first two years of the festival, the costs were carried by the Sowetan newspaper, but it soon became apparent that we needed a title sponsor. By 1991, Caltex came on board in this role, with the Sowetan as the media partner. Roy Wright, who was the Caltex representative, was a model sponsor. He supported, cajoled, and guided, but left the artistic direction and decisions in the hands of the founders of the festival.

The festival continued to be sponsored by Caltex until 1998. At the 1998 festival, when there was a strike on at Caltex, a representative of one of the strikers' unions was given permission to speak at the festival. He denounced Caltex in no uncertain terms, and the Chief Executive of Caltex at the time, who was present at the concert, decided there and then that they would not continue with their sponsorship.

Fortunately, Transnet came on board the following year; but, as sponsors in the later years of the festival, they became increasingly prescriptive about what should and should not be included in the program, as well as what type of music should be sung, and which soloists should be part of the festival.

While Prof. was on the committee, he resisted any attempts to add "lighter" music and performers to the program, as he always maintained that commercial music could look after itself. Traditional music was the primary focus of the festival, and that is what needed support, both to preserve the music and its integrity, and promote its use in the various communities which we served.

A new element of commercialism entered the dealings of the festival after Transnet came on board, where choirs wanted to be paid for their participation. It was no longer enough just to be part of this amazing celebration of our Nation Building.

Another important sponsorship element was television, particularly for the title sponsor Caltex and subsequently Transnet. This very important addition gave them a much wider exposure. SABC TV filmed the event in 1993, and from 1997, they became partners in the entire production.

Logo

The first logo of the Nation Building Massed Choir Festival was intended to depict the idea of the power being in the hands of the people, and the slogan said exactly that: "The power is in your hands." The logo, showing a hand holding a world displaying the continent of Africa, spoke to Aggrey's vision of picking up pieces and rebuilding, supporting communities, providing leadership for the people, and all the other unifying concepts he had conceived. The logo only appeared on the first three program and music books. Thereafter, the theme and look of the program and books changed to reflect the corporate colors of Caltex as the main sponsor, and, to a lesser extent, the Sowetan. In fact, the front covers of the books changed every two to four years. They changed in 1994, where a more African design was introduced, and then again in 1999 when Transnet replaced Caltex as the main sponsor, and a more music-focused logo was introduced. This logo was modified slightly in 2002, having had the human elements (singers and conductor's hands) removed.

Choirs

We soon decided that the choirs needed to rotate so that more people could take part in the festival. We had a maximum capacity of twenty choirs. We decided that two or three should be rotated out each time and new ones brought in. One of the interesting aspects of so many different choirs taking part was that Prof. and I traveled around the country visiting each of the choirs in turn. It was on these journeys that Prof. and I got to know each other very well. We traveled as far afield as Sebokeng, Mohlakeng, Atteridgeville, Mamelodi, Daveyton, and of course there were many choirs locally in Soweto itself.

We shared experiences and stories of our families, and I heard from him of the indignities that he had suffered under the apartheid system, how he had overcome them, and how positive he was for the future not only of his own family, who were all educated to a very high standard, but also of South Africa, which we both loved so deeply. We realized that with Nation Building, we were playing a small part in the growth and development of a new vision for South Africa.

Visiting the choirs was an enriching experience for both of us, but eventually the task became too big for just the two of us, so we had to appoint regional coordinators who then did that work.

It became a badge of honor to take part in the Massed Choir Festival, and there was never a shortage of choirs from which to choose. From time to time, we also had visiting choirs and some of the more notable of these were Imilonji kaNtu, a choir from Lesotho, a marimba group from Botswana, the St. Vincent's Choir for the Deaf, and the Papaya Choir from Norway who specialized in African songs. I remember Prof. saying that if you shut your eyes, you wouldn't know they were white!

Soloists

The first Massed Choir Festival in 1989 had a quartet of soloists. We soon realized that there was an untapped reservoir of very talented young singers who were potential soloists, and so we expanded our team of soloists to include eight singers, rotating four each year. We held whole-day auditions at the SABC where we would audition up to fifty singers. In the beginning, the auditions were adjudicated by Prof. and myself, but once again the entire process grew beyond our capacity. Slowly we started including external adjudicators to assist with the process. The Sowetan newspaper was incredibly helpful in publicizing the festival itself and the auditions for soloists. It was one of the few times that I made it into a cartoon in a major newspaper.

Potential soloists would often travel long distances to attend auditions and singing at the festival became a very prestigious achievement, particularly once television became involved.

Orchestra

When we started the festival in 1989, the orchestra in residence was the Transvaal Chamber Orchestra. We were able to add other groups to the orchestra to supplement it. Linda Mngoma ran a small group of orchestral musicians in Soweto and brought several players to join the orchestra in the first festival. Among those players was Sibongile Khumalo, Linda's sister, who played the violin. She subsequently sang as a soloist in the concert the following year. In the years that followed, we expanded the orchestra and its membership, including players from the Johannesburg Youth Orchestra, Buskaid Soweto

String Ensemble, and many other ensembles, and eventually the orchestra was renamed the Nation Building Orchestra.

As the years went by, we commissioned new arrangements of traditional African songs for the orchestra, as well as new compositions by local composers. Interestingly, we had arrangements made that could be used both with a choir and without a choir, as just orchestral pieces. These were recorded and released on the Marco Polo label and are played frequently on radio stations around South Africa. These also inspired, in more recent years, the recordings of the music of SJ Khosa in two different formats: orchestra alone and orchestra and choir together.

When the SABC brought its orchestra back from Pretoria in December 1991, that orchestra then became the core of the Nation Building Orchestra and remained so until its demise in 1999 when the Johannesburg Festival Orchestra took over that role.

Music and Notation

We decided from the beginning that all choirs had to have one book of music. Traditionally, Black choirs learned music via tonic sol-fa while white choirs used staff notation. The first Festival music pack had two versions of each song—one in tonic sol-fa and one in staff notation. We realized that this was a rather clumsy way of presenting it, and we soon developed a dual-notation system so that everyone was reading from the same song-sheet literally! Singers could choose which system to use depending on their preference. We hoped that this would develop people's flexibility in reading the two different systems. This notation first appeared in the 1996 music book.

The Massed Choir Festival music books became resources for many choirs who used them for their own purposes. They are still a sought-after resource. The process of dual notation eventually led to the production of several volumes of South African choral music edited by Prof. and published by the Southern African Music Rights Organisation (SAMRO). Much of this material had first appeared at the Massed Choir Festival.

After 1994, when eleven languages in South Africa held equal stature, we decided that we needed to include all eleven languages in the music that was sung. Some of these appeared in the first half of the concert, performed by individual choirs, but we also commissioned arrangements of songs in the less-prevalent languages such as Xitsonga and Tshivenda.

Many local composers were requested to do arrangements or write compositions in the latter years. These included Ludumo Magangane, Phelelani Mnomiya, Mokale Koapeng, Bongani Ndodana-Breen, and Prof. himself. In fact, on our journeys around Gauteng visiting choirs, Prof. used to sing excerpts that he was working on at the time, and it turned out that many of these were the beginnings of movements from *UShaka KaSenzangakhona*, which eventually developed into the musical epic orchestrated by Christopher James and Robert Maxym, and which we recorded in the SABC studios after its first performance. Several movements of it were sung at the Massed Choir Festival before it was completed.

National Anthem

In 1990, we sang the African National Anthem at the Massed Choir Festival—the original version of "Nkosi Sikelel' iAfrika." I have a feeling that according to the laws at the time it was illegal. After 1994, Prof. realized that leading into a new era would mean that we needed a new national anthem, and he had already been turning it over in his mind when he and I were approached to serve on the National Anthem Committee. By the time of the first meeting, I think he had already worked out the structure in his head. One of the committee members (Dr. Jeanne Zaidel-Rudolph) had suggested new wording for the English section which included the line "*Let us live and die for freedom.*" Prof. *strongly* objected to this, saying that there had been enough dying. Similarly, the word "fight" for freedom was also dismissed as being too aggressive. I eventually suggested the word "strive" in place of the word "die," which was accepted by the committee. So, with some changes in the wording, it was a relatively simple process to produce the final version. Prof. pointed out that the text included the four main language groups in South Africa: Nguni, Sotho, English, and Afrikaans. He sang it to the cabinet once it had been finalized by the committee, and I clearly remember him returning after that episode and telling us how cabinet had cheered.

This is the national anthem which we still sing today, and although the attribution is "The National Anthem Committee," structurally it was Prof.'s work (see Khumalo, Chapter 3). The premiere performance was at the Sowetan Nation Building Massed Choir Festival in September 1996, more than a year before it was officially gazetted. From the interest generated using the African

National Anthem and the development of a new National Anthem for South Africa, a committee was established which included Prof. and me, to try to find the grave of the late Enoch Sontonga. We eventually located it in Braamfontein Cemetery. At a ceremony on Heritage Day, September 24, 1996, a monument was unveiled to Enoch Sontonga, and our two choirs sang the various versions of "Nkosi Sikelel' iAfrika" which had developed over the years, including what is now the South African national anthem, along with other traditional African songs. The National Symphony Orchestra and the Buskaid Soweto String Ensemble accompanied the choirs. We were all astonished that at the end of the ceremony at which President Nelson Mandela spoke, he shook the hand of every single person present.

Conductors

Eventually, Prof. and I realized that we could no longer cope with all the rehearsals of the choirs on our own, so we divided the Gauteng area into several regions and appointed regional coordinators. This gave us the opportunity to use them as co-conductors in the main festival event. We were developing a pool of conductors whom we could use to conduct either unaccompanied choral pieces or, in some cases, pieces with choir and orchestra. This was expanded in the years ahead. Some of the people who assisted with the conducting were Ludumo Magangane, Mokale Koapeng, and Danny Pooe. Many of them have gone on to be successful conductors independent of the Massed Choir Festival.

Prof. had no experience of conducting orchestras prior to the festival, and he and I had many very happy shared experiences as I mentored him in the tasks of conducting an orchestra. Eventually, he became quite skilled at this and really seemed to enjoy it. The fact that some of the arrangements we had done were direct transcriptions of choral pieces of course helped, because he conducted the orchestra like a choir. He never really mastered staff notation, but he taught me a lot about tonic sol-fa and about the interesting aspects of traditional African music, and the movements that accompany it. He often laughed at my improvised movements for certain pieces. Very often in the massed choir pieces, he would conduct, and I would "choreograph" and direct the choir in their movements.

Audience Participation

From the very first concert in 1989, we realized that audience participation was a *crucial* element in the success of these concerts, subsequently allowing specifically for audience participation in some songs. In the first half of each program, where the choirs were singing their own traditional numbers, the audience was not allowed to join in. That was for each choir to perform and show what they could do. However, in the second half of each concert, for the massed choir items, the audience knew that they could join in, and many knew the pieces that were chosen due to the strong practice of aural transfer.

For the first few years, Prof. himself did new arrangements of traditional songs, very often combining two or three folk songs into one arrangement—a medley, so to speak. He knew intimately which songs the audience would know well enough to join, and he therefore allowed more repeats than strictly necessary so that they could really get into the music.

These audience participation numbers eventually proved to be the highlight of the festival, especially when we had orchestral accompaniment for them as well. It is not something you can easily imagine, but four thousand people singing lustily and moving as one was truly something to behold. Very often, the favorite song of the afternoon would be sung as people exited the stadium after the concert. This absolutely demonstrated the spirit of unity and Nation Building that we were trying to promote and unleashed the energies that went with it.

Spinoffs

Once the Nation Building Massed Choir Festival had become more established, other centers around South Africa were calling for it to be introduced in their cities. From 1994 to 1998, the Massed Choir Festival happened in Cape Town, where the repertoire was slightly different because we had choirs that sang in Afrikaans. Up to this point, Afrikaans songs had not been included in the festival concerts, but in the Western Cape it seemed appropriate. It gave us the opportunity to use composers from the Western Cape, and to commission a new piece for the festival from Grant MacLachlan, *Laat Ons Hierdie Land Uitbou*, with words by Hein Willemse. Furthermore, it created the opportunity for a new sponsor, as the Sowetan was not so active in Cape Town. From 1997, the

Cape Argus became the media partner in Cape Town (the Sowetan and the Cape Argus were part of the same stable of newspapers). This opened the way for conductors and soloists from the Cape to enjoy the same opportunities as their counterparts in Gauteng. In 1998, an attempt was made to start the festival in KwaZulu-Natal, and although the book of music was printed, the festival never got off the ground. The discontinuation of the Caltex sponsorship subsequently put paid to the festivals in Cape Town and KwaZulu-Natal as Transnet was not interested in continuing the festival in these regions.

However, a smaller festival was started in Limpopo. The Northern Province Massed Choir Festival started in 2000 and continued for three years, supported by Standard Bank, Transnet, and Business and Arts South Africa. For those three years it was very successful. In the third year, it was taken over by the Limpopo provincial government and was never held again.

Starting in 1998, we wanted to make commemorative recordings in CD and cassette format to celebrate ten years of the festival. The SABC provided us with facilities to record free of charge. At that stage, I was in charge of the National Symphony Orchestra, and their services were also given free of charge. We recorded a full CD's worth of music, including highlights from the first ten years.

All of the conducting on the CD was done by Prof. and Ludumo Magangane, and they provided the cover leaflet notes which included background information on all the songs included in the recording. The choirs involved were the Soweto Songsters and the Bonisudumo Choristers. Soloists included Busi Nkosi, Jabulani Simelane, Joyce Mogolagae, Mlungisi Qwabe, Nomthandazo Mkhize, Peter Mcebi, Sibongile Khumalo, Sibongile Mngoma, Themba Mkwani, and Vusi Mokhitli.

The recording process itself was relatively quick as these things go. The CD provides a good reflection of the type of music sung at the festival for the first ten years.

Unfortunately, this was all happening around the time that Caltex discontinued their sponsorship, and I ended up carrying all the costs of the CD and cassette tape production personally, despite the CD cover still carrying the Caltex logo. Although the studio and the orchestra were free, I had to pay soloists, choirs, transport, and production costs, all of which came to R40,142.00, which in those days was a small fortune! Eventually, I ended up paying the choirs in CDs and cassettes. It took four years just to recover the costs with income from sales. As far as I know, this was the only quasi-commercial recording done of the Nation Building Massed Choir Festival.

Legacy

It is amazing how the good news of the Massed Choir Festival spread around South Africa. Wherever I traveled people asked about the festival and how they could participate, especially once it was on television. It was not easy to reproduce in other centers; without a sponsor, it was an extremely expensive operation. But, as mentioned previously, the music books that were printed for each festival became extremely valuable resources and led to the production of three volumes of music by SAMRO called *South Africa Sings*. All of the music in Volumes I and II was sung at the Massed Choir Festival. In each volume, a background note was given on each piece as well as a translation, and all the music was printed using the dual notation that Prof. and I had pioneered for the Massed Choir Festival music books.

Another important legacy aspect was the development of soloists, many of whom gained extremely useful experience and exposure by singing at the festivals. Several of them went on to very distinguished careers in music.

Prof.'s Retirement and My Departure from the Massed Choir Festival

Having reached the age of seventy, Prof. decided it was time for him to retire from the more active participation in the Massed Choir Festival because he wanted to concentrate on his opera *Princess Magogo* and his composing. His final year as an official Music Director was 2003. I had paid tribute to him on his seventieth birthday in 2002, and at the 2003 concert, for his final appearance as Music Director, Prof. was honored with gifts and tributes and a collage of photographs from the previous years of the festival.

Without the guiding hands of Prof. and Aggrey, who had passed away in June 2004, we lost a significant influence on the Massed Choir Festival, and the subsequent years saw the introduction of a more commercial element into the programs. After an unfortunate incident in the lead up to the 2005 festival, I resigned, and this marked the end of my association with the Massed Choir Festival after sixteen years. The festival continued for another four years until its twentieth anniversary in 2009, and then it ceased.

New Directions

Since 2009, choral music patterns have changed somewhat in South Africa, and there are now more African black choirs singing in noncompetitive events. This was a trend started by the Massed Choir Festival. In my opinion, it has been a positive development because of the wider repertoire sung by choirs and the opportunity for more cooperation between choirs rather than rivalries against other choirs. Since the days of the festival, there has been a divergence in the focus of performance and singing away from competitions, including youth choirs, show choirs, gospel choirs, and musicals such as *Umoja* and *African Footprint*, all of which have enriched the choral music scene in South Africa. All these elements have also helped to establish South African choral music as an enviable player on the world stage.

More recently, Jerome Klaaste, Aggrey's son, has set up the Aggrey Klaaste Trust, and the revival of the Massed Choir Festival has been discussed, but to date, nothing has been confirmed.

I still feel that the Nation Building Massed Choir Festival was one of the most challenging, and, at the same time, rewarding things I have done in my career. It came at a critical time in South African history and in a small way contributed to the change that was coming in 1994.

The friendship between Prof. and me and the musical partnership have surely been a highlight of my life, and I cherish the memories and the many lessons I learned from this giant in the history of music in South Africa.

Professor Mzilikazi Khumalo.
Halala Prof., Halala!

5

The Use of Tonic Sol-fa Notation by Professor Mzilikazi Khumalo

Ludumo Magangane

Professor Mzilikazi Khumalo composed almost exclusively in tonic sol-fa notation which is commonly used by composers of choral music in South Africa. This shows the influence of missionaries on the region beginning in the nineteenth century. I worked with Prof. Khumalo as a choral conductor and director for many years. I was trained at the University of Zululand under Professor Khabi Mngoma and learned both staff notation and tonic sol-fa. When Prof. Khumalo was working with the Nation Building Massed Choir Festivals, I was involved as a conductor. I assisted him and Maestro Richard Cock in setting songs in dual notation. My collaboration with Prof. Khumalo continued with the setting of his major works, including the song cycle *Haya Mntwan' Omkhulu*, as well as the epic *UShaka KaSenzangakhona*, and the opera *Princess Magogo KaDinuzulu*. I transcribed the tonic sol-fa into staff notation, working at first by hand and later with notation software. My transcriptions would be sent to the orchestrators who would then harmonize and orchestrate the music for the performances. I was also involved in editing the publication of choral music scores in the series published by SAMRO, *South Africa Sings* (in three volumes). This chapter provides a brief explanation and overview of Prof. Khumalo's use of tonic sol-fa. For a more detailed exploration of tonic sol-fa in particular, the reader is referred to Christine Lucia's *Music Notation: A South African Guide*.[1]

Background: Tonic Sol-fa Notation

"Tonic sol-fa is a pedagogical technique for teaching sight-singing, invented by Sarah Ann Glover of Norwich, England and popularized by John Curwen who adapted it from a number of earlier musical systems."[2] It is used for representing music that is sung by choirs and is a system that is in common use on the African continent, having been brought by missionaries. It is also in use in some parts of Europe like France.[3] Missionary education in Southern Africa targeted reading, writing, and arithmetic.[4] After passing what was then known as Standard Six, an external examination in the primary school (which would be equivalent to Grade 8 today), graduates could then go to colleges (like the Kilnerton Training Institution) to train as teachers and preachers and to take the Native Teachers' Higher Certificate. This is where future teachers were trained in music theory—mainly reading tonic sol-fa and staff notation—choir training and conducting. Some of those teachers became composers, and they were able to write in both the tonic sol-fa and staff notation systems (Enoch Sontonga wrote "Nkosi Sikelel' iAfrika" in tonic sol-fa notation. It was transcribed into staff notation probably by him or by some other musician).

The Black African composers (like Sontonga and Tyamzashe) improved their knowledge of tonic sol-fa notation by registering with tonic sol-fa colleges such as the Tonic Sol-fa College of Music in Earlham Grove, which was founded by Reverend John Curwen.[5] This could explain why Black African composers and choirs almost exclusively used tonic sol-fa notation. This began toward the end of the nineteenth century. Several Black African conductors and choristers who have studied music at tertiary institutions are able to use both tonic sol-fa and staff notation in composing and in singing.[6]

Tuning forks were used to establish pitch. A tuning fork would have to be hit on a hard surface to produce a tonic sound, so you would find a tuning fork in C major, F major, D major, and so on. Even if a choir conductor had one tuning fork, he/she would use the modulator to get to the required pitch. The later period in the development of choral music in Southern Africa saw the introduction of the pitch pipe or melodica, which replaced the tuning fork. Choirs started in the mission schools, and the first choir conductors were teachers.[7] The next section outlines the practice of tonic sol-fa and explains how it is transcribed into staff notation. There follows a discussion of Prof. Khumalo's practice with reference to his music.

Comparison between Tonic Sol-fa Notation and Staff Notation

In tonic sol-fa, the semibreve will be represented this way:

{I d: - I - : - I

The three pulls (hyphens) indicate how long you have to sustain d (doh), which is in the first beat.

{I d: - I represents a minim

{I d: I represents a crotchet

The empty space between the colon and the bar line is a rest. The absence of a symbol and punctuation in that space makes it a full rest (one-beat rest). There is no symbol that represents rests in tonic sol-fa notation.

a) {I . d: I or b) {I d . : I or c) {I d: - . d I

Each of the above examples is in duple time.

The first beat in example a) above represents a quaver rest and a quaver. A dot in the space of a beat divides the beat into two halves. So, example a) represents a quaver rest, a quaver, and a crotchet rest in the second beat.

Example b) represents a quaver, followed by a quaver rest (the space between the dot and the colon), and followed by a crotchet rest.

Example c) represents a dotted crotchet and a quaver. The d (doh) in the first beat represents a crotchet value. The pull (hyphen) in the second beat indicates that the crotchet must be sustained for a quaver value (the dot divides the second beat into two halves—quaver values), and the d (doh) in the second beat is a quaver.

{I . , d: I represents a semiquaver

It was indicated above that a dot divides a beat into two halves. So, the space between the bar line and the dot is half of the first beat—meaning that it is a quaver rest. The space on the right-hand side of the dot is further reduced by the comma. The space between the dot and the comma is a quarter of the first beat—meaning that it is a semiquaver rest. This then makes d (doh) a semiquaver.

{I d . , d: d I represents a dotted quaver and a semiquaver in the first beat, and a full beat (crotchet) in the second. It is assumed that the sound is sustained between the dot and the comma. Some composers who wanted to clearly indicate that it is definitely a dotted quaver and semiquaver would represent it this way:

{I d . - , d: d I

In other words, they would put a pull (hyphen) between the dot and the comma to indicate that the sound continues from the quaver to the semiquaver. Without the pull, it would be a quaver, a semiquaver rest, and a semiquaver.

Thirds or triplets are represented by three notes separated by commas. At first, the commas were written upside down, but composers later wrote them as regular commas:

{I d,r,m: f I m: r,m,r I d: - I : II}.

The above are two four-beat bars. The first three notes are thirds (three quavers which are thirds); f (fah) in the second beat is a full note or equal to one beat (crotchet); m (me) in the third beat is also a full note; r,m,r is a fourth beat composed of thirds; d (doh) in the first beat of the second bar extends in value to the second beat. It therefore is a minim. Beats three and four are rests.

There are no demisemiquaver and hemidemisemiquaver equivalents in tonic sol-fa notation. Songs written in dual notation place the lyrics below the stave, tonic sol-fa notes are written in full. This is to help a person who reads staff notation only to understand the comparison between tonic sol-fa notation and staff notation.

The Use of Tonic Sol-fa Notation by Professor Mzilikazi Khumalo

The early Black African compositions were mainly Christian, like "Vuka Deborah" (Wake up Deborah) by John Knox Bokwe and "Nkosi Sikelel' iAfrika" (Lord bless Africa in isiXhosa) by Enoch Mankayi Sontonga. African composers wrote their songs exclusively in tonic sol-fa notation. Alfred Assegai Kumalo was one such composer whose song "Nkosi Busisa iAfrika" (Lord bless Africa in isiZulu) was Christian and completely hymnal. In due course, secular songs were also composed. The melodic lines, even if songs were secular, would be hymnal. The composers mainly made use of the diatonic major scale and followed Baroque harmony, which was the influence of the missionaries.

Some of Professor Mzilikazi's forerunners would still use the hymnal approach, but they would have a section (usually a short midsection of the song) that would be rhythmic and quicker than the opening and closing sections, for example, "Sylvia Mntakwethu" (Sylvia my beloved) by Michael Moerane. The midsection is the "Vuthuza moya" (Blow wind) section, which represents the beating of the sea waves against the sailing ship, caused by a strong wind at sea. Composers from the Cape colony would repeat each section in their compositions, like "Isitandwa sam" (My love) by Tyamzashe or "Rosie" by B.B. Myataza. Compare this with J.P. Mohapeloa from Lesotho, who had a different style. In his song "U ea kae?" (Where are you going to?), he has an inbuilt threshing rhythm with strong first and third beats in quadruple beat bars. Other compositions of his would incorporate sounds that he heard, for example, "Linoto" (sounds produced by hitting objects). In this song, the choir imitates sounds that Mohapeloa heard in a factory. We can safely say his approach was eclectic. Another composer who was Professor Mzilikazi Khumalo's predecessor was Reuben Tholakele Caluza, who also made use of tonic sol-fa to compose his songs. His music was very syncopated, for example, "Ixhegwana" (An oldish man—actually referring to a rickshaw), "Umntakababa" (My sibling), "Umshado" (A wedding). Caluza's syncopated rhythms were influenced by his exposure to American Ragtime music. In Zulu Ragtime music, this was called "Ukureka" (to sing in Ragtime style).[8]

All of Professor Mzilikazi Khumalo's compositions are written in the tonic sol-fa notation. Only occasionally would Professor Khumalo have syncopation in his music, for example, "He! He! He!" (a chanting sound; in spoken language it would follow a question) in "Izibongo ZikaShaka" (The praises of King Shaka). Most of the time, the lyrics were about the history of the Zulu nation. He also followed the hymnal approach, even though at times he would be eclectic, for example, "UGqozi" (Power of Inspiration). Later, the composers still kept the hymnal aspect—in what we would refer to as part one and part three of the songs. The midsection would be especially rhythmic—the rhythms being essentially African in this case. In many instances, these would imitate African dance rhythms. The rhythms would be accurately captured by using the tonic sol-fa notation. Todd Matshikiza's "Hamba Kahle" (Fare thee well) is one such example. The "Hay' ngenene phakama" (Yes indeed rise) section represents an isiXhosa traditional dance movement. One such example by Professor Khumalo is his "Ma Ngificwa Ukufa" (When death comes upon me). Part one of the song is hymnal (see score at the end of this volume). The English translation of the words is:

Ngimbeleni—bury me
Phansi—below
Kotshani—the grass
Duze—near
Nezihlahla zomnyezane—the willow trees

This hymnal section goes on for twenty-eight bars, with a time change from quadruple to triple time and back to quadruple time. From bar 9, the key changes from F major to C major.

> Ngozwa nami—I will hear
> Lapho—when
> Ngilele—I am asleep (in death)

As indicated in the earlier sections above, the "r" (ray) above "s" (soh) in bar 9 is the bridge note which is in the key F major, and it gives "s" (soh) its sound. "S" (soh) is therefore in the key C major, and all the other ensuing notes will be in the key C major until the composer indicates otherwise.

This section is followed by a rhythmic section—"Ziyagiya ziqethuke" (they dance and perform acrobatics)—which depicts a syncopated African rhythm. This is the only section that truly represents the African rhythmic style in the song. After this section, the song goes back to the hymnal style.

Some twenty years later, Professor Khumalo broke new terrain by using some isiZulu idioms to compose an entire song, without using Western hymnody. He also took into account the isiZulu speech tone patterns and depicted those patterns in many of his later songs. In a word like "e-hhe" (yes), the voice glides from a lower pitch to a higher one on the "hhe" part, in spoken language. In "woza" (come), there is no glide if the vowel "o" is shortened. But if the vowel is long, then there will be a glide from the top to a lower pitch. Songs like "S'khala kini makhos'ohlanga" (We are asking for help from you traditional kings), "Imvukuzane" (a mole), "Insizw'endala" (the old guy—referring to Nelson Mandela after his release), "Inkondlo kaMnkabayi" (Mnkabayi's love song [Shaka's aunt]) were written around that time. "Xola Hleziphi" (Be forgiving, Hleziphi) is another. To represent the glide, Mzilikazi Khumalo would write the main note and then write a short diagonal line on the left top side above the main note. This would indicate that the singer first has to sound a pitch below the note and glide upward to the actual or main note. In other cases, the note will have two diagonal lines on either side of it. This would mean that the glide happens on either side of the note, for example,

> I . , m : l , - , ′l I
> Ng'-ba---mbe,

The Ng' (nasal) is sung to the mediant, the "ba" to the submediant, and the "mbe" is sung to the second submediant but the singer first glides from below the submediant. In other cases in the song, the glide happens on either side of the note, for example,

l , , d : m , - , ʹmˈ l
Ng'-ba-----mbe,

In this case, the singer glides from below the mediant, onto the mediant, and glides back again. The next note r (ray) will determine how far back the singer has to glide. In the next example, "Xola Hleziphi," Professor Khumalo took the glides a step further by indicating the pitch from which the voice should glide, linking it with a curved line to the main note (Figure 5.1).

In the example above, the glides happen in "Na- of 'Nango' (there is), and also in -she" (pronounced sheh) of "Washesha" (the name of a bus service in Zululand). The tonic sol-fa indicates d (doh) with a tie to r (ray), meaning that the singer starts with the sound of the tonic in B♭ major, then glides up to the supertonic. The staff notation has a quaver tied on to the crotchet with a straight short line. The next glide is from l_1 (lah) to m_1. Each of the glides is executed to the value of one beat (crotchet value).

In some instances, Professor Khumalo would mix styles, for example, "Amahubo Esizwe Esimnyama" (The reverential songs of the Black nation—written after the 1976 riots). In this song he combines different isiZulu idioms

Figure 5.1 "Xola Hleziphi" by J. S. M. Khumalo.

plus the political slogans of the time, ending with a short hymnal passage. The "Ihubo" section that he uses in this song is "IsoBivane" (he—the king—is at Bivane—a place), "Inkosi yenqab'ukubuyekhaya" (the king refuses to come back home), "zwan'isidumo sempi" (listen to the rumblings of war). Professor Khumalo comfortably uses tonic sol-fa notation to capture the rhythms of this ihubo which has a deliberate slow tempo.

Another song with mixed styles is the chorus *Izibongo ZikaShaka* (Shaka's praise songs) (see score included at the end of this volume) which forms part three of his epic *UShaka KaSenzangakhona* (Shaka, son of Senzangakhona). In the opening of the song, he uses a pentatonic scale: d: r: f : s: l (tonic; supertonic; subdominant; dominant; submediant). All four voices of the chorus use this pentatonic scale until the end of this section. The next section is hymnal, ending up with a tenor solo with female voices accompanying. The next section goes back to a Zulu idiom introduced by a bass solo also with female voices accompanying. Then, it breaks into a very rhythmic African dance movement with hand clapping: "Waqeda qed'izizw'uyakuhlaselaphi na?" (you go around destroying tribes, where are you going to attack?), with choral vocal responses having glides (He! He! He! referred to above). A descant solo voice joins this movement until its end. This is followed by a moving hymnal section, and the chorus culminates in yet another African dance section. Parts one, two, and four of *UShaka KaSenzangakhona* follow purely isiZulu idioms. Professor Khumalo would say that when he would write solo music in some of his songs, he would write with a particular soloist in mind. For example, he would write for a dramatic soprano, a lyric tenor, or for a true bass who could reach low registers. He would use tonic sol-fa to achieve these results. When writing a song that he felt would not be well represented by Western simple or compound time, he would write it and use what I would refer to as an extension of compound time. This would be music that does not fit into 6/8, 9/8, or even 12/8. He would then write notes on how to sing the music. In cases where some of the music should involve demisemiquavers or hemidemisemiquavers (values that are not represented by tonic sol-fa), he would write the notes—say he has to write four hemidemisemi-quavers—in the space of a semiquaver (which is equal to a quarter note [semiquaver] in tonic sol-fah), and write footnotes to guide the performer. In short, Professor Khumalo did not allow the shortcomings of tonic sol-fa to disadvantage him.

When Professor Khumalo started writing his music using isiZulu idioms, some choir conductors found his music too challenging, and this was a problem because his music was often prescribed for choir competitions.

One exception was his friend, the late Jabulani Mazibuko of the Soweto Teachers' Choir. Professor Khumalo and Mazibuko had an arrangement that as soon as Prof. Khumalo finished a song, he would give it to Mazibuko to teach it to his choir. That is how choirs got to know about *Izibongo ZikaShaka* (King Shaka's praises).

Not only did Professor Khumalo display knowledge of tonic sol-fa notation in his compositions, he also made arrangements of African folk songs in tonic sol-fa. These were largely used at the Massed Choir Festival which was held between 1989 and 2009 at the Standard Bank Arena. Folk songs are generally taught orally in various African communities. Professor Khumalo would take a known folk song and arrange it in tonic sol-fa for a mixed choir of sopranos, altos, tenors, and basses. He would capture the rhythms and meter of the folk song accurately. Most of the time he would also add an introduction of a solo voice or a quartet at the beginning of the annotated folk song. This addition would therefore be composed. At times, Professor Khumalo would embellish the folk song by changing some of the rhythms just to make the song more interesting. The folk songs would be the highlight of the festival, where the massed choir of about a thousand voices would perform the folk songs with choreography. The audience would be on its feet joining the massed choir. (The writer of this chapter experienced this throughout the years of the Massed Choir Festival, having been an assistant to Professor Khumalo and Richard Cock, and having conducted two of the participating choirs—the Kwa Thema Youth Choir and Bonisudumo Choristers). One of the folk songs that he arranged is "Sizongena Laph'emzini" (We will come into this homestead). He first composed music for a quartet, which was inspired by the folk song. The end of the quartet section flows into the chorus part, where he represents the folk song the way it is usually performed. To accurately capture the rhythm, Professor Khumalo uses sixteen semiquavers arranged in groups of four, conducted in quadruple time. In the chorus section, he uses twelve semiquavers also arranged in groups of four, conducted in triple time.

Conclusion

Professor Khumalo was a composer who wrote predominantly in tonic sol-fa. His style developed gradually during his career so that many African indigenous practices were included. This required him to make innovations in notation, such as the use of glides to depict speech tones. He wrote and arranged many songs and ensembles. In addition to the epic *UShaka KaSenzangakhona* (1996), Professor Khumalo also wrote a complete isiZulu opera—*Princess Magogo KaDinuzulu* (Princess Magogo, DinuZulu's daughter) in 2002, and a song cycle based on Princess Magogo, *Haya Mntwan' Omkhulu* (Sing Princess), composed in 1999, all in tonic sol-fa notation. I collaborated with Prof. Khumalo and Richard Cock in developing a system of dual notation that is now used as a practical way of teaching his music to choirs in South Africa, many of whom still rely on tonic sol-fa rather than staff notation. The fact that most Black choristers rely on tonic sol-fa suggests that this method of notation remains relevant in South Africa today, and Khumalo's innovations enable a more accurate performance practice for African music.

6

The Music for A Cappella Choir

David Smith

The choral art of Mzilikazi Khumalo has been widely appreciated, both in South Africa and beyond.[1] His eminence as a cultural leader as well as a composer is unquestioned, and his passing in 2021 was an occasion of profound grief and respect.[2] Yet simply locating and defining his choral output poses a challenge to researchers, even if it is unlikely to need the kind of full-scale restoration that has recently been afforded the creative work of Joshua Mohapeloa and Michael Moerane, in the comprehensive critical editions that have been researched and published by Christine Lucia.[3] The labor behind these unusual trophies of scholarship rests, however, on the nature and extent of public, personal, and family archives. In Khumalo's case, that legacy remains under investigation rather than being definitively established.

Music archives in South Africa, as elsewhere, reflect institutional capacities and biases. "A lack of funding, staff shortages, and time constraints in the archives, libraries and document centers environment are all factors that inhibit research" is a cry echoed in many quarters; in this case, it heads an introduction to a directory of music collections held in this country.[4] A survey of the holdings yields a strangely fractured view of this historical activity: the contents of repositories rely heavily on personal donations, which can yield idiosyncratic emphases, and have decisively favored the work of white composers at the expense of their Black counterparts.

At present, there is no centralized collection of Khumalo's work. Nevertheless, his revered status at the end of his career was supported by various forms of documentation, the most important for this chapter being *Izingoma zikaMzilikazi Khumalo*,[5] consisting of thirty-six of his choral compositions, either original or arrangements, published in dual notation. A set of three volumes entitled *South Africa Sings*[6] represents the work of an editorial committee headed by Khumalo and includes two of his well-established arrangements and his song honoring Nelson Mandela ("Insizw'endala"). The *South African Sings* albums provide the most accessible window on the historic Black choral-song tradition and contains invaluable notes on the composers and translations of their texts. The fact that others besides Khumalo were involved in compiling this anthology strengthens the view of it as presenting a "mainstream" perspective on the style.

The evidence of the composer's ear is collected on three commercially released recordings made by Khumalo and his choir, the Soweto Songsters. Their digital cassette recorded in Tampa, Florida (Regal Zonophone 1993), includes six songs whose arrangements are expressly attributed to Khumalo.[7] Another release that is also closely related to its Salvation Army identity is the choir's *Lwandle Loyiso* (Ukhozi FM, 1999), where six items are listed as his arrangements.[8] The compact disc marking a decade of Massed Choir Festivals (Sowetan, 1999) includes among its eighteen tracks ten from the *South Africa Sings* collection, making it something of an exemplar of these songs. It is also less personally self-effacing than the other recordings mentioned, since it contains an important original work by Khumalo, "Izibongo ZikaShaka" (The traditional praises of King Shaka; also included in this book), along with five of his arrangements.[9]

The duplication of materials across the published scores and the recordings represents a narrowing of the scope of Khumalo's works for choir. The *Izingoma* collection ranges more widely and must for the time being be considered the core of what Khumalo saw as his *a cappella* choral legacy. But the volume is not widely known, most likely because it has been advertised as a resource for Zulu-language high schools rather than the market at large. In addition, its material has been overshadowed by the "old faithfuls" in *South Africa Sings*, and by the music of Khumalo's own epic cantata *UShaka KaSenzangakhona* (1996) and his opera *Princess Magogo KaDinuzulu* (2002). This applies to both YouTube uploads and to recent choral competitions. The hope must be that this defective preservation and skewed dissemination of his compositional materials will eventually be remedied, perhaps through efforts like the present study.

Khumalo's early career output is associated with three songs based on poems by the eminent Zulu novelist and Romantic poet, Benedict Wallet Vilakazi (1906–47) who, like Khumalo later, taught African languages at Wits University. "Ma Ngificwa Ukufa" (When death is upon me) has been identified as the composer's first publicly acknowledged work; it had the distinction of being selected for the first National Choral Eisteddfod of the African Teachers' Association of South Africa held in Bloemfontein in 1962.[10] Its tender refrain, "Lala sithandwa, lal'uphumule" (Sleep, dear one; sleep and rest in peace), is familiar to every Black chorister (see score included in this volume).

Typically, for the repetition of the melody in the second statement (bars 64–71), fresh movement in the inner voices intensifies the affection. Tenderness is one of the cardinal points of Khumalo's world; another is delivery "with passion," appropriate to the middle section of the song in "traditional Zulu dance rhythm"—an early indication of the composer's ambition to write into choral idiom various aspects of indigenous musical practice.

It should be noted that Vilakazi's poem, published in the collection *Inkondlo kaZulu* (1935), is much shortened in the song, and that the references to the freedom in heaven from the white man and from pass laws appear to be Khumalo's own invention. For all that, the tone of the verse (based on a Romantic trope of conversation with the beloved dead) is well expressed in the music's post-Victorian language—an apt consolatory match.

The challenge of this song in performance arises from the composer's scrupulous adherence to the sense of the words, a compressed type of word-painting that easily yields a mosaic at the cost of architectural unity. The two other Vilakazi songs ("UGqozi" [Power of Inspiration] and "KwaDedangendlale" [Valley of a Thousand Hills])[11] are more extended and feel more continuous, and some of the thematic inflections are managed by changes in the texture (soli or a solo in combination with choral parts), rather than by sharp changes of mood and tempo.

For the better part of his work, Khumalo relied on Themba Msimang for his texts. This meant a freer, more rhetorical approach, with the actual incorporation of the stylized speech of the *imbongi*; it was this linguistic direction that permitted the projection of musical lines that displayed the Zulu language with both flair and fidelity to local "styles." The "Haya" style thus comes to the fore, an emphatic and dramatic solo manner with recitative-like repeated notes and decorated cadences in a flexible meter, against punctuations from the choral background (Figure 6.1).

This widening of resources in his mature work (post-1980) meant that Khumalo embraced modes rather than the strict adherence to keys of his earlier works. Melodic material became starker: he was not afraid to employ extensive unison passages (with theatrical effect), pentatonic formations over adjacent root notes brought the sounds of seventh and fourth intervals to prominence, and vocal lines changed from mellifluously charming to energetically mobile. These factors provided him with a new coherence that owed little to the Western

Figure 6.1 Mzilikazi Khumalo, "Inkondlo KaMnkabayi," bars 26–33.

Figure 6.2 Mzilikazi Khumalo, "Insizw'endala," bars 58–62.

musical language from which he had emerged, and the songs are never too long to induce the sense of uniformity that at times emanates from his two large-scale compositions (Figure 6.2).

It would be helpful to know the precise date and intention behind "IZulu Elisha," a mainly four-voice setting of a biblical pericope, Revelation 21:1-4. It "belongs," if anywhere, to the third phase of the European motet tradition (Randel 1986: 512): compact, through-composed settings of a textual unit, the vernacular indicating a Protestant context, the theme a liturgical pointer (most likely a funeral or memorial service). The agreement of text and music is again manifest. The general frame is of tranquil comfort, and the memory of musical pathos is summoned by quotation from the admired "Intermezzo" in Mascagni's opera *Cavalleria rusticana* (Figure 6.3).[12]

But the vision of a new heaven and earth (bars 9–12) sets off a vigorous dotted passage, complete with echo effects, and a measured cadence to mark the obliteration of the sea. The "new Jerusalem" has its own *espressivo* section; it gives way to a strong, initially unison, representation of the "voice from the

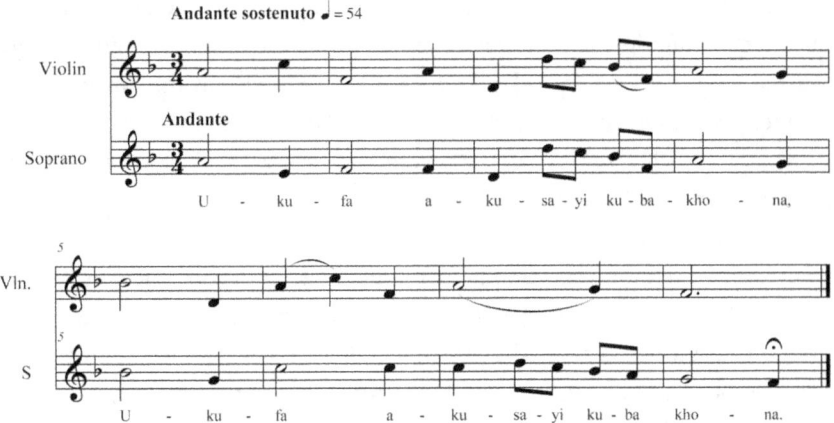

Figure 6.3 Mzilikazi Khumalo, "IZulu Elisha," bars 1–8.

Figure 6.4 Mzilikazi Khumalo, "IZulu Elisha," bars 36–41.

throne" (at bar 36) that climaxes in a fanfare figure appropriate to the familiar scriptural imagery of music in the Book of Revelation: the trumpets sounded by the seven angels (chapter 8), or even the voice of the Spirit, "a loud voice like a trumpet" (1: 10) (Figure 6.4).

Male voices around a bass solo in A-flat major (bar 45)–Khumalo departs from F major only to its three flatter keys (E-flat, B-flat, and A-flat majors)—praise the "tabernacle [home] of God ... among mortals," before a three-voice setting of the promise to "wipe every tear from their eyes" (v.4). The final sentences (referring to the cessation of death and sorrow with the extinction of the "first things") return to and extend the calm triple-meter homophony of the introduction and its melodic inspiration, marking the idea of "the first things" passing away with a final *calando*. It is disappointing that this finely crafted composition has not become a staple of South African memorials.

Khumalo's 1981 setting of the traditional praises of Shaka published in *Izingoma* (pp. 56–73) demands separate discussion. It may well be the only such setting—for choral forces—of a typically African oral art originally far removed from multivoice motivic/harmonic manipulations. In this instance, the praises are arguably a central example of the form.[13] The text used is only part of the praises as preserved, chiefly the opening address and a few closing lines, with two interpolations by another hand (see bars 13–20 and 101–117). Khumalo used a largely through-composed format, with repetitions of musical material confined to its constituent sections. These in turn are distinguished by metrical, tonal, and textural contrasts, always in relation to changes in the text.[14] Table 6.1 is based on the sections proposed by Mugovhani and Oluranti.[15]

The dissection by Mugovhani and Oluranti (2015, pp. 2–13, "the analysis") reveals a large binary structure within which alternate two distinct approaches to tonality, one modal and colored by pentatony (X sections in the table), the other diatonic by major/minor orientation with notable chromatic touches, and thus clearly beholden to Western functional harmony (Y sections).

Other factors reinforce the impression that Khumalo was here intent on using indigenous and Western polarities in "conversation":

- Melodic contours that fall in conformity with typical isiZulu cadence. These are manifested in all voices in X sections, but only in leading lines (usually soprano) in Y sections;
- Textural differentiation, the greatest number of voices enriching traditional chordal harmony (Y), versus the "polyphonic" spreading of the motives in a more aerated idiom (X);
- The prevailing syllabic delivery of the text, which lends itself to spurts of "recitative" inspired by isiZulu speech rhythms.

The analysis presses the musical dichotomy hard to make the case for the clear-cut expression of cultural identities. Indeed, the examples from which the authors argue constitute compelling evidence of the differentiation of traditions. Yet, they are related as well as defined. For one thing, syllabic setting is a widespread manner of treating text; the clear isiZulu speech approximations occupy one end of a spectrum and the arrangement of phrases in periodic symmetry the other

Table 6.1 Sections Proposed by Mugovhani and Oluranti (2015)

	Section	Bars	Text	Description	Remarks
A	X1*	1–20	Ndabezitha! UDlungwane kaNdaba	Nonsimultaneous entry; strong unison, bars 8–10	Textually "leading" and "following" parts are identical[16]
	Y1	21–28	UShaka ngiyesaba	Fully harmonized homophony	G major
	Y2	29–40	Uteku lwabafazi	Mainly homophonic	Key-change: D major
	Transition 1	41–44	UShaka, Ushaka	Four-voice, sequential	Harmonic climax
	Y3	45–52	Ushaka, ngiyesab'ukuthi	Solo tenor with 2-pt women	Here & in Y4, women lightly harmonize; G major
	Y4	53–68	Utekulwabafazi	Solo bass with SAA fills	Text repeat of Y2 with new music; A minor
B	Transition 2	69–72	Ilembe leq'amany'amalembe	Tutti basses, then adding tenors	Unison
	X2	73–100	Waqedaqed'izizw'uyakuhlasela	*Ndlamu* dance rhythm B then B+T, SA added	Text repetition; tonal glides important
	Y5	101–113	Uyakuhlasela phina?	TTBB	Strict homophony
	X3	113–125	Umoy'omzansi	Bonga style Purely pentatonic	Repetition involved; the entire section may be repeated

*See discussion below.

end. The most telling departure from strictly syllabic writing is a chromatic sequential passage (Transition 1), where the text is frozen (six repetitions of "UShaka"), but the choral acclamation is quite unlike anything else in the work (see score included in this volume).

A subtlety that binds the piece together, despite its fidelity to textual variety, is its underlying 12/8 meter, very pronounced in the X sections where syncopations abound but also implied in the more flowing Y sections. The analysis fails to note that the concluding Bonga-style section pursues a different dance, also syncopated but decisively in 4/4. It is natural to consider this a coda in an African accent, and to view this infectious winding-up as a praise of the spirit of "Praises."

Another point of interest is the "gendered" quality of various stretches, both in X and Y sections. Some of it hints at a societal inspiration that is confirmed by the many instances of male/female division of the choir in Khumalo's arrangements of traditional (or "popular") material. It also runs through his tribute to Mandela, "Insizw'endala." More interesting is the way in which he "borrows" tenor voices to combine with sopranos and altos against an independent bass line. Altos are also included in three-part low-voice responses to a soprano lead.[17]

Reflections on Khumalo's Arrangements

The principle behind these creations is the transfer of music that is (or was) shared by many people in an orally learned form to a notated standard that (a) constitutes a composer's stylization of the source material; (b) renders the song available to others who participate in a formal process of choral performance. How does he treat and recommend these songs?

"Ndikhokhele, bawo!" is both "anonymous" and very popular. A song that affirms faith and God's protection, his version exudes restraint: over a cushioned chorus, the leader provides the emotional color. Its stages are:

Bars 1–17: women's voices (solo S + SAA)
Bars 17–29: men's voices (tenor lead), expanding to full choir for cadencing (bar 33)
SATB is established with S as the corporate leader. Passages add or pare away voices for the emphasis of a single phrase, or for its delicate ending.

"Woza, Mmeli Wami"

Khumalo marks this traditional gospel song "Passionately"; he is formalizing what spontaneous church performance, through an orally learned experience, would achieve. Thus, tonal glides are required throughout to reflect the characteristic lingual roots, and the editorial notes to *South Africa Sings*, Vol. 1, pertain to this group execution of an inherent pattern of pronunciation.[18] The call-and-response opening, allotted to a soprano solo and SATB, is reconfigured at bar 33 as an SAA semi-chorus in front of the choir, allowing for harmonizing of the lead part.

The rhythmic interest—one might say the kinesthetic point—is contained in both the pervasive syncopation and the elusive way in which the phrase unfolds across seven bars (Figure 6.5).

"Iph'indlela" adds to the familiar characteristics (call-and-response structure, circling primary harmonies) an early modulation to the subdominant key (F major to B-flat major). The choral tessitura is thereby moved (upward) to highlight the expansive soprano part in a resonant range. The circling material is resolved by the only truly homophonic material in the whole song (bars 65–66), an understated "tipping of the hat" to finish.

Figure 6.5 Mzilikazi Khumalo, "Woza, Mmeli Wami!", bars 33–39.

The most contrapuntally complex of the arrangements is "Sizongena Laph'Emzini!" (We will enter this homestead!). It is "a composition based on two Zulu traditional wedding songs," and that descriptive subtitle is justified as much by an episode of playful two-voice outlines (bars 13–36, "Sivulen'singene sonke") as by the remarkable degree of assertive elaboration among all the voices that follows. At points in the recapitulation of the first song ("Sizongena"), as many as three melodic foci are present simultaneously (Figure 6.6).

The ringing conclusion is an integral aspect of the arranger's art in satisfactorily rounding off a cyclical or looped song that by its nature would either fade or simply break up. Khumalo's "exits" are worth a study in themselves. The terminations of his songs cannot be considered in isolation: they may sometimes quote or vary an internal cadence, or by contrast consciously depart from the prevailing ideas to make their point. His propensity for arranging "traditional" songs that employ various forms of repetition to maintain their groove typically involves concluding them by freezing the music on one, or, more often, two chords to complete the text. In general, his approach is unfussy though it can sometimes seem rather abrupt. In these cases, the form of the cadence stems from a cardinal linguistic feature of Nguni poetry, especially at the ends of lines. Unlike, say, the tendency of poetry in English to favor iambic patterns (unstressed–stressed), so that the stressed syllable and last note typically coincide with the strongest pulse of a measure, Nguni meters mostly end with a marked trochaic effect (stressed–unstressed). In musical terms, this translates into an agogic accent

Figure 6.6 Mzilikazi Khumalo, "Sizongena Laph'Emzini," bars 49–51.

on the penultimate syllable and a trailing chord thereafter. Khumalo naturally respects the speech model but introduces subtleties—like changing the voicing of a sustained harmony or dropping the final syllable in imitation of colloquial delivery—to give the necessary ending a directed quality.

Despite their variety and depth of emotion, the choral songs broadly exhibit a highly personal discretion, indeed, a modesty of design: their core and interest lie in the subtle, often intricate unfolding of a song, and the deft execution that it requires. For Khumalo, it seems, the four-part choir was an obligatory vehicle. However, this choice includes a range of enrichment allowed by part pairings and divisions, by chordal directness and motivic play, and the ranging of sound across all the available registers. In his hands these were sufficiently supple means to communicate all the feelings and sounds of his imagination.

It is easy to underestimate an achievement based on a type of poise and aesthetic restraint. And the projection of his music onto massed choral forces or luxuriant orchestral settings seems to contradict that perception. But a comparison with the style of African American spirituals—which cover overlapping content—quickly shows how completely he foreswore the towering arrangements to which the spirituals are often subject.[19] In compositional terms, this divergence represents life choices: an elaborately projected theatrical summation versus a quieter, more straightforward celebration of the continuity of communal life with its faith, joys, and griefs.

This survey has concentrated on "supply-side" investigation, that is, on the sources of Khumalo's inspirations and the creative ends to which he put them. The ever-changing demand for music is an equally complex matter: the reliance of a large percentage of the public on technological access to the arts has moved consumption and appreciation far beyond live performance venues, especially in burgeoning radio and other streaming services. Contemporary economic trends are also proving decisive: thus, the national choral eisteddfod among South African state schools is now indebted to a private family trust for its continuation, while the National Choir Festival, for so long sustained by business sponsorship, has closed its operations.

Such changes have implications for the choral scene, which now has both the means of wider dissemination as well as stiff competition from many rival forms of music. That choirs will continue to hone their skills, tackle new material, compete, and collaborate seems certain. But a body of choral writing like Khumalo's—the expression of a man in his time—is currently suspended between its value as a legacy and its prospects in a society passing through forceful changes. Furthering its stylistic innovations (the stylization of oral traditions, the mingling of musical worlds) demands a professional competence in future composers that was hard-won by its originator, and its traffic with poetic texts involved collaboration with noteworthy writers, not to mention the composer's own grasp of literary (and linguistic) dimensions. On the side of reception, critical esteem is insufficient as a preservative: only a widely prevailing enthusiasm and continuing engagement can carry this repertoire into the future.

The Evolution of *UShaka* as an African Epic

Robert Maxym

Ndabezitha!

In Zulu culture, it is customary that when one wishes to address the king, to speak about the king, or even when one wishes to sing about him, he must first be saluted. This traditional royal salute is *"Ndabezitha!"* (Your Majesty!).

UShaka, KaSenzangakhona (isiZulu: Shaka, Son of Senzangakhona) traces the life and times of Shaka (1787–1828), king of the Zulus. Shaka is recognized worldwide as a military genius, nation-builder, and leader of his people. Without dealing either in the positive or negative aspects of his life, reign, or acts, historically, opinions on Shaka have been based, one might almost say biased, on a primarily European perception of the Zulu king.

The composer Professor Mzilikazi Khumalo and the poet Professor Themba Msimang, through their epic collaboration on *UShaka*, attempted by means of music and praise poetry to correct misconceptions in this perception, presenting, as they put it, "the Zulu people's history from the Zulu people's point of view." In so doing, they have also presented a moving mosaic of the traditional Zulu worldview, from the ancestors of creation unto implications for the Zulus of the present day.

The original musical composition was written a cappella for SATB Soli, Traditional Praise Poet, and Choir, between 1979 and 1995, in tonic sol-fa notation (see Magangane, Chapter 5, and Mhlambi, Chapter 8, this volume).

UShaka is, in the composer's own words, "my life's work." Mzilikazi Khumalo is the most deeply revered composer of serious indigenous music in South Africa, a guiding light of its choral tradition, and guardian of the culture of his Zulu people through music. His work used traditional and original praise poetry written by his colleague, Themba Msimang, doyen of Zulu poetry and literature, compiler of the current Zulu grammar, biographer of the Zulu royal house, himself a guardian of the tradition of Zulu praise poets. These are two giants of the South African cultural stage, whom I have long affectionately and respectfully referred to as the "South African" Beethoven and the "South African" Homer. Let me elaborate a bit on this comparison.

Beethoven was once invited to perform as pianist at the palace of some or other prince in Vienna: when presenting himself at the door, he was advised by the doorman that he should go around back to the servants' entrance. Beethoven replied: "If the Prince wants music this evening, you will let me in by way of the front door: my name is Beethoven!" Mozart was happy to go around back; he saw it as his lot—Beethoven was not!

As far as Homer is concerned, today we appreciate the history and culture of the Greeks largely through his poetic epics, the story of his people. It is no less applicable to the poetry written by Msimang for the story of *his* people. In much the same way, Khumalo's quest for "equal treatment" as a creative artist must be appreciated in the context of South Africa's recent past, both culturally and politically. Mzilikazi Khumalo was someone who would not accept "going around back to the servants' entrance." From early on, his wish for an orchestral accompaniment to his original work was manifested.

What is now Part III of *UShaka* was completed in 1981, and (standing under the possibility of correction) an initial instrumental accompaniment was attempted by Péter Louis van Dijk, but this work, however, did not proceed further. Some years later, in 1987, excerpts of Part III were orchestrated by Professor Carl van Wyk and Walter Mony, Khumalo's colleagues at Wits University, and performed there, but this work also did not proceed any further. As Khumalo told me in later years, these orchestrations sounded "too European."

Several years passed, and the composer expanded, refined, and revised his work. During the early 1990s, there emerged a complete African epic, including a preamble, four parts, and an epilogue. SAMRO granted funds for the third attempt at an orchestral accompaniment to Dr. Christopher James, a composer and lecturer in music at Unisa, which proceeded from 1992 to 1994.

My first exposure to the work came in mid-1993, when Khumalo invited me to a trial performance of Part IV of the James orchestration, conducted by the composer himself in the Great Hall at Wits University. I reserved opinion, as it was indeed only a "trial" performance.

Over a year later, in October 1994, the composer phoned me, stating simply, "I have a problem with my *UShaka*, Robert." Two performances were scheduled for late November with the Transvaal Philharmonic Orchestra in Johannesburg and Soweto. The first read-through rehearsal had broken off within 30 minutes, and he was concerned that the performances seemed to be endangered.

I agreed to have a look. The computerized orchestral score was prepared in a rudimentary manner. Choral staves were incompletely notated, with many complex rhythms remaining unbeamed, and the original Zulu text was missing in the choral parts. It was very difficult to assess the situation; however, Khumalo, upon my request for a score with at least the text included, delivered to me the same score with the complete text written out in his own hand the very next day.

Some weeks later, rehearsals began. The rehearsal situation could not be compared in any way with professional working environments to which I had become accustomed during my conducting career in Europe. The choir and soloists were singing from copies of Khumalo's original tonic sol-fa manuscript, into which had been added indications as to just how many "bars orchestra" (i.e., rests) were in between the sections they had been used to singing without accompaniment. There were no "cue notes" in their parts to assist in finding tones within this new musical situation. The orchestral musicians, for their part, were faced with orchestral material devoid of reference points to the vocal text in Zulu, which almost none of them understood. With all due respect to the stalwart efforts of all the parties involved, this was an extremely difficult task for all the musicians and singers, and for the conductor of the work.

Mzilikazi's Khumalo's great friend, Professor Khabi Mngoma, esteemed musician and mentor from the University of Zululand in KwaZulu-Natal, was the conductor. Despite his unmistakable musical talents and voluminous knowledge, he had not, to my knowledge, ever conducted a full-scale symphonic/choral apparatus before. His daughter Sibongile Khumalo, a leading South African vocalist, was the alto soloist. Of the group of soloists, none other than Sibongile had ever, to my knowledge, had the experience of singing together with the orchestra.

The four participating choirs all had long-standing associations with Mzilikazi Khumalo. They had accompanied the composition and initial performances of *UShaka* for years, with unstinting artistic commitment during years of hardship throughout the land in the time of apartheid.

Initially, I was engaged by Stephen Wikner, orchestra director of the Transvaal Philharmonic, as a musical consultant. With a view toward the musical picture as a whole, and indeed no different than would have been expected of me in earlier days of my conducting career in European opera houses, when I also "assisted," I prepared simultaneously to be able to conduct the work, should it become necessary. It did.

Mngoma began the rehearsal resolutely with *Ndabezitha!* which is a slow, solemn, and steady piece. It took the choirs three tries to get the first entrance right, then there was an attempt at a run-through, which, however, was not completed. Three or four musicians had questions about notes or rhythms in their parts. Khumalo beckoned me to join him and Chris James to consult with Khabi Mngoma. With three copies of the orchestral score and the original tonic sol-fa manuscript at our disposal, I noticed to my great consternation that Mngoma's score was still lacking the Zulu text for choirs and soloists. Mngoma, bless his heart, never had a realistic chance. We consulted our scores and had a small meeting. It took us 3 or 4 minutes to solve the questions and communicate the answers to the musicians. This scenario repeated itself numerous times, but just from this initial example, it will be clear where this was going.

The rehearsal situation was in its very essence untenable, as the materials were faulty and incomplete. Two systems of musical notation not easily reconcilable with one another were in play in the same musical work.

Some limited progress was made by the end of the first rehearsal, and after gathering to plan out our strategy for the morrow, we all agreed that two particular and most unusual methods would be tried. First, Mngoma and I would divide our attentions, with him rehearsing Parts II and IV, and myself rehearsing Parts I and III. At that time, it was intended that there should be two conductors for the performances. Second, we decided that I would begin the second rehearsal by rehearsing Part I, then hand over to Mngoma for Part II, and so forth.

Before the start of the next day's rehearsal, Khumalo explained the substance of our deliberations to all present, whereupon I began the rehearsal. Simply stated, the beginning of this rehearsal also brought a sea change in the course of my own personal musical destiny.

Having set the scene, I will now be brief about the course of the remaining rehearsals and these 1994 performances. By the close of the second evening's rehearsal and subsequent deliberations, I had been nominated to conduct the performances of *UShaka*. Khabi Mngoma, Khumalo's wise and magnanimous friend, had voluntarily ceded the conductorship to me with the words: "'*Mfowethu*' (my brother), the ancestors have sent this young man to us to do justice to your *UShaka*." This comment has, over the course of the last thirty years, assumed prophetic proportions.

Later that week, with effectively two full rehearsals under our belts, we gave a rendition of the work which in essence started at the first note, ended at the last note, and avoided any blatant and noticeable breakdowns. The efforts of all concerned were extraordinary, and indeed the performances went off successfully enough, considering the unique musical circumstances.

I can state confidently that at the time, with 20 years of conducting experience behind me, having performed over 150 different stage works in over 2,000 public performances, including numerous world premieres and operas as difficult as *Lulu*, this was the hardest performance challenge I had ever faced. And this indeed was the core of the problem.

Personally, I was deeply troubled after those performances. Knowing that Khumalo's wish was that *UShaka* should be performed not only in South Africa but around the world, my view was that the work in its current material form was doomed to languish. Serious musicians and conductors would likely not give this score much consideration.

Orchestrally, I felt there were grave weaknesses, characterized by large gaps of empty spaces which complicated rather than simplified coordination of the musical forces. The orchestra seldom provided the choir with references for their entrance notes, nor reacted in any meaningful way to what they sang. The musicians were essentially bored and needed substantially more to play, in particular some technically demanding passages, to keep their interest challenged. The orchestra was treated as a "passive" entity, with effectively no dialogue occurring between itself and the choir, with no independent musical work to do. There was thus effectively no musical "line." One of my favorite composers, Ermanno Wolf-Ferrari, once said: "If the musicians don't enjoy playing the music, the chances are it won't often be played."

In consequence, I felt there was a scant performance future for the work. I felt honor-bound to communicate these reservations to Khumalo, especially since I thought that his magnificent original work deserved a better fate.

In December 1994 and early January 1995, intense consultations took place among Khumalo, Msimang, Chris James, and myself, in which I gave expression to my feelings in this regard. I explained to Khumalo that, if he wanted *UShaka* to be played around the world, he needed an orchestration which would solve the problems which I have outlined above. After I had finished, he surprised me by asking simply, "Robert, could you write this type of orchestration?" Nonplussed, I replied that I thought that I could. He then asked me, "Would you write this type of orchestration?" I replied that I would. Chris James assented to this assessment and agreed to our course of action. Thus, by mutual consensus, Khumalo entrusted and authorized me, in a simple letter of one sentence, with the "orchestral enrichment and enhancement" of *UShaka*, based upon James's orchestration. The next day, I began work.

This was to be an orchestration of *UShaka*, which, while based loosely on the James score, in the end effectively became a thorough reworking of every bar of the music, without altering a single note of the original vocal composition nor its musical structure. It was my task to create an enhanced orchestral accompaniment to the vocal text, to compose transitional material between numbers within each of the four parts of the epic, and to provide an overture, the major themes of which were chosen by Khumalo.

One day in late January 1995, Khumalo came over to my place in Bryanston. We sat down together for the whole day, during which I played for him many recordings of music, ranging from Bach through all of the major classical and romantic composers, into the moderns as far as Shostakovich. My question for him throughout this exercise was, "Mzilikazi, what kind of orchestra do you want for this new version of *UShaka*?" At the end he stated, "Somewhere between this man Mahler and this Zemlinsky; I like the way they handle the orchestra."

Considering that some critics have commented negatively on the nature of my orchestration (though perhaps more have commented positively), I feel it necessary to put this on the record: Mzilikazi Khumalo got exactly what he wanted. Had he wanted a Beethovenian or Brahmsian orchestration, he would have received this, likewise with any other composer and their orchestral characteristics. Mahler/Zemlinsky—this motivated everything I wrote for the orchestra.

Unquestionably, the most significant milestone in my orchestral realization of the work was early on when I requested and received Khumalo's permission to "harmonize" the work within the confines of the orchestral forces.

Chris James's orchestration had been mostly "intervallic," and this severely limited orchestral expression. When Khumalo pressed me to elaborate on this concept, I sat down at the piano and, improvising from Part I, Nr. 3: "Imbizo Yezinyandezulu," said "well, it could sound something like this." He liked it and gave me permission to proceed in this vein (Figures 7.1 and 7.2).

Khumalo was intimately involved at every stage of this work. Once I had completed a section, we met at Wits, reserved room 9 in the Music Department Building, and I played everything for him at the piano—"the flutes are doing this, the strings are doing this, and so forth"—for his approval. Whenever he

Figure 7.1 *UShaka*, Part 1, no. 3, "Imbizo Yezinyandezulu" (An assembly of the ancestral spirits). Khumalo, Msimang, James, and with orchestration and enhancement by Robert Maxym. Copyright SAMRO.

Figure 7.2 *UShaka*, Part 1, No. 3, "Imbizo Yezinyandezulu" (An assembly of the ancestral spirits), Khumalo, Msimang, James, with piano-vocal score by Robert Maxym. Copyright Maxym Music CC.

had reservations, we threshed this out. If he disapproved of anything, it was corrected to his satisfaction. Every single bar of the work was validated in this manner, by Khumalo himself.

It was in October 1995, well along in my orchestration, that I received for the first time a copy of Khumalo's original tonic sol-fa score. While teaching myself this notation, I became aware that the original score and the James score had quite a number of discrepancies, in both rhythms and the actual notes. Every one of these discrepancies was discussed with Mzilikazi to arrive at the correct interpretation. They were all thus subsequently corrected.

It was also in late 1995 when SAMRO granted funding to allow the orchestration to proceed more rapidly. Richard Cock, director of the National Symphony Orchestra of the SABC (NSO), committed the NSO to a CD recording for May 1996, and thus the work progressed more rapidly to its conclusion. With the dire straits in which South African orchestras found themselves at the time, Richard Cock said "if we don't do it now, we may not get another chance." The orchestration was completed in March 1996, after fifteen months' work. In April 1996, SONY SA committed to producing and distributing the recording on CD and music cassette. Recording sessions took place during May and September of 1996.

At this point, I would like to acknowledge and pay tribute to all the people and forces who made this work possible, both in 1994 and 1996:

Sibongile Khumalo, Themba Mkhwani, Peter Mcebi, Sibongile Mngoma, Phindile Shongwe, Soweto Songsters, Bonisudumo Choristers (Choirmaster Ludumo Magangane), Daveyton Adult Choir (Choirmaster Abiah Mahlase), Cenestra Male Choir (Choirmaster Themba Madlopha), Transvaal Philharmonic Orchestra (Stephen Wikner), National Symphony Orchestra (Richard Cock), Daphne Kramers, SAMRO, and the Foundation for the Creative Arts. If I have inadvertently forgotten anyone, I beg their forgiveness.

The first public performance of this final orchestration took place on September 24, 1996, Heritage Day (formerly known as Shaka Day, commemorating the day of his assassination in 1828) at Johannesburg's City Hall and was broadcast nationwide by SABC 3.

In the intervening twenty-eight years, there have been to the best of my knowledge more than twenty-five performances of the complete work, in Johannesburg, Pretoria, Cape Town, Durban, Chicago, Rome, Vienna, Madrid, Basel, Geneva, Zürich, Brussels, Charleroi, Antwerp, and Linz. Excerpts have been performed in several of these cities, most notably at the state banquet for the Non-Aligned Movement summit in Durban in September 1998, hosted by then president Nelson Mandela. Excerpts of *UShaka* were required material for the 2002 "Nation Building" Massed Choir Festival and the 2007 POLMUSCA Festival. Apart from myself, five other conductors have conducted the work in public.

However, as of the 1996 performances, the evolution of this epic work was not yet complete. How could *UShaka* possibly fare on the world's stages, still effectively a musical torso? Without Black South African choirs and soloists, singing from copies of the original tonic sol-fa manuscript, the work still remained inaccessible to choirs, soloists, choirmasters, stage managers, and rehearsal pianists trained in Western staff notation. The conductor and the orchestra were already provided for, but one vital element was still missing before *UShaka* could stand on its own in the wider world of music.

Having enhanced *UShaka* to its orchestral maturity, and with Khumalo's, Msimang's, and James's permission, I set about in late 1996 to reduce *UShaka* to its necessary lowest common denominator, the piano vocal score. This was the sole reason for the establishment of my company, Maxym Music CC. There was no source of funding for the creation of the piano vocal score, and simply put, if I didn't do it, no one else would.

This was, however, no ordinary task of a piano reduction from an orchestral score. My musical experience brought to light three notable precedents for the type of work which I had been doing up to now on *UShaka* and which was now imperative for the impending work on the piano vocal score:

1) The long musicological history of the reconstruction of Mahler's 10th symphony, which involved Zemlinsky, Shostakovich, and a number of other musical personages before finding its culmination in the work of Derryck Cooke and his associates.[1]
2) Pavel Lamm's exemplary work on the original version of Moussorgsky's "Boris Godunov,"[2] and
3) Raymond Leppard's realization of Monteverdi's "*L'Incoronazione di Poppea.*"[3]

These scores were each accompanied by extensive historical and stylistic notes, which provided invaluable information in study and performance. If there was to be a comparable international standard musical volume on *UShaka*, an extended introduction was needed, providing linguistic, historical, and cultural information, thus enabling the sensitive musician to gain insight into the work.

As their publisher now, I was privy to the wealth of information which Khumalo and Msimang contributed to this end, for their accumulated knowledge had been straining to be shared out into the world.

The components of the introduction were crystallized to:

a) A complete and accurate version of the epic poetic text in Zulu and its English translation. This volume provides the only definitive Zulu orthography, corrected from all earlier versions, by the poet himself. The English translation is jointly by the composer and the poet;
b) Extensive historical and cultural commentaries by the poet, including some truly remarkable historical poetic excerpts;
c) Commentaries by the composer on traditional Zulu music styles, interpretation, and techniques; and
d) A glossary of terms and symbols used in the tonic sol-fa score of the original music, as the piano vocal score is in dual notation.

Dual notation was a cultural imperative, for the piano score had to remain accessible to musicians conversant only with tonic sol-fa notation, starting with Mzilikazi Khumalo himself, and extending to all those who had learned it from the original tonic sol-fa manuscript copies still in circulation in South Africa.

In compiling the volume, original tonic sol-fa and staff notation transcriptions of the complete vocal text have finally been unified, smoothing out all the inconsistencies which had come to light among the three primary sources. Khumalo's word was final as to any and all questions in this regard. The "red book" represents the fruit of this musicological work, and is thus the only definitive musical text to *UShaka* in both systems of notation.

The task was completed in May 1999, after two and a half years' work. Since its completion, it has been used successfully by choirs, soloists, choirmasters, and pianists, both Black and white, in performances of *UShaka* in South Africa and in many other countries. Finally, the full range of professional standard materials is available for capable musical forces anywhere in the world.

As an artistic work, *UShaka* is simply unparalleled in the history of African music, indeed in the history of music. It is the single most extensive musico-dramatic work by an African composer and his librettist. It is the only "Epic in Music and Praise Poetry" (*UShaka*'s official subtitle—not an opera, not a musical, not an oratorio—an epic) in the history of music, thus establishing its own "genre." For many years, it was the only symphonic/choral repertoire work in Zulu. In performance, it presents a breathtaking musical challenge to choirs, soloists, and orchestras, and it has moved audiences to tears, exultation, ululation, whistling, and other spontaneous expressions of deep involvement.

Finally, it is not only musically, but also in a deeply spiritual/social sense that *UShaka* is significant, for it is self-evident that great music can bring great healing. Msimang and Khumalo perceived that the Zulu people, indeed many African peoples, have suffered greatly under Shaka's "curse," uttered at the moment of his death: "You will never reign, you will be reigned over by the whites." Thus, in the final chorus, "Siyashweleza, Nodumehlezi" (We beg your pardon, Nodumehlezi), they call upon the entire Zulu nation to go down upon their knees at Shaka's grave. In an act of collective contrition, they are to implore Shaka's forgiveness, that he may revert upon his words and revoke the curse, freeing his people from the cloud which has darkened their way for almost 200 years.

Msimang and Khumalo know that *UShaka*'s message of inner reconciliation is intended not only for the Zulus, but by extension for all the peoples of South Africa. Taking this line of reasoning to its logical conclusion, *UShaka* should also prove to be a message of reconciliation for the world. "Shwele, Ndabezitha!"

8

Sigiya Ngengoma[1]

Music Dancing History and Politics in *UShaka KaSenzangakhona* (1996)

Innocentia Mhlambi

Introduction

UShaka KaSenzangakhona (Shaka, Son of Senzangakhona, 1996) is a musical rendition of Shaka kaSenzangakhona's life history set against the heroic but painful history of the Zulu people. Mzilikazi Khumalo epically represents some of the fertile sites demonstrating ingenuity in how indigenous Zulu verbal art, musical genres, songs, and dance movements are enmeshed into a musical tapestry. Khumalo experimented with the form in his earlier choral music, in a poem, "Ma Ngificwa Ukufa" ("When Death Overcomes Me," 1934), by Benedict Bhambatha Vilakazi. *UShaka* complicates his deployment of African oral and performance aesthetics by showing how oral art forms and the dancing body come together in a musical sonic–somatic dalliance. In "Ma Ngificwa Ukufa," a poem turned choral piece, he approached this sonic–somatic flirtation by adding these lines:

> *Akukho mlungu akukho pasi* (There is no white man there is no dompass)
> *Kulele izinkulungwane zakithi* (Sleeping are thousands of our people)
> *Ziyagiya ziyagiya ziqethuke* (Who are dancing until they fall to the ground)
> *Ziyagiya zonke* (They are all dancing)
> (Mzilikazi Khumalo's "Ma Ngificwa Ukufa," 1959)

The last two lines convoke visual images of departed souls "dancing" through musical sounds. *UShaka*, composed many decades after this poem, returns us to this earlier feat. Arguably, in *UShaka* the singing–dancing body plays on several developments which include the continued search for an African idiom and its deployment in choral repertoire with a symphony orchestra. In addition, endorsement of African heritage in Black-composed serious music by commissioning bodies is crucial for reaffirming the centrality of African idioms in contemporary choral literature and orchestral music. In *UShaka*, the singing–dancing movements are noticeably bolder and more mature compared to "Ma Ngificwa Ukufa." Khumalo infuses a wider range of Zulu oral arts and performance traditions into strains that can be felt at once by an interpretative community that shares in the epistemic and rhythmic tapestry of Zulu traditional and modern art music genres.

The Zulu oral arts and performance traditions embodied in the oratorio together present a spectacle of theatricality and complexity when added to the orchestra. The vocal timbres and orchestral sounds are made to resonate in familiar ways with the linguistic cadences of isiZulu. The effect is that the entire musical piece is a "speaking" and "singing print" which is isiZulu in linguistic inflections and cultural flair. Additionally, in *UShaka*, the etymological and modern epistemes that interconnect with various performance cultures and histories of Zulu-speaking people are summoned through cultural cognitively-derived dance–music inflections and prosodic features that have been wrought into it. Khumalo's compositional style seeks to deploy the African heritage beyond making such work merely distinctively African. By allowing solfege transgressive experimentations, identified as the high and low flowing grace tones, he goes on to capture certain prosodic features of the isiZulu language which are regarded as impossible to represent using the tonic solfa system, which he uses nonetheless in some of the traditional singing genres in this oratorio. This chapter explores how Khumalo's linguistic and musical background informs interplays of sonic–somatic repertoires and Zulu epistemes to provoke and reflect on Zulu political history in contemporary South Africa.

Symbolic Capital: Commissioning Art Music and the Zulu Song–Dance Genres

Khumalo's conceptualization of *UShaka* in 1981 and earlier draft compositions of his oratorio coincided with the national broadcaster's production of a drama series, *Shaka Zulu* (1986), which portrays Zulu cultural history and the legendary Shaka in awkward ways. Some of the constructions of the history of the Zulu people and their king in this series prompted the past Zulu monarch, His Royal Majesty King Zwelithini, to lodge a complaint, which saw a temporary suspension of this drama series. At the Khumalo symposium in August 2018 at the University of South Africa, Themba Msimang, the oratorio's librettist, commented on how he, together with Mzilikazi Khumalo, were approached by the SABC to be part of the production team of this version of history. After a few plenary sessions, they discovered that the SABC's version was based on formal South African historiography which introduced aspects that were uncomfortable to them as cultural scholars, and perhaps custodians, and linguists of the Zulu ethnic group. In view of the problematic representation of the SABC's version of this part of Zulu history, they both withdrew their participation, and the television series went on to be premiered in 1986.[2] Their near involvement with this filmic production awoke in them a desire to tell this version of history from the inside, as *non-officialese* cultural history. The commissioning process afforded them a platform through which to consider the African heritage in the oratorio.

Christine Lucia, using Bourdieu's notion of the field of cultural production, maps out the South African musical landscape over three decades to 2005, which also affects *UShaka* and other African cultural productions beyond it.[3] Through Bourdieu's constructs, she analyzes preconditions that cause a piece of work to be produced and consumed. These constructs include an analysis of how a field assigns value to works as symbolic capital (cultural signification) as opposed to artistic (aesthetic) or economic (income-generating) capital.[4] Work which results from commissions has a greater symbolic value as capital. Commissioning bodies lend symbolic support (in some cases, or resistance in others) to imperatives emanating from the larger field of socioeconomic power. They are more conscious of the economic logic of class and race in a shifting historical and political landscape and may even prescribe the style of a piece. Khumalo's oratorio was commissioned together with a number of other large-scale works composed by established white male, middle-class classical composers in South Africa. These commissioned works also displayed awareness of societal realities as they related to class, race, and gender; music politics, and conventions. Nonetheless, many of these compositions were leaning toward overwhelmingly instrumental traditions of Western classical style.

After 1994, commissioned works by the National Arts Council and SAMRO reflected changes in tandem with the broader sociopolitical directions of the country. Genres of music provided for also showed some expansion, as jazz and African orchestral arrangements of traditional African music by white, middle-class male arrangers were supported. The shifts toward African musical genres reflected a cross-cultural prerequisite: an imperative of an African aesthetic requirement which accorded symbolic capital to a long-standing indigenization project. The African aesthetic requirement created new debates around the national identity of the arts in the country. The diversity sought by such debates saw the recycling of older hierarchies, albeit in new gear, an aspect that continued to promote the status quo, with minimal spaces given to newness. Thus, by 2000, an interesting nomenclature for commissioned works emerged: *Five African Sketches* for guitar, *Inyanga* for solo marimba, *Mass for Africa*, *Metamorphosis on an African Wedding Song* for violin, *Music for the Rainbow People* for chamber orchestra, *Nonyana. The Ceremonial Dancer* for piano, which increasingly had musical grammars that leaned toward Western composition.[5]

South African Western-derived orchestral music began in the 1980s, quite belatedly in experimenting with African idioms. Their approach to it was constrained as composers worked intuitively whereas in the choral tradition, the indigenization of Western music was by this time a convention approaching almost 150 years, which included composers from earlier missionary periods. Yet, up to that point choral composers were not wholly pleased with effects produced, seeking to move beyond constraints they identified, such as the limitation of the tonic solfa notation which did not allow for representation of the prosodic features as found in the spoken language, from which music in African conceptualization proceeds. Music choices made by Western-trained composers reflect interlinks between music and training.[6] Composers trained in staff notation operated on a different plane from choral composers, who largely had no formal training and nuanced studies in European classical repertoires. The first time there was a concerted effort to bring the two musical traditions for combined performances was around 1988, when the very first national Massed Choir Festival was staged in Johannesburg under the directorship of Mzilikazi Khumalo and Richard Cock. Out of these combined experimental performances a new, more unifying idiom syncretizing choral tradition and European classical conventions was formulated. Choral composers brought into this space over a century and a half of knowledge of molding modern music which drew copiously from the African heritage. Western music practitioners also brought into this space advanced understandings of formalized European music canons and expertise. Unlike some Western-based South African white composers' approach to African elements, Khumalo's deployment of indigenous materials is not intravenous, but these are wrought from within the linguistic patterns and insider knowledge of the historic and cultural traditions of the Zulu people specifically.

Singing-Body Rhythms' Intersubjectivity with Sociocultural Politics

The interplay of music and social variables within a nation-state is a subject that has engaged an older generation of anthropological scholars such as Schechner and Turner and contemporary cultural scholars such as McNally, Meintjes, Gunner, and Mbembe.[7] These studies offer descriptions and interpretations of visualities of singing–dancing bodies within terrains of popular everyday culture and can be extended to provide insights on the aestheticization of serious or art music when sonic–somatic repertoires are deployed. Khumalo's conceptualization of this work has a dancing body as a precursor to the laying out of the music and can contribute to African music and performance studies, mapping a trajectory that links most types of music performances to sociopolitical and cultural contexts from which the musics emerged. Anthropologists, cultural studies scholars, and ethnomusicologists argue that if other dimensions of music add to it being a pleasurable experience to audiences and as such provide these audiences with power, these dimensions are crucial to the meaning of the music and its effect on publics.[8] This radical move bestows authority on anyone who belongs to the interpretive community of a particular type of music, anyone who understands how its audiences appreciate it, and who is able to identify aspects that make a piece of music powerful, to conduct an analysis.

Earlier rejoinders to Khumalo's epic mainly emphasize musicological and ethnomusicological aspects of its composition. Sociocultural dimensions that transgress music-oriented constructs are addressed minimally, or not at all.[9] Choral literature, while it acknowledges the uniqueness of *amakwaya* choral traditions in South Africa, nonetheless continues to insist on focusing on issues of authenticity, borrowing on models that appraise African choralism along mutually exclusive binaries of the modern versus traditional.[10] Nonetheless, Mugovhani, though proceeding from an ethnomusicological perspective, holds fascinating views seen to be transgressing the confines of ethnomusicology.

Mugovhani's contribution begins to set into motion views suggested by cultural scholars because it links choral music to its cultural, historical, and broader political economy of music production in the country.

This chapter develops from Mugovhani's views and locates Khumalo's works within models whose vantage points are African popular arts. The indigenization project at the heart of Khumalo's music situates his musical craftsmanship within features germane to the constitution of African popular art forms. Interplays of sonic–somatic expressions are linked to questions raised by Khumalo's rendition of Zulu political and cultural history within the context of its composition in the decade of the 1980s and its premiere in the middle of the 1990s. These questions are fundamental to unlocking specific sonic acts and somatic vocabularies he deployed to give the oratorio authoritative weight compared to any other renditions of this epoch of Zulu history. The following questions structure this chapter: What power is in Shaka's life history that gives it traction? Or what is it in the past of the Zulu people that makes it a history that can be tied to feelings of post-1994 national belonging? What forms of signifying practices are enacted through the deployment of selected verbal art and performance traditions that enable an understanding of South African political history?

Praising, Singing, and the Dancing Body

The singing–dancing features framing the epic draw on intrinsic cultural-cognitive and aesthetic elements. These elements are also broadly arranged around other ritual elements and a cosmological mise-en-scène that refract a deeply spiritual Zulu outlook on life. Cultural-cognitive in this discussion entails observations of experiences that best fit and promote the interests of a group. In the oratorio, an array of singing and dancing genres such as the traditional salutation, *Bayede*; song genres such as *ukuhaya* (flowing melodic form of singing); *isililo* (a dirge-like singing); *izibongo* (praise singing); *amahubo* (ancestral songs); *amahubo empi* (war-like rhythmic beat songs); and the traditional dancing styles such as *ukugiya*, *indlamu*, and *ingoma*, as well as the ancestral ritual of placation (*ukuthetha amadlozi*) all together proceed from being conceptualized around the interplay of prosodic elements of the speaking voice and the moving body. These performance elements are saturated with symbolic metaphors that intertextually resonate with ontological epistemologies characterizing Zulu people's knowledge of their world. In this section, only the aesthetic inclusion of three performance genres will be discussed: the deployment of the *ukuhaya* singing genre, *izibongo* performance, and the admixture of *indlamu-ingoma* dance. The major aspect with the nominated genres is that Khumalo has directed in his own handwriting in the tonic solfa copy for choristers how those sections of the oratorio ought to be sung.[11]

Two major instances bring into play the dialectics of the sonic–somatic acts in the oratorio: circumstances leading to the conception of Shaka, and Echo number 20, *Izibongo ZikaShaka* (Shaka's Praises). The preamble sets the tone for courtly observances, one of which is the salutation, *Ndabezitha!* The composer's note indicates how this section should be approached: "In keeping with accepted cultural norms; the choir first pays its respect to the King, in the form of this royal salute, before the story begins." The salutation is central to the rewriting of Zulu royal political history and therefore for Black National politics by extension. During the colonial period, after King Cetshwayo's deposition and the dividing of Zululand into thirteen districts, the colonial administration attempted to abolish this salutation and aimed to reserve it instead for addressing colonial officials only. In defiance, Chief Mankulumana Mnyamana of the Buthelezi clan, Zululand's traditional prime minister, openly defied the English colonialists by addressing King Dinuzulu with this royal salutation when he returned from exile in St. Helena. Msimang, who is a historian and an avid scholar of the isiZulu literary canon, would have experienced firsthand how the Zulu popular imagination appraised this aspect of their history. He had a firm understanding of the Zulu people's activism in cultural and national politics in their reclamation of the autonomy of the Zulu monarchy and how they questioned its marginalization. This question of the empire's control of the Zulu monarchy is a trope in isiZulu literature; likewise, Zondi's play *Insumansumane* (1983) registers this sentiment.[12] This play reconstructs creatively the historical fallout between Inkosi uBhambatha KaMancinza, a Zondi chief, and the colonial officer Theophilus Shepstone, a self-proclaimed paramount chief of the Zulu people during the Poll Tax War of 1906 (*Impi Yamakhanda*). In the play, the central conflict revolves around this salutation and is put across as the cause of Bhambatha KaMancinza's *Impi Yamakhanda*. Msimang and Khumalo's convocation of this historical moment, more than a century after the demise of the Zulu empire, registers continuities of Zulu peoples' struggle for freer existences and reclamation of their history. In the music, Khumalo is cautionary and specific on how this salutation is to be sung:

he instructs, "slowly, with deliberation and great respect," as in the singing of the ancestral *amahubo* musical genre.

The salutation is followed by the unfolding of the story, which is represented by *Ikloba Lothando* (A Fiery Love), which concerns the pronouncement by ancestors about Shaka's forthcoming birth. The directives on how this part is to be sung echo those given for the *Ndabezitha* section. The introduction commences slowly, picking up a tempo which scaffolds into a powerful, broader musical buildup. This sequential development leads up to the first sonic and somatic dialogue introduced by the singing style of *ukuhaya* (Figure 8.1):

Ikloba Lothando (pages 5–8)

> Call: *ILembe lehla ngezilulu zabaphansi nabaphezulu* (The Lembe came down from above riding reed-crafted boats)
> Response: *Ngezilulu zabaphansi nabaphezulu* (Reed-crafted boats of the ancestors and heavenly bodies)
> Call: *Kwazamazam' iziziba* (Ponds shook)
> Response: *Iziziba* (Ponds)
> Call: *Abaphansi banyenyez' emichachazweni yamanzi* (Ancestors whispered in the streams of water)
> Response: *Emichachazweni yamanzi* (In the streams of water)
> Call: *Abaphansi banyenyez' eziziben' ezizonzobele* (Ancestors whispered in the still ponds)
> Response: *Eziziben'ezizonzobele* (In the still ponds)
> Call: *ILembe lehla ngezinhlaka zabaphansi nabaphezulu* (The Lembe came down using frames of ancestors and heavenly bodies)
> Response: *Ngezinhlaka zabaphansi nabaphezulu* (Using frames of ancestors and heavenly bodies)
> Call: *Belul' izandla neminwe, Badob' inhliziyw' emnandi,* (They stretched out their hands and fingers, fished out a sweet heart)
> Call: *KaNandi weNguga ongumnandi weNguga* (Of Nandi, daughter of Nguga, the sweet one of Nguga)
> Response: *Nandi weNguga* (Nandi, daughter of Nguga)
> Call: *Baphehl' uzwath' ezibilini ezinzulu zenhliziyo* (They blew into fire-causing sticks, in the depth of hearts)
> Response: *Ikloba lothando* (A fiery love)
> Call: *Kwasuk'ikloba lothando, lavuth' ubuhanguhangu, lamhangula* (Then began a fiery love, it burnt wildly, and scorched)
> Response: *Ikloba lothando, Nandi weNgug' uzolala kanjani? Nandi weNgug'uzolala kanjani?* (A fiery love, Nandi, daughter of Nguga, how will you sleep?)

Call: *Nandi weNguga* (Nandi, daughter of Nguga)
Response: *Uzolala kanjani? Nandi weNgug' uzolala kanjani?* (How will you sleep? Nandi, daughter of Nguga, how will you sleep?)
Call: *Nekloba lothando!* (Consumed by fiery love)
Response: *Nandi weNgug'uzolala kanjani?* (Nandi, daughter of Nguga, how will you sleep?)

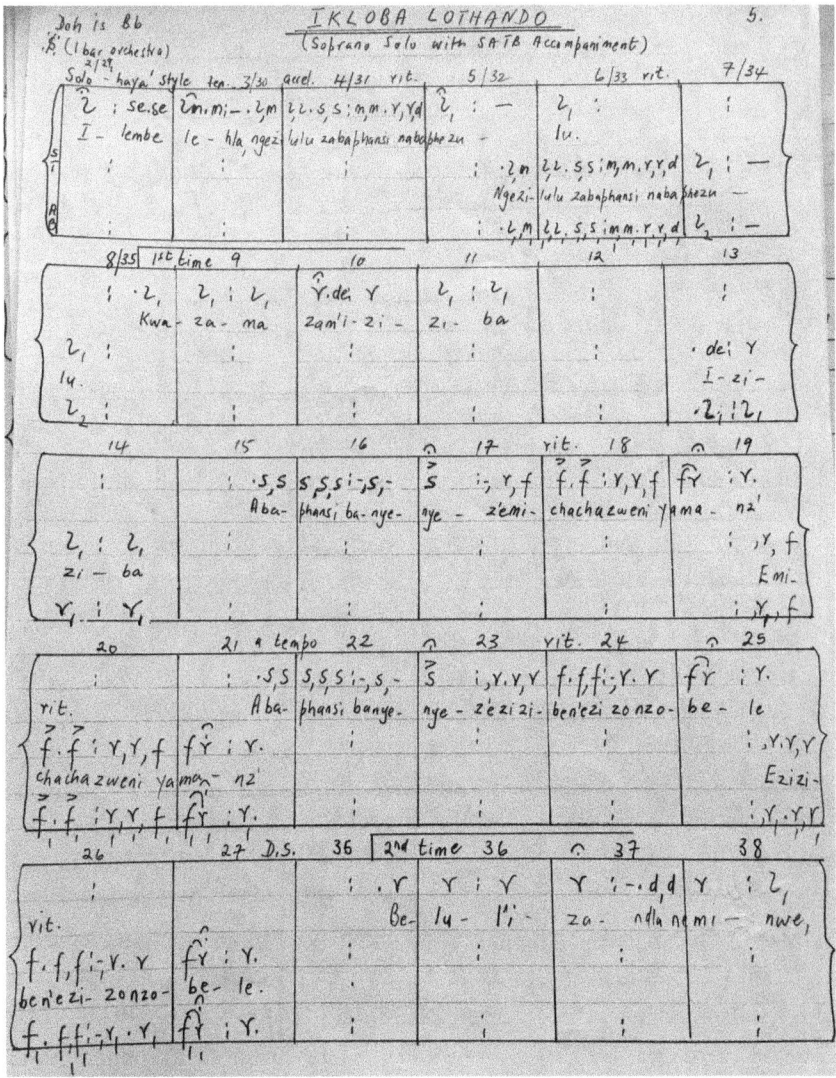

Figure 8.1 "Ikloba Lothando" from *UShaka KaSenzangakhona*, by Mzilikazi Khumalo and Themba Msimang.

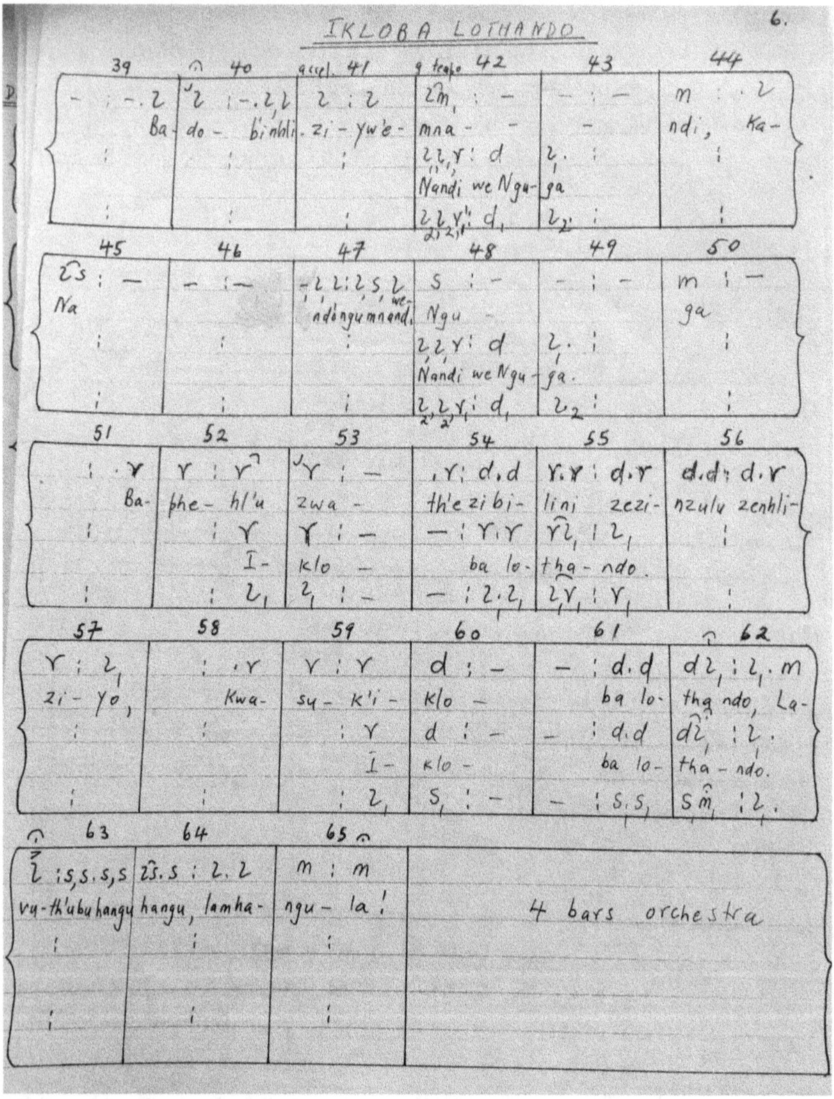

Figure 8.1 (Continued).

In this introductory part, Khumalo plays with voice timbres and dancing styles which introduce a dialectical play that conjures up images of personified love with hands and fingers that capture Nandi's heart and consume it in a fiery passion. The dance itself is not physically enacted in the conventional sense, but it is articulated through singing styles which flow from natural speech acts

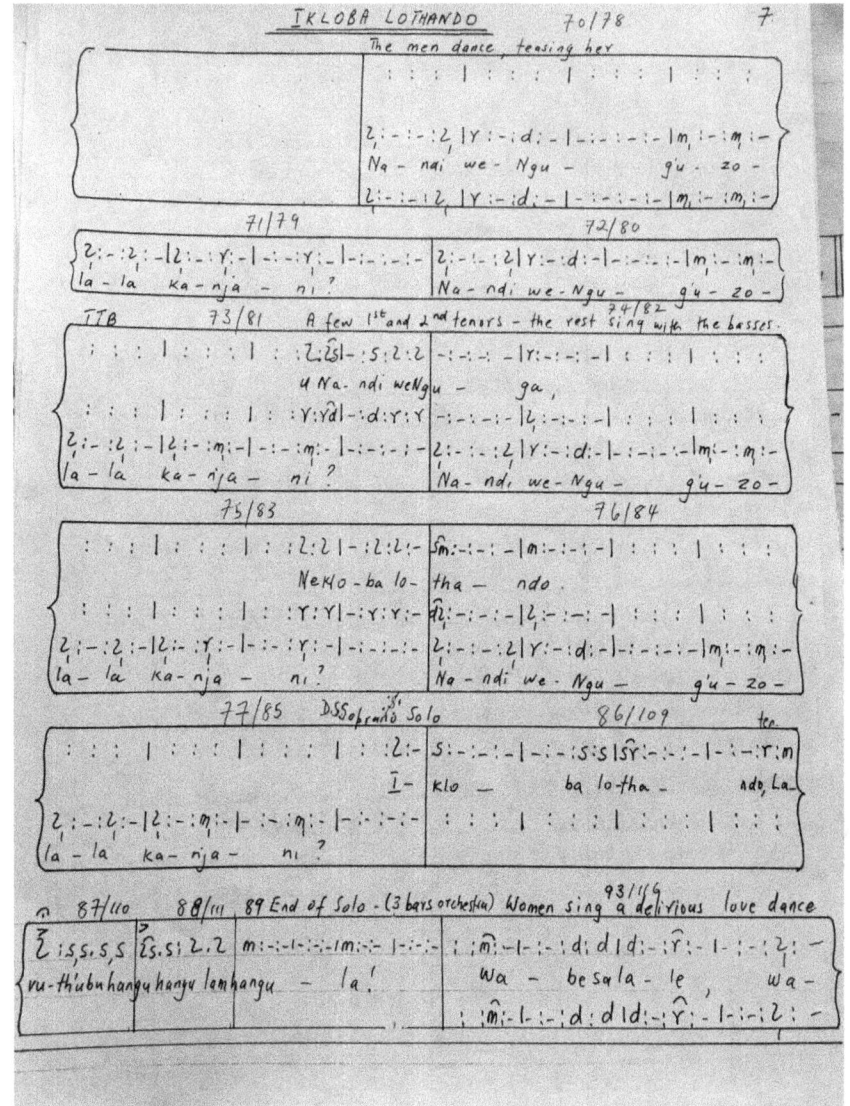

Figure 8.1 (Continued).

of isiZulu-speaking interlocution. In the last five lines of this call and response, "men join in the dance, singing teasing her about her uncontrollable feelings" (see the score bar 70/78 below). This sequence is looped onto by women who join in the sing–dance sequence, registering "a delirious love dance" (see the

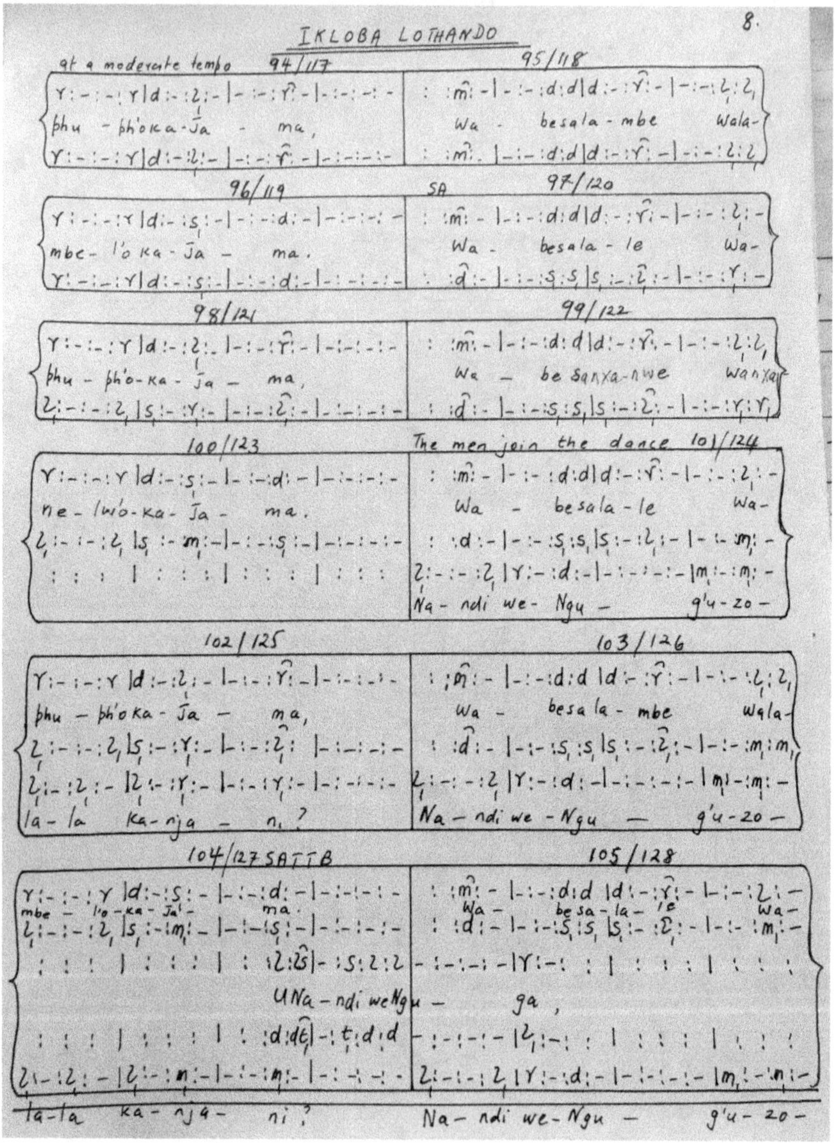

Figure 8.1 (Continued).

score bar 93/116 below), which again is looped onto by the call and response by men's jovial singing–dancing (see the score bar 101/124 below), all of which have been performed without any body movement, in standstill; however, with the sonic and somatic relationship strongly "concretely visible" and "intensely audible" in the song:

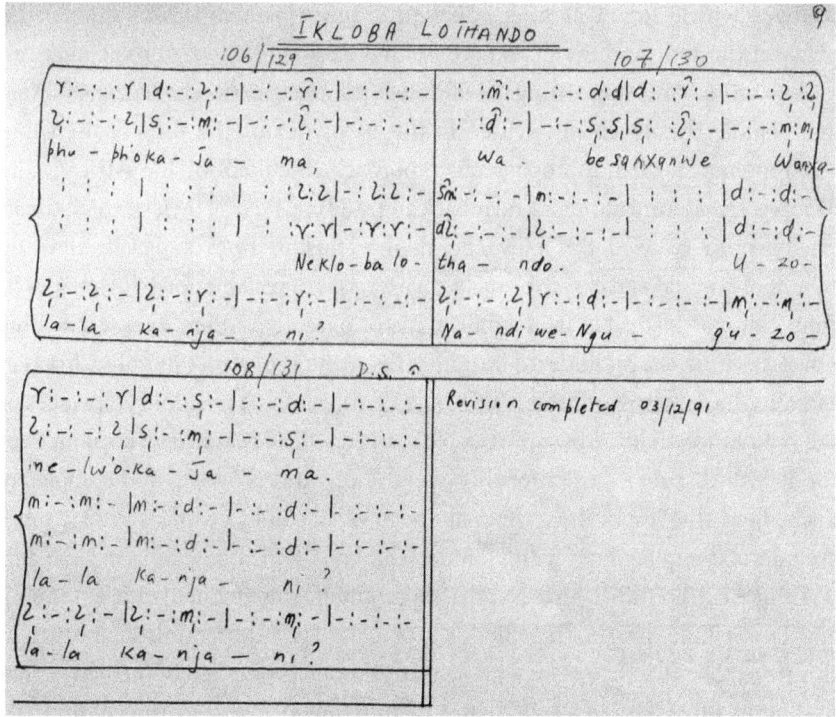

Figure 8.1 (Continued).

Call: *Ikloba lothando, lavuth' ubuhanguhangu lamhangula!* (A fiery love, burnt wildly and scorched her!)
Wabesalalale, waphuph' okaJama (She tried sleeping but dreamt of the son of Jama)
Wabesalambe walambel' okaJama (She hungered for the son of Jama)
Wabasalale waphuph' okaJama (She tried sleeping but dreamt of the son of Jama)
Wabasanxanwe wanxanelw' okaJama (She thirsted for the son of Jama)
Response: *Nandi weNgug' uzolala kanjani?* (Nandi, daughter of Nguga, how will you sleep?)
Response 1: *Nekloba lothando* (Consumed by fiery love)
Response 2: *Nandi weNgug' uzolala kanjani?* (Nandi, daughter of Nguga, how will you sleep?)

The above sequence conjures "moving" dancing bodies fused into sung parts. It describes Nandi's passion, how her heart was scorched by the flames of Senzangakhona's love. The entire section enters into an unmistakable intertextual dialogue with R.R.R. Dhlomo's *UShaka KaSenzangakhona* (1937). Similarities between the song and the fiction are minutely brought down to basic nuances: a consuming fire, forecasting an ill-fated romance between Senzangakhona and Nandi. The novel was written in the 1930s during the time of the white anthropological turn, a propagandist approach intended for the African elite to forego modernization and turn back to tradition.[13] Nonetheless, the African intelligentsia realized this ploy and their exclusion from a racialized white monopoly capital and opted to engage in exercises of reclamation of history away from colonial-instigated white, official historiography in their own terms. This novel was further a rejoinder to the rather disturbing constructions of a Christian morality-based novel of Mofolo's *Chaka* (1923). Mofolo's reactions to ravages of the Zulu Empire on the Basotho people worked within Manichean discourses of the British discourses of rationality, civilization, and progress, and completely discredited this important historical epoch of the Zulu people. Further, there are intertextual dialogues with Donnie Mhlongo's *Ilanga LaseLangeni* (The Sun of Langeni, 1991), in which Nandi's representation is imbued with autonomy and power that characterized her as a precolonial Zulu feministic apostle. In this novel, Nandi's encounter with Senzangakhona is emptied of the patriarchal undertones that saw her as a victim of unrequited love and the coldhearted members of the royal house. Instead, she is portrayed as a woman of strength and perceptiveness—a character consistent with the mantle of Zulu royal women—who took responsibility for her actions as she single-handedly raised one of the most powerful kings. Mhlongo's take on Nandi reinscribes the powerful position royal women enjoyed in precolonial patriarchal-based Zulu society, an aspect lost to modern Africans because of missionary's tampering with gender roles during their proselytizing moments.[14]

In Mzilikazi Khumalo's *UShaka*, the analogy established by the musical sequence with these literary narratives is concluded in yet another courtly transaction, which ties Shaka's birth to ancestral sanctioning of his existence: *Imbizo yeziNyandezulu* (The meeting of the Nyandezulu) and *Imbizo Yajub' uMjokwane* (The meeting selected Mjokwane). Taken together, the literary pieces and these musical sequences detail the circumstances around Shaka's extraordinary conception and the cultural reverence bestowed upon those occupying positions of power among Zulu society. However, underlying this simple reading is complexity introduced by certain oral narrations which speak of Zulu epistemologies tied to oral ontologies that take us further back, beyond colonially obliterated histories of Zulu forefathers that predate the history of Shaka. Colonial historiography has repeatedly presented a dimension of the Zulu past that mainly corresponded with Shaka's rise to power because it marked the period of their settlement in Natal. In the oratorio, Phunga noMageba and Jama are names that suggest historical constructions which are longer than the two hundred years of Zulu history conventionally provided by *officialese* historiography.[15] The oral histories refracted by allusion to these Zulu monarchs within this context require a journey back to pre-European-based history, to the founding ancestors of the Zulu people under one group, the Nguni people constituted by Qwabe and Zulu, and how they are then followed by almost nineteen Zulu monarchs. The epistemological narrative of genesis introduced by the myth of creation is suggestive of how within this cultural system, existence among Zulu society is a spiritual affair. It proceeds from careful unfoldings of cyclical repetitions of historical events and deliberations sanctioned by the ancestors at the *Imbizo YeziNyandezulu*, a gathering of past kings believed to have powers to also identify key personnel to execute its assignments, as the next sequence, *Imbizo Yamjub'okaMjokwane*, indicates. Both *Imbizo YeziNyandezulu* and *Imbizo Yajub'uMjokwane* present intersubjective relationships between this metaphysical world of ancestors and earthly beings introduced by the song in *Ikloba Lothando*. The former sequences are playful overlayings of *ukuhaya* and *ukubonga* genres at particular junctures in the melody, but all of which are preludes, signaling a disastrous courtship, the aftermath of which, among other things, is the birth of the Zulu Empire, which was destined to witness many calamities in the hands of its founding ruler and other rulers thereafter in its collision with other nations. At this juncture, the oratorio signals its awareness of this history through intertextuality and other meaning-making processes that have been repeatedly derived from an array of oral historical sources, all of which are presented in an interplay between singing and dancing.

From Prosodic Cadences to Bodily Movements: *Izibongo*, Sonic–Somatic Dialectics

The summoned myth of genesis in this oratorio is also corroborated by verbatim inscriptions of history in the form of narrative flows and *izibongo* introduced as echoes in the oratorio. *Izibongo* are repositories of persons, family, clan, and an entire nation's naming practices, genealogies, events, and historical inscriptions.

Where these oral art forms act as archives for the public sphere, they are normally recordings of events and national highlights attending to the political elite in traditional society. In the recitation of *izibongo*, generally, both the sonic and somatic acts are involved. The *imbongi* (praise singer) recites genealogies of the Zulu royal house and King Shaka's interspersed with *izithakazelo* (the honorific names), *izithopho* (personal praises and attributes), and historical triumphant events. At the same time, sequences move on to include traditional dance routines for which Zulu people are celebrated, including: *indlamu*, which in this oratorio is interchanged with its modern variant, *ingoma*. *Indlamu* is a percussion-based spirited traditional war dance which both women and men perform accompanied by heavy drumming in traditional Zulu communities. In traditional contexts, uniformly costumed performers in traditional attire execute precision-based bodily movements, with elements of solo self-stylization performed at intervals. *Ingoma*, on the other hand, though an evolving category of a dance style, takes many of its features from *indlamu*, but added to it are those aspects that refract contemporary contextual factors that have since affected Zulu people.

The *ingoma* dance genre covers a broad range of male team dances such as *isikhuze, isicathulo, ukukomika, isiZulu, isiBhaca, umzansi* and *isishameni, ukhwaxa/ubhaca* of Nongoma and Kwa-Hlabisa, *ukhwaxa/ubhaca* of Mzimkhulu, *isikhomazi* of Umkhomazi.[16] Erlmann posits that *ingoma* developed out of overwhelming changes of traditional rural Zulu culture through impoverishment, dispossession, and labor migration around the First World War.[17] He adds that the kinesic patterns of *ingoma* are inseparably linked to choral songs in call-and-response structure and, as such, constitute a complex statement of unity of dance and song in Zulu performance culture. Vusabantu Ngema describes what dance means for a Zulu person, stating that "it is a body of history that embodies an explanation and a justification of the existence of the Zulu people and a process through which Zulu people have preserved, evolved and transformed themselves."[18]

In the oratorio, the Echoes (1–20) are rich historical narrations linking up huge segments of Shaka's life experiences which at some sections are sung parts and at others recited. *Izibongo* brings to narrative frames large sections of secondary plane structures into the primary plane of the sung narrative. Echo number 20 is preceded by the narrator's rendition of vast historical timelines in concentrated forms which then flow into a recitation of *izibongo* after which are sung a rendition of the actual praises of Shaka:

Narrator: *Bayamemeza ngaphesheya kweGwa* (They are howling from across the iGwa river)
Bath'emakhosanen'uwafakel'uxhuxhu (Saying that he instils fear among small chiefs)
Kuze kwas'exhuxhuma (Until dawn they were shuddering)
Kuze kwas'exhuxhuzela/ (Until dawn they were trembling)
Kuxhuxhuzel'uNgoza kubaThembu (Even Ngoza of the abaThembu was shivering)
Kuxhuxhuzel'uMacingwan'eNgonyameni (Macingwane of Ngonyameni shook)
Amakhos'abhincela nxanye (The chief lost all hope)
Kwaw'ibheshu kwawi'usiphenama (The back and front covering loincloths fell)
Edl'ejeqeza okwamadlanga (They ate glancing about in fear like vultures)
Ethi lukhulu luyeza luyanyelela (Saying something huge is stealthily coming)
Silufanisa noPhunga (We liken it to Phunga)
Silufanisa noMageba (We liken it to Mageba)

Fascinating though is how the narrator embellishes this historical reality by what is rumored to have been thoughts and happenings in other chiefs when they heard of Shaka's approaching legions. All are said to have suffered uncontrollable shivers, with some even losing their garbs in their state of flight. The narrated segment is followed by another, couched in the tradition of *izibongo*, which is accompanied by the *imbongi* performance dance style. This narrative braids together imagined historical internecine and colonial encounters with vignettes of real praises from Shaka's *izibongo*:

Imbongi: *Makhos'anoxhuxhu ngokuxhuxhuma* (You chiefs who are trembling because of fear)
Nin'elize lashona nidla nijeqeza (You who until dusk ate glancing about in fear)
Abanye sebethath'imithwalo bayetshatha (Others picked up their baggage and carried it on their backs)
Okandaba akaxabene namuntu (The son of Ndaba is not quarrelling with anyone)
Uthi Ndlu emnyama hlanganani (He is saying House of Black people unite)
Ukhoz'olumaphik'abanzi; (The hawk with wide wings)

> *Lufukamel'uZihlandlo kaGcwabe* (Covered Zihlandlo of Gcwabe)
> *Lufukamel'uMzilikazi kaMashobana* (Covered Mzilikazi of Mashobane)
> *Lufukamel'omnyama nomhlophe* (Covered both white and black)
> *Ngoba lufukamel'uFini* (Because it covered Fynn)
> *Kwabandlebe zikhany'ilanga* (Among the white people)
> *Ngoba lufukamel'uFebana* (Because it covered Farewell)
> *Kwabandlebe zikhany' ilanga* (Among the white people)
> *Ngabona sekugiy'amathongo* (I even saw ancestors dancing)

Significant from this praise singing is how the above segment leads to Echo 20, which now provides a full rendition in SATB (soprano, alto, tenor, and bass) choral arrangement of selected Shakan praise poems:

> Choir: *UDlungwane kaNdaba* (Dlungwane son of Ndaba)
> *UDlungwane woMbelebele* (Ferocious one of the Mbelebele regiment)
> *Odlunge emanxulumeni* (Who raged among great homes)
> *Kwaze kwasa amanxulum'esibekelana* (Until dawn great homes were turned upside down)
> *UMjokwane kaNdaba* (Mjokwane, son of Ndaba)
> *Usala kutshelwa, usala kunyenyezelwa* (The one who refuses to be told, who refuses to be whispered to)
> *Usishaka kasishayeki* (He who beats but is not beaten)
> *UNodumehlezi kaMenzi* (He who is famous without effort, Son of Menzi)
> *Ushaka ngiyesaba ukuthi wuShaka* (Shaka, to whom I am afraid to call Shaka)
> *UShaka wayeyinkosi yaseMashobeni* (Shaka was the king of Mashobeni)
> *Uteku lwabafazi bakwaNomgabi* (The laughter of the women of Nomgabi)
> *Betekula behlezi emlovini* (Who mocked basking in the sun)
> *Bethi uShaka, kayikubusa, kayikubankosi* (Saying Shaka will never rule, that he will never be king)
> *Kanti yilaph'ezakunethezeka* (When actually he will be comfortable)
> *Ilemb'eleqa amanye ngokukhalipha* (The Axe that surpasses other axes by being sharp)

In the tradition of reciting *izibongo*, these can be entered from any segment in its entire body. In this oratorio, the segment used as an entry point is not that which emphasizes his lineage or genealogy, but that which highlights his triumphs and stature. This melodic flow is interrupted by the entry of a sung narrative imagining a dancing body in music; this dance is *indlamu* (bar 77). *Indlamu* is the sung dancing rhythmic pattern that takes up the momentum of the melodic line, which on its repetition adds on a clapping patterning to the musical texture. The clapping brings *ingoma* kinetic dancing patterns. With the clapping, there are variations which conjecture up images of rhythmic accentuations effected by the falling thud of the dancer's feet in his dance pattern.[19] The following sequence brings visualities of this dance, however in music:

SATB:	*Waqedaqed' izizw'uyakuhlaselaphi na*? (You go about exterminating nations, where next are you attacking? (*indlamu-ingoma* dance sequence introduced)
	He, he, he, uyakuhlaselapphi na? (He, he, he, where next are you attacking?)
	Waqedaqed' izizw'uyakuhlaselaphi na? (You go about exterminating nations, where next are you attacking?)
	He, he, he, uyakuhlaselaphi na? (He, he, he, where next are you attacking?)
	Soprano solo: *Umlilo wothate kaMjokwane* (The wild fire of dry grass of Mjokwane) (sequence repeated twice)
	Umlilo wothathe wubuhanguhangu (The wild fire of dry grass burns wildly)
	Oshis'izikhova zaseDlebe, (And burnt the owls of Dlebe)
	Kwaye kwasha nezaseMabedlana (Even the place of Mabedlana was burnt down)
SATB:	*Uyakuhlaselaphi na*? (When next are you attacking?)
	Uyakuhlaselpahi na? (When next are you attacking?)
	Osifuba sinenqaba (He whose chest is like a fortress)
	UBayede kaNdaba (Bayede son of Ndaba)
	UBayede kaNdaba (Bayede son of Ndaba)
	UNdaba ngiyemesaba, ngimuka naye (Ndaba I am afraid of you, I am carried away with him)
	Ngimbuka kwehle izinyembezi (I look at him and tears roll down)
	Umoy'omzansi wongenelo (The cold wind from the east that breeze)
	Ohlez'ubangenela nangomnyango (That always comes in even through the door)
Soprano:	*Oth'esadl'ezinye wadl'ezinye* (One who while devouring some devoured others)
	(repeated until the end of the melodic sequence)
SATB:	*Ndabezitha! Ndabezitha! Ndabezitha!*

In highlighting the confluence *izibongo* and *indlamu-ingoma* have in the creation of an unmistakable Zulu idiomatic aesthetic effect in the oratorio, Meintjes's work on *ingoma* performance at Keates Drift, eMsinga on December 25, 2000, is illustrative. Symmetrical features exist with the dance performance she describes, and which the oratorio recreates musically:

> *gqi!* is an aural icon of the thud of the foot hitting the ground after a high frontal kick in the Zulu men's dance style called *ingoma*. After a preparatory sequence, the dancer's right knee bends, his back arches, his head tilts back. He extends his right arm over his head as his left leg stretches back to prepare for the pick-up to the beat. The forward thrust of his left arm balances his taut and arching body. Then, as if a spring suddenly triggered, he kicks his left leg into the sky, curls his torso and shoots his right arm forward to balance his one-legged stance. His skyward foot thunders down onto the ground on the beat *gqi!* Dust flies. He throws away the movement with his hands, in the recoil of his torso, with a flick of his head, and he saunters off.[20]

The brief description above is a textual recreation of visual sequences of *ingoma* dance. Its description is not radically different from that of kinetic high kicking motions of *indlamu* dance. *Indlamu* involves a performer's lifting up one foot over his head and then landing it on the ground with a big thundering sound on a downward beat and at times falling backward. The bodily movements are almost similar in both *indlamu* and *ingoma* dances. In team dances, performers shadow each other's moves in synchronized perfect patterns. Both dances allow for solo exhibitions, normally self-stylized improvisations. In terms of accompaniments, *ingoma*'s rhythms are organized around chanting and clapping of hands while *indlamu* percussion-derived rhythms are sourced from multiple drumming being played in contrapuntal beats. In both dance styles, repetitive dance routines signal structural subtleties: complexities of rhythmic patterns, intricate foot negotiations, play with shifts of body weight, and counterpoint of juxtaposed body parts. Khumalo's epic recreates these dance patterns when Shaka's *izibongo* are introduced.

The sequence introduced by the praise poet in Echo 20 and thereafter looped onto by the SATB choir from bar 9 until bar 138 recreates in musical terms these dance routines described above. Bar 9 commences with the *izibongo* of King Shaka; the prosodic elements of the spoken word then progress into the singing. These praises are sung as in their recitation dictum until bar 76. As these praises are introduced, Khumalo is clear regarding how they must be sung, "slow and reverential, with rhythm strongly marked." These melodic features are maintained from bar 9 until bar 23, when there is another instruction given about how to proceed with the remainder of the sequence. From the last note of bar 23 to bar 47, the singing is urged on the "same tempo, but rhythm less marked." This sequence is thereafter followed by the solo Tenor from bar 48 to 56, looped onto by the Bass solo from bar 57 to 76, serving as the penultimate before the *indlamu-ingoma* dance rhythms commence and the full power of the sonic emphasis of its music is felt.

The *indlamu* dance sequence is sung by the entire SATB from bar 77 to 96 and with a dramatic coloratura soprano solo accompanied by the TB (97–105). The Soprano soloist is dropped off altogether with the entire soprano part as the TTBB picks up at "Tempo Primo" from bar 105 to 108, and then joined in again by the entire soprano voice from bar 109 to 116, only to be dropped again from bar 117 to 120. The entire SATB voice is brought back again for the ultimate punch line which is also drawn from real Shakan praises presented in call and response. The Soprano's call, "*Oth'esadl'ezinye wabedl'ezinye*" and the ATB response, "*Ndabezitha*" (bar 121–138), alternates with the Alto voice looping from the Soprano calls of "*wath'esadl'ezinye wadl'ezinye*," however pushing from the middle between the Soprano's call and the TB's response. The aesthetic effect of this rondo convokes images of sea-waves of relentless attacking armies, which plays on the Shakan military stratagem of *izimpondo zempi* (horns of the armies) attacking from both sides and with the midpoint called *isifuba sempi* (the chest of the army) advancing from the middle. In the recreation of this metaphor musically, the Soprano attacks from the left-hand side with the beginning of the call, which is repeated and given a boost in the middle by the Alto voice and rounded off from the right-hand side by the Tenor and the Bass voices. The entire singing sequence aurally recreates the Shakan Zulu military strategy of the wings of both armies placed on either side of the horns of the armies and having the thrusting middle army occupying its chest in its synchronized collaboration to enclose the enemy completely.

It is thus no wonder that *indlamu* dance becomes the aesthetic effect for describing Shaka's wars of conquest and his triumphs in this oratorio. *Indlamu* originated from war dances from battlefronts and became prominent with Shaka's war drills. From then on, it became a marked performance feature in celebratory events after winning wars and in inaugurations of kings in Zulu traditional society. Within the Shakan context of this dance, it projects power, preparedness for war, and underscores military prowess and the organizational capabilities of

Zulu armies. The dance as a war drill exercised, taught, and instilled discipline in Zulu men, and also symbolized self-control and dominance. In the oratorio, this stature of being in control and dominant is captured in the entire section of *Izibongo ZikaShaka* (bars 9–138): its narrative interplay with *izibongo* and the sonic force of its musicality establish the sense of self-control and dominance which is reinforced by a particularized clapping of hands by choristers and the drumming by the orchestra. The clapping itself helps conjecture bodily movements of the performer's landing kick with *isiqgi*. This sequence, introduced by the call of the TB, "*waqed' aqed' íziwe uyakuhlaselaphi na?*" is accompanied by contrapuntal hand clapping of the TB beginning from the end of bar 76 to 88 to which the SA joins from the end of bar 84 to 88. The opening two bars emulate the fast-dancing rhythms effected by the stamping of the feet, but from the end of bar 78 through to 80, "*he, he, he, uyakuhlaselaphi na?*" conjures up the image of a swaying torso with arms outstretched as the dancer prepares to bring down the skyward kick back onto the ground which falls squarely on a downward beat. This movement and its image are continued again from the end of bar 80 through to 84. The repetition of this sequence with the entire SATB voice from bar 85 to 88 anticipates a second pattern in contrapuntal clapping which now alternates between the TB and the SA from bar 89 to 96. This alternative contrapuntal clapping ends a dance sequence which has movements that bring to mind *ingoma* dance movements. The last clapping pattern from bar 97 to 108 is a single beat pattern which emulates the rapid rhythm of downward thudding of the *indlamu* dancer's feet before he throws away the movement altogether. The contrasting movements, which are built into the *ingoma*'s slower and the faster *indlamu*-rhythm producing beats, introduce complex subtleties endemic to dance cultures of Zulu people, and yet at the same time amplify the kinds of historical performance cultures Zulu men have gone through since precolonial times until in the contemporary era when so much had changed and affected their cultural lives.

Conclusion

Khumalo's craftsmanship and experimentations within a larger, international Black art music history draw from a conscious effort by African artists of different persuasions on the continent and in the African diaspora. His *UShaka* engaged existing compositions that attempted mergers between Western and

African stylistics and stamped a symbolic capital on these efforts. In terms of the history they address, Msimang and Khumalo's deployment of this epoch of the Zulu past, using these singing and dancing genres, is significant for the kinds of claims they postulate for the Zulu nation. The recreation of traditional Zulu performance sensibilities in this oratorio accentuates ideas of how the values of *ubuZulu* (Zuluness), its authority and power, are continually reinscribed into unfolding contemporary politics, aspects which many renditions of Shakan history have failed to signal. Khumalo's musical stylistics reflect continued attempts to reinscribe Zulu political and cultural pasts for the contemporary African society, and his attempts are a testament to how art music can be a site for self-representation.

9

The Unique Collaboration Behind the Opera *Princess Magogo KaDinuzulu*

Sandra de Villiers

This is the story of how the opera, *Princess Magogo KaDinuzulu*, was created. It begins with the formation of Opera Africa in 1992 and the development of what the artist Andrew Verster later described as "Africanized" productions of operas in South Africa. I was the founding Chief Executive Officer at Opera Africa working in collaboration with my husband, Hein de Villiers,[1] and a board of leading musicians, artists, and business personalities in South Africa. I had returned to South Africa following my operatic studies in Austria and was keen to develop opera locally.[2] During the early years of Opera Africa, we focused on creating African productions of European operas for a local audience. We recognized the wealth of vocal talent in the country and the rich tradition of choral singing. Handel's *Messiah*, Mendelssohn's *Elijah*, and other choral works by Haydn and Mozart were popular with community choirs, but even so, opera had not taken root in communities and was too expensive for many to attend. The first work that Opera Africa staged was two productions of *Die Zauberflöte* (*The Magic Flute*) by W. A. Mozart. The first was adapted to an African setting on the plains of Kenya by the director Jacky Vermaas and costume designer Patti Slavin. The second production, directed by Themi Venturas and designed by Andrew Verster, probably had the greatest impact on the artistic team's approach to the making of the *Princess Magogo* opera. An early production that also impacted our approach to touring with productions was Gounod's *Faust*. It was initiated by the Opera Africa chairman, Professor Khabi Mngoma, who taught at the University of Zululand and opened at the 5000-seater King Bhekuzulu Hall at the University of Zululand. The production was directed in the round with visual projections as backdrops in place of fixed sets. Soloists were selected from national auditions. The KwaZulu-Natal Philharmonic Orchestra rehearsed and performed the work at the King Bhekuzulu Hall, as well as at the Playhouse in Durban. The tricky contrapuntal chorus parts were transcribed into tonic sol-fa for the local choir, Cantata Chorale from eSikhawini, a township outside Empangeni. It was a dangerous time with a great deal of unrest in the townships. We had to be met at the entrance of the township by the management of the choir to accompany us to the rehearsal venue. We toured *Faust* with the same cast nationally to Bloemfontein, Roodepoort, Johannesburg, and the Playhouse in Durban, using a local orchestra at each venue. It was beautiful and a great encouragement to experience how easily the rural choir adjusted to this sophisticated art form—and this via tonic sol-fa.

Opera Africa always focused on developing an African identity for the productions which were greatly influenced by the well-known painter Andrew Verster, who designed most of our opera productions. Our initial productions of Western operas had set out to create "Africanized" works. In the beginning, there was a negative connotation to this approach as it was an approach well ahead of the times, but the word stuck. We wanted to make operas accessible to the man or woman in the street, and particularly to Black audiences. In 1992, we decided to take the next step and ask: Is it possible to initiate and develop a genre of African opera?

The positive reception of these early productions encouraged us to go ahead and commission a new work built on indigenous African principles. *Princess Magogo*, as it is affectionately known, was commissioned by Opera Africa in 1998.[3] It was an ambitious project that brought together some of the country's leading intellectuals involved with Zulu music, culture, and history. The African identity of *Princess Magogo* is evident in the language, the choral idiom, the history conveyed in the libretto, the costume designs, and the dance styles. These cultural elements came together in our production for an entirely new approach to African opera. Just as you have Italian, German, and French opera, we aimed to establish an African operatic genre. That is where I started researching ideas for the new work. It began with a visit to Professor Mazisi Kunene at the University of KwaZulu-Natal.[4] Professor Kunene was a famous poet who had lived a big part of his life overseas because of the political situation in South Africa. He returned to South Africa in 1992 and had published an epic on Shaka. He said to me, "Sandra, why don't you write an opera on *Princess Magogo*." Prof. Kunene proposed that I meet Princess Magogo's son, Dr. Mangosuthu Buthelezi,[5] and he wrote to Dr. Buthelezi by way of introduction. When I took the proposal to the Opera Africa board, Prof. Khabi Mngoma, retired professor of music at the University of Zululand and chairman of our board, was keen to take the matter forward. He happened to have a longtime friendship with Dr. Buthelezi and set up an initial meeting at Ulundi with himself, the Opera Africa artistic director, Hein de Villiers, and me.

Prof. Mngoma was a humble person who was an established figure in the development of music in Soweto, Johannesburg, and in Zululand, where he founded the music department at the University of Zululand. He started the Soweto String Quartet and was involved with the establishment of orchestras and ensembles for Black musicians in Johannesburg. I had met Prof. Mngoma in 1992 when he agreed to join the Opera Africa board. As a close friend of Dr. Buthelezi, he was crucial in brokering that relationship by organizing regular meetings with myself and the rest of our artistic team at Mahlabathini and Ulundi.[6] Hein and I would stay at the Holiday Inn in Ulundi, and we met Dr. Buthelezi at his home at KwaPhindangene where he showed us around the Princess's home and took us to her grave. His unstinting and enthusiastic support throughout every facet of the research and writing of the opera was invaluable, especially to Andrew Verster when he started on the set and costume designs for the opera and to the composer Mzilikazi Khumalo where Dr. Buthelezi frequently sang his mother's songs to explain and elaborate on musical questions from the composer and on historical facts from the librettist, Themba Msimang (I still have tapes of many of these meetings with Dr. Buthelezi singing!).

The idea for the designate composer came to me on listening to a CD of the epic *UShaka KaSenzangakhona* by Professor Mzilikazi Khumalo (1996). I remember that moment, saying to Hein, "I've got our composer!" (Figure 9.1) The renowned South African singer Sibongile Khumalo was Prof. Mngoma's daughter, and she also served on the Opera Africa board. Her recommendation was that we approach Duma Ndlovu to write the libretto. However, since Prof. Khumalo was used to finding inspiration in poetry rather than prose we ultimately turned to his longtime collaborator and friend, Professor Themba Msimang, a well-known linguist, historian, and poet, to write the libretto for the *Princess Magogo KaDinuzulu* opera.[7] Deciding on an orchestrator was also quite a process, starting with composer Bongani Ndodana-Breen—then still a young and upcoming talent. Kevin Volans, the internationally renowned South African composer then living in Ireland, happened to be a friend of Andrew Verster, and he was also considered. But we settled on Michael Hankinson, who had a

Figure 9.1 Professor Mzilikazi Khumalo and Prince Mangosuthu Buthelezi. Photo Credit: Opera Africa.

successful career in musical theater, arranging, and composing and had worked under Hein de Villiers during his time as Inspector of Music in the KwaZulu Natal Education Department. Together they formed the core of the artistic team who worked on the opera. Each of Khumalo, Msimang, and Hankinson was based in the Gauteng province, which made the collaboration easier. Since Khumalo wrote exclusively in tonic solfa, it was necessary to include a transcriber, the conductor and choral director Ludumo Magangane, who would set Khumalo's music in staff notation for Michael Hankinson to orchestrate.

The rest of the artistic team included the internationally acclaimed South African painter Andrew Verster, an eclectic artist who would do the set and costume designs, and Themi Venturas, an experienced theater director who spoke Zulu fluently.[8] The choice of conductor for the world premiere fell on Gerhard Geist, a German now living in Durban who had also worked with us beforehand.[9] I remember the team sitting on the balcony at our house in Durban on a regular basis, deciding on the choice of the musical format, for example, "durch komponiert" versus a number opera, what original songs by Princess Magogo to leave untouched (for instance, unaccompanied); or Hein and I meeting at Andrew's house with him and Themi sitting on the floor with designs spread all over. Andrew's designs for the set were inspired by our visits to Mahlabathini where he saw the aloes that play such an important iconic role in the opera. It is also where he got the inspiration for the plumes on the warriors' heads. All of this was initiated by the scenery of Zululand in northern KwaZulu-Natal. But there are also scenes that depict the colonial setting at the time and some of this is unexpected for audiences who arrive to see a Zulu opera. For instance, Prince Solomon, before he became king, is profiled wearing jodhpurs on stage! When questioned, Dr. Buthelezi would say, "but that is the way they dressed in St Helena," and the habit remained when they returned after their ban was lifted.

Dr. Buthelezi always made himself available to our artistic team, despite being national Minister of Home Affairs at the time, and he met with the artistic team either in Pretoria at his offices or at his home in Mahlabathini in Zululand. This enabled them to check on historical facts and to get his valued opinion and the go-ahead when artistic decisions had to be taken, keeping in mind that we were writing an opera and not making a documentary. Sadly, Prof. Khabi Mngoma passed away in 2001 and was not there to see the work through. It was left to me to take over the responsibility of driving the project, and I am eternally grateful to Dr. Buthelezi, as son of his beloved mother, Princess Magogo, supporting me throughout. He was always a phone call away, and always ready to assist the team to ensure that the opera retained its authentic indigenous character. This close and on-hand collaboration among everyone in the team was essential but also most enriching for everyone with their passion to ensure the success of this unique and historical opera. Khumalo and Msimang were learning how to do their first opera, but we learned from them, too. We were trained in the European tradition of opera, and it was quite exciting learning about Zulu music and culture along the way. For instance, the use of Khumalo's Bonga style was translated in operatic terms as recitative, thus demonstrating an important linkage between the traditions.

There were some logistical challenges with a team this large. The combination of the Durban- and Gauteng-based artists meant that we had to use a range of technologies to communicate. With Prof. Khumalo, Michael Hankinson, and Ludumo Magangane in Johannesburg, and Prof. Msimang in northern Zululand, the team had to correspond in letters and faxes before computers and cell phones came along!

Princess Magogo was herself very unusual because of the important role she played in Zulu politics despite being a woman and with a huge influence on her brother, King Solomon. Her story is told in a Prologue, two acts leading up to her marriage, and an Epilogue. Prof. Msimang wrote a beautiful libretto for an aria to open the Epilogue about Dr. Buthelezi's father which was left out for political reasons at the time, but Prof. Msimang and I are still very interested in eventually having this inserted. It would be a unifying element in an opera that documents the life and tragic love story between Princess Magogo and her lover Ndwandwe as told to the artistic team at his round table in his office in Pretoria by Dr. Buthelezi himself. This has all the elements of a classic operatic plot and still authentically mirrors the history of the time, as President Mandela told the audience when he attended a performance of the opera at the South African State Theatre in Pretoria.

The musical collaboration between Prof. Khumalo and Michael Hankinson was crucial as Prof. Khumalo only wrote in tonic sol-fa. Ludumo Magangane, choral conductor and director, transcribed his music into staff notation, and Michael Hankinson had to compile the piano score and write the orchestration, arrangements, and additional incidental music to link the numbers, keeping in mind at all times to stay as close as possible to Prof. Khumalo's style of writing. Prof. Khumalo and Michael Hankinson did a great job considering the many elements they had to work with. Our choice of the musical format of a *number opera* turned out to be a stroke of genius, making it easier for Prof. Khumalo in composing his first opera. A note of interest is that at that time there was no software for music notation, and Ludumo Magangane and Prof. Khumalo's work was all handwritten, still preserved in the Opera Africa archives today. Prof. Khumalo always said that he was heartsore that he was not able to do his own orchestration. This was a lingering regret for him.

The World Premiere of the opera was scheduled for May 4, 2002, in Durban. As the music came in, we handed it to the singers to learn. It was fortuitous that we had the tonic sol-fa version by the composer available while the piano score and orchestration were still being written, because this made it possible for Hein de Villiers, together with the conductor Gerhard Geist at the piano, to start music rehearsals timeously as choristers as well as soloists were all competent tonic sol-fa sight readers. Two weeks before opening night, the Finale of the opera was not yet finished, which is not unusual in a newly commissioned work. Prof. Khumalo took a hands-on role during rehearsals, demonstrating to the cast his very specific stylistic requirements regarding musical interpretation, certain technical requirements, and as a linguist himself, in assuring that the "high" Zulu was pronounced correctly and understood. It was an enriching experience not only for the "Western" team but also for the isiZulu-speaking artists who learned a great deal about the Zulu culture. Michael Hankinson's attendance at the stage rehearsals in Durban and his willingness to work under huge pressure to produce incidental music between numbers when needed by Themi Venturas during the staging was of great value.

The eight Shembe and eight Zulu dancers with their Shembe horns were led by Bongani Zulu, who did the choreography and was also the magnificent lead Shembe dancer. He played a very hands-on role during the rehearsals as well as performances, and toured with us wherever the opera was performed. His Shembe and Zulu dancers were extraordinary and a great hit throughout, actually causing a problem by reacting to the encouragement of the audiences (especially Black audiences) by always extending their allotted performing time. The in-house filming at the Oslo Opera House of probably our best production has been and still is of great value to document these authentic dances, making it possible for professional dancers to replicate the choreography although they will probably never be able to express the same raw passion and enthusiasm of the original team. During our Ravinia Festival run in Chicago in the United States, the director of the festival, Welz Kaufman, played a critical role in putting on the opera. His assistant Christine Taylor and her team put in a lot of work to develop a broader audience with extensive visits and exchanges to schools, universities, churches, community centers and collaboration between Bongani Zulu and his dancers with the Joffrey Ballet. African American audiences attended the performances of *Princess Magogo* in large numbers and later Opera Africa's performances of Prof. Khumalo's epic *UShaka*. Andrew Verster's unique graphics and handwritten surtitles projected on screens were specifically designed for these tours.

The inclusion of Shembe elements in the opera was important because of the history of the Zulu royal house. The British had banished the Zulu Royal House into exile on the island of Saint Helena in the South Atlantic Ocean. When Princess Magogo was expecting her son, Mangosuthu Buthelezi, she found refuge with the Shembe in Zululand. The link to Shembe in the *Princess Magogo* opera was made through the dancing, costumes, and musical elements. For instance, we decided to include their distinctive musical horn. This instrument creates a loud, guttural sound that is quite unlike Western brass instruments. Andrew Verster wanted to create costumes in the style of Shembe, and this required permission. With Bongani Zulu accompanying me, I had to go to the head of the Shembe religion in KwaMashu to formally ask for his blessing. We had to take our shoes off and stand on our knees outside his front door. When he appeared, a ceremony took place, and part of the ritual was to pay a minimal sum. Usually, these costumes are only worn for religious purposes, but Bongani Zulu and I were eventually able to secure permission to use them as part of the opera.

Regarding the orchestration, decisions had to be taken on whether the Shembe horns should be integrated into the orchestra or left out? How? And should these cultural elements be amalgamated with a Western orchestra? The decision eventually was to keep the Western style and cultural elements separate in dance, using their indigenous instruments, and in wedding songs to be sung a cappella. This is also the case where the ugubu is used by the Princess. It turned out to be a decision of genius as it kept the true Zulu culture and historic elements of the opera intact, allowing us to create an opera and not a short-lived documentary. The traditional *ugubhu* bow played by Princess Magogo was specially made for us by Brother Clement Sithole from iNkamana Abbey and where required in the score, the accompaniment was recorded on a CD for use in the opera performances when Princess Magogo was miming playing the bow.

The traditional Zulu indunas from Zululand, whom Dr. Buthelezi had designated to come quietly attending stage rehearsals at the Playhouse, Durban, played a positive role. Although tricky for the stage director to handle during his rehearsals, a very authentic opera was being created, enabling former president Mandela, who attended a performance at the South African State Theatre in Pretoria in 2003, to say, "this is how it really happened." Active research was involved in getting the traditional songs included in the opera and whenever there was a dispute, we could go to Dr. Buthelezi, who was himself an authority on these matters.

Many people wonder if *Princess Magogo* was the first African opera. This depends on how you define the terms. Some say that Wole Soyinka wrote the first African opera, *Opera Wonyosi*. This was a dramatic work with music. But *Magogo* is the first in many ways because of how it incorporates African languages, culture, history, and dance; and not least because it was designed and conceived for an operatic stage. Crucial to its authenticity was having

Dr. Buthelezi sign off since the opera is based on the life and music of his mother. He was very passionate about the project.

Princess Magogo has had several performances nationally as well as internationally since its World Premiere in 2002. The opera can still be licensed for productions locally and globally, and I am optimistic that it will receive more exposure once the scores have been published.

10

The Music of *Princess Magogo KaDinuzulu*

Megan Quilliam

In 2002, just eighteen years after her death, Zulu music icon Princess Magogo kaDinuzulu (1900–1984) became the eponymous heroine of a distinctly South African opera. The result of a commission by Opera Africa and the subsequent collaboration between Mzilikazi Khumalo (composer), Themba Msimang (librettist), and Michael Hankinson (composer and orchestrator) that took several years and manifested several different iterations and evolutions to reach the operatic stage, *Princess Magogo KaDinuzulu* is a singular cultural landmark in several ways. Not only does it hold the dual distinctions of being the first Zulu language opera and the first South African opera to reach commercial and international success, the nature of the collaboration (especially the joint effort between Khumalo and Hankinson) was unique in South African musical history at the time of its premiere. Finished just eight years after the end of apartheid, a period during which the country had attempted to heal divisions through Desmond Tutu's idea of the "rainbow nation," *Princess Magogo KaDinuzulu* is also one of the first operas to establish a postapartheid South African operatic identity that embraced not only indigenous music, but also important historical figures who had contributed to the formation of national and cultural identity.

In her 2002 study of the person Princess Magogo, Liz Gunner comments on how much the princess loved opera. Gunner writes, "perhaps, then, there was something deeply fitting in presenting Princess Magogo through a musical medium that could resist any narrow essentializing, that gave a sense of the sweep of her life in a turbulent history, and its creative links both with the past and with many presents."[1] Despite Gunner's suggestion that opera as a formal distinction avoids confined categorization, the word "opera" is still almost universally laden with a perceived association with European culture, influence, and artistic elitism. In the twenty-first century, however, the postcolonial world has seen numerous attempts to exert the political power of opera in order "to transform a person's (and a culture's) status and recognition," "challenge the durability of Eurocentric [opera]," and to elicit conversations around decolonization.[2] What do we make, then, of the music of a twenty-first century, postapartheid opera which showcases a heroine whom David Rycroft has called the greatest authority on Zulu music?[3]

In this chapter, I analyze the music of the opera by examining Khumalo's compositional techniques, by investigating the nature of the artistic collaboration between Khumalo and Michael Hankinson, and by addressing the presence of original music by Princess Magogo as a third posthumous compositional voice within the musical fabric of the opera. By analyzing aspects of the opera's music, I provide a musicological component to the work already begun by Innocentia Mhlambi in her 2015 analysis of the opera. In addition, I borrow the analytical techniques employed by Ndwamato George Mugovhani and Ayodamope Oluranti in their analysis of Khumalo's choral works to understand the musical language and fabric of this work. In doing so, I question the cultural implications of portraying an important Zulu musical icon through the lens of European operatic conventions, as well as the ongoing discourse surrounding the role of art music and opera in postapartheid South Africa. Ultimately, I argue that both the musical content of the opera and the circumstances surrounding its creation combine to form an ideal metaphor which speaks to the cultural context into which the opera was founded: the immediate postapartheid euphoria attached to the rainbow nation ideology.

A Zulu Opera? Streams of Influence

Innocentia Mhlambi provides an important outline of how the opera came about, noting that it was the real Princess Magogo's songs that provided the initial creative impetus.[4] She documents that it was South African composer Peter Klatzow who first arranged the songs for voice and piano using staff notation, which resulted in a performance and recording in 2000 and 2001, respectively. Afterward, librettist Themba Msimang, himself an *imbongi*, "wove these songs into extensive praises of past Zulu Monarchs and important moments in Zulu history."[5] With a commission from Opera Africa, Khumalo then began to compose original vocal music alongside Msimang's construction of a narrative that centered on the princess within the context of Zulu history in the early twentieth century. Michael Hankinson, a British-South African composer commissioned by Opera Africa to harmonize Khumalo's melodies, compose original incidental music, and orchestrate, cemented the operatic process by working with Khumalo to fill in some of the musical gaps.

The final product is an opera in every sense of the term. It communicates the drama of Magogo's life through a combination of words, music, spectacle, and detailed mise-en-scène. It is sung through by a cast of lead characters and chorus members who are accompanied by a thirty-four-piece orchestra. Indeed, each singer on stage has been trained to sing in the Western sense of operatic style. Created in the form of a classic number opera, the opera is made up of individual pieces of music that are connected by the narrative but may stand alone if detached from the larger concept of the opera. True to operatic form, Khumalo reserves arias for introspective musical soliloquies and recitative for periods of action or conversational dialogue between two or more characters. Khumalo incorporates leitmotifs and uses standard operatic conventions to build and relieve tension and drama. Like Violetta, Lucia, and Carmen before her, our heroine is doomed from the beginning of the narrative. In the style of the tragic heroine given to us by nineteenth-century European operas, her eventual death, where she sings until her last breath, provides the story's conclusion at the end of Act 2.

While Khumalo adheres to these rules of standard operatic practice and recalls trends found in the European operatic canon, the opera cannot be viewed simply as a South African version of European operatic style because there are far more complex frameworks that have coalesced to create the context into which *Princess Magogo KaDinuzulu* was born. Various musical traditions that are historically syncretic have consistently played roles in communicating and mediating intercultural ideals in South Africa. While this work is called an opera, other cultural traditions, or streams of influence, have contributed on varying levels to the creation of this work.

South African Choral Music

Unlike those of West Africa, art music trends and traditions in South Africa tended to fall along racial lines. Whereas white composers were afforded the opportunity to receive training in the style of their European counterparts, Black composers, for most of the twentieth century, received little in the way of formal music education. Instead, Black students were restricted to learning tonic sol-fa notation instead of staff notation.⁶ Accordingly, very few Black composers wrote orchestral or operatic music. Instead, the primary medium through which Black composers expressed themselves was choral music in the hymnodic style.

Over the course of the twentieth century, choral composers began increasingly injecting elements of indigenous music into the framework of Western-style hymns. By the 1950s, a more meticulous and organized effort among composers like Mohapeloa and Caluza arose to link choral music to African nationalism. We need look no further than the professional experience of Khumalo himself for this most obvious musical influence on *Princess Magogo*.

Traditional Zulu and *Ugubhu* Bow Music

Ndwamato George Mugovhani and Ayodamope Oluranti have written about the influence of indigenous/traditional elements in the many choral pieces by Khumalo, establishing a theoretical framework with which we may understand some of the techniques and approaches Khumalo takes in *Princess Magogo KaDinuzulu* (Figure 10.1).⁷ In addition, David Rycroft and Dave Dargie have

Figure 10.1 Sibongile Khumalo (as Princess Magogo kaDinuzulu) with Ntsikelelo Mali. Photo Credit: Opera Africa.

contributed much in the way of understanding Zulu music as it relates to Zulu bow music in particular.⁸ Through these analyses, we can extract a succinct understanding of some of the predominant elements associated with Zulu traditional music and *ugubhu* music:

- In keeping with the tonology of Zulu, as well as typical Zulu phrase structure, melodies in Zulu music are typically descending in contour.
- Zulu music typically maintains one key center. In often using pentatonic or hexatonic modes, the rules associated with functional harmony in Western music typically do not apply. In cases where there are elements similar to functional harmony, we tend to see progressions from the dominant chord to the tonic chord that do not have a leading tone.
- Rhythm in traditional Zulu music is often characterized by complex polyrhythms and interlocking rhythms.
- The process of adding homophonic choral accompaniment to existing traditional indigenous melodies has become an important part of Zulu composition. Occasionally, a homophonic texture is "loosened" into heterophony. A heterophonic texture sees the primary melody accompanied by variations of that same melody.
- Much traditional Zulu music is typically governed by a pattern of call-and-response.

(Music) Theater in South Africa

South Africa's long history of urban theater has traditionally been a fertile space in which politics, messages of social change and, in many cases, music have intermingled to create an important body of work that has reflected the various tribulations of apartheid and postapartheid society. Historically mixing together elements of indigenous music and popular styles that had been developed in the Black urban centers and townships of South Africa from the early 1900s onward, urban theater aimed to recall the tradition of the "old concert-and-dances of the black community" with the added element of a socially significant plotline.⁹ The canon of theatrical works developed during apartheid was simultaneously reactive and proactive in its didactic dimension: it exposed while at the same time attempting to resolve the problems, contradictions, and politics of South African life. Musical theater is an indirect musical influence on the opera; however, the structural model of telling a didactic and inherently political story using cultural and musical amalgamation is reflected in the score and libretto of *Princess Magogo KaDinuzulu*.

Opera in South Africa

Prior to the end of apartheid, the white middle and upper classes used operas from the European canon as a means of maintaining strong cultural ties to Europe and, in doing so, of declaring and maintaining their own European identity. Performed either by white South Africans or visiting European troupes, singers and musicians staged strict interpretations of unadapted and unedited European operas.

The end of apartheid in 1994, however, opened new realms of operatic expression that endeavored to articulate an emerging national identity which was inherently different from the pre-1994 era. This includes adaptations of operas from the European canon that were changed to communicate with and reflect South African society. Highly publicized adaptations include Cape Town Opera's production of *La Bohème: Noir* in 1998; *uCarmen eKhayelitsha*, produced by the Isango Ensemble in 2001; and *Impempe Yomlingo* ("*Magic Flute*" in isiXhosa), which was produced by the Isango Ensemble in 2007.

The immediate postapartheid period also saw several original operas based on indigenous topics composed by South African composers. The first full-length opera by a South African was *Enoch, Prophet of God*, composed in 1994 by Roelof Temmingh (composer) and Michael Williams (librettist). Temmingh, an Afrikaans composer, described the music as being "based in a 'new tonality' which draws on the heritage of Western, African and Asian music, and which abandons the esoteric nature of much late 20th century 'serious' music in favor of a more readily accessible style."[10] Indeed, the soundscape Temmingh established in *Enoch, Prophet of God* was revolutionary and indicative of the changing state of South African society by incorporating choral hymns and praise songs into the fabric of the opera, effectively pioneering the bonding of two musical cultures that had previously been separated by race. The post-1994 operatic landscape in South Africa has proven to be a fruitful environment where music has been used to highlight national conversations regarding the nature of postapartheid identity and culture.

It is with this contextual matrix of influences in mind that I sought to understand the music of *Princess Magogo KaDinuzulu*. At the heart of this matrix is the symbiotic relationship and interplay between European and African musical elements. My goal in this chapter is to consider Khumalo's interlacing of the real Princess Magogo's songs into the fabric of the opera, his original music, Hankinson's contributions, and the various moments of traditional Zulu music injected into the opera's narrative on stage in light of this syncretism. To do this, I shall focus on several case studies.

First, a note regarding the collaboration between Khumalo and Hankinson is needed, considering the uniqueness of the cultural context surrounding the opera's creation and because Hankinson's role and the cooperation between the two composers is often outshone by the fact that this history-making opera was helmed by one of South Africa's foremost Black composers within the decade after the end of apartheid. Given the fact that Khumalo did not have experience in composing for instruments or in orchestrating for an entire opera, Hankinson's role within the creation of the work is significant. Hankinson, therefore, shares copyright with Khumalo while acknowledging that it was Khumalo who held creative authority over ultimate musical decisions.[11] According to Hankinson, Khumalo would compose original vocal lines and choruses using tonic sol-fa notation, which would then be transcribed into staff notation by Ludumo Magangane. These transcriptions would then be sent to Hankinson to be harmonized first into a piano vocal score and later orchestrated into a complete score. Hankinson also composed all the scene change music. Hankinson told me:

> I tried to create a musical support that would enhance the vocal line(s) and the dramatic content of each scene. . . . I spent time memorizing the melody and the English translation of the relevant part of the libretto—then I'd allow it all to settle in my mind. I would let it rumble around my head—frequently at night. The emotional content of the libretto was key to figuring out an accompaniment both in terms of harmonic structure and style of orchestration, counter melodic material would often appear mentally at this point.[12]

While on some level Hankinson viewed the vocal melodies that he received from Khumalo as a canvas onto which he could contribute his own artistic voice, Khumalo was included at all points during Hankinson's compositional process and at each step of the orchestration. Khumalo always had the final say.

Reimagining Princess Magogo's Songs for the Operatic Stage

The opera begins with a prologue scene, an introduction where we meet the Princess on her deathbed. Struggling and anxious, she begins to reminisce about her youth. Her recollections eventually lead us into the action of the opera's narrative which is, we discover, merely a reenactment of her memories. Before launching into her flashbacks, however, she sings the first aria of the opera, an arrangement of "Uyephi Na?"—the traditional lullaby which was performed by the real Princess Magogo that Khumalo here adapts to illustrate the princess' unease on her deathbed (Figure 10.2). In the original version of this song, the princess accompanies herself on the *ugubhu* musical bow. Looking at the transcription of her recording done by David Rycroft,[13] an excerpt of which is reproduced below, several elements of the song stand out.

First are the two notes produced by the *ugubhu* on the top line, in this case B and C. This is the semitone shift that characterizes all *ugubhu* music. Rycroft speaks of the semitone relationship of the two notes produced on an *ugubhu* as providing an equivalent for the Western concept of functional harmonic progressions, and that these two notes should be thought of as "root notes" providing a sense of harmonic progression.[14] The instrumental part is made up of a phrase that continues to repeat itself. The vocal part consists of two different repeating phrases (A and B). Indicative of all Zulu bow songs (according to Rycroft) is that the instrumental part and vocal part never appear to match up. Instead, they are staggered, somewhat independent of each other. In addition, the contour of Magogo's melody descends. Each phrase begins up high and aims down low. Furthermore, there is an audible pattern of the accompanying strikes against the bow that emphasizes groupings of three notes. While I do not wish to impose a Western system of music theory

Figure 10.2 Transcribed excerpt from "Uyephi na?" by Princess Magogo kaDinuzulu (by Megan Quilliam from David Rycroft's original transcription).

onto traditional Zulu music, David Rycroft's transcription notates this song into a compound meter wherein we have three beats per "measure."

Khumalo, in the operatic version, maintains several of these traditional Zulu elements in the aria version of this song. He also approximates the basic melodic contour of the original melody, even down to the notation of the vocal ornaments Magogo uses in the recording. In doing so, he preserves that downward trajectory that Rycroft, Mugovhani, and others have noted as an important and prevalent feature of traditional Zulu music (Figure 10.3).

The operatic version maintains a similar pentatonic approach to the tonality that we hear in the original recording, even though here the tonal center hovers around B-flat rather than C (see example). Hankinson's accompaniment lacks what we would call functional harmonic progressions in the European sense of the word. Instead, he chooses to create the feel of a drone on B-flat rather than risk losing the feel of the original song with a forced harmonic progression. Occasionally, in the B section of the melody, the drone switches to focus on a C major chord. This alternation between B-flat and C is rather interesting, considering that the original recording features that alternation between B and C. Khumalo also keeps the basic shape of the original form, but he shortens it significantly. Instead of having a chorus provide a counterpart, he has the princess sing what was originally the chorus line as part of the aria.

Hankinson, in his orchestration, retains two features from the original recording: he emphasizes the groupings of three beats in a compound meter (which is here 6/8 rather than 3/8) primarily in the clarinet, kalimba, and viola lines.

Figure 10.3 Excerpt from "Uyephi na?" Prologue Scene 1, No. 2, bars 4–12.

Figure 10.4 Excerpt from "Uyephi na?" Prologue Scene 1, No. 2, bars 1–7.

He also gives us the impression of the *ugubhu* accompaniment we heard in Princess Magogo's recording. In this version, however, this presents as a whole tone shift instead of a semitone shift, although there are instances where he "wobbles" between notes a semitone apart. This triplet figure that appears throughout the aria (beginning on the tonic, B-flat, and moving up to the supertonic, C) also interestingly reverses the natural melodic tendencies found in the *ugubhu* accompaniment of the original, where the shift should be moving up from the leading tone to the tonic, and then back down.

Hankinson and Khumalo also retain the sense of the independency between the melody and the rest of the orchestra, demonstrating a general rule of *ugubhu* music: that the melodic pattern and the instrumental pattern never begin or end together, that they form more of an "overlapping" relationship, according to Rycroft.[15] As in the recording, the operatic Magogo's melody seems to start in the middle of an existing accompanying phrase.

In terms of what is added, what is untraditional, in this adaptation, we can look beyond the obvious dimensions like instrumentation and tonality to focus on original contributions. Hankinson provides several instances of a melodic counterpoint to Magogo's melody. In fact, an oboe melody seems to begin the melody for her in the bars preceding her first words. Notice as well that it, too, preserves that descending trajectory. The oboe melody returns in measure 11, creating a sense of polyphonic texture as it overlays Magogo's song. In measure 16, a descending flute melody appears just as Magogo finishes her phrase, leading into a counterpoint between the oboe and clarinet before Magogo picks up the next phrase. This process of layering seemingly independent melodies on top of Magogo's melody continues throughout the aria.

The addition of Hankinson's nonvocal melodies gestures toward the kind of polyphonic melodic layering found in Khumalo's choral music repertoire. As a result, his orchestration adds further sonic complexity to the music and aligns the aria's music with techniques found commonly throughout choral and operatic literature.

"Sabulawa KwaZulu"—Act 1, Narrative Interlude

If we were to establish a spectrum of the adaptations of Magogo's original songs, the aria "Sabulawa KwaZulu" would fall on the opposite end of "Uyephi Na?". "Sabulawa KwaZulu" is an adaptation of Princess Magogo's performance of "Kwabase Sabulawa nguDingane," which, in Rycroft's words, is a "lament for a national calamity, the downfall of the Zulu nation, and the main object of blame here appears to be Dingane."[16] We hear the older version of the princess sing this song in the narrative interlude toward the middle of Act 1, just after her father tasks her with "recording the nation's history" in a flashback. Innocentia Mhlambi informs us that this aria, within the context of the opera, invokes the Bhambatha rebellion and allegorically references South African politics during apartheid.[17]

The mood Hankinson sets up in this aria and the one that came immediately before are a stark juxtaposition of each other. "Sabulawa KwaZulu" begins with an ominous descending chromatic pattern in the English horn and bass clarinet before an unsettling accompaniment of *col legno* bowing, reflecting the distress the princess now feels. Hankinson indicated to me that the *col legno* bowing here was specifically meant to imitate the sound of Zulu spears hitting their shields as an intimidation technique while at war.[18]

Figure 10.5 Excerpt from "Sabulawa KwaZulu," Act 1, scene 5, no. 23, bars 1–14.

When the princess does begin singing, the first phrase is fairly similar to the original melody, although it amplifies and elaborates on the vocal ornament we see here for dramatic effect, under which what I'm calling the "distress" chromatic motif reappears. Thereafter, Khumalo's melody deviates quite a bit from the original recording. Note also that the libretto in this aria deviates slightly from the original version to suit the requirements of the narrative.

The rest of the aria takes its cues from twentieth- and twenty-first-century opera and is characterized by melodic figures and accompaniments that reflect

Figure 10.5 (Continued).

the tension of the lyrics: moments of dissonance; chromaticism; and a low, alarming tuba march. This is an example of Hankinson crafting the orchestration to serve the drama, and of Khumalo harnessing the power of the princess's original melody and transforming it into one of the most powerfully emotive arias of the opera.

The above examples indicate the complexity of the creative forces at work in this opera. Setting aside the presence of Themba Msimang's libretto, there are three distinct compositional voices contributing to the operatic renderings of the real Princess Magogo's songs. Of course, Princess Magogo herself provided the impetus with her original compositions. Michael Hankinson supported and enhanced the drama of the princess' songs. His harmonies and orchestrations created the context in which her melodies and words would fit within an operatic context. Khumalo, one might argue, had less direct compositional influence since these were adaptations of existing vocal melodies; however, it is important to remember that he had ultimate control over the final product. He presided over the degree to which traditionalisms from Princess Magogo's original compositions were transferred to their operatic form, including form, melody, and libretto.

Khumalo's Original Contributions to the Opera and Traditional Zulu Music Staged within the Narrative

The varying degrees to which traditional Zulu musical elements interact with European operatic conventions in the songs that Khumalo adapted for new purposes extend to his original contributions within the opera as well. The association of this opera with Zulu traditional culture and music, however, is most obvious in the many instances of onstage performances of traditional Zulu music that break away from the operatic environment we see throughout the work. I have decided to discuss these two aspects of the opera together because they are so intertwined.

Prologue into Act 1

Just after the princess sings "Uyephi Na?" in the opera's Prologue, she is visited by a chorus of the ancestral warriors who have come to invite her back to the realm of the ancestors. In this chorus, "Woza S'ambe," Khumalo separates the tenors and basses into independent, repetitive musical lines that alternate between antiphony and polyphony. The shape of these melodic lines is descending, as is typical of Zulu music.

At the end of "Woza S'ambe," the male chorus of ancestral warriors begins to kneel while a brass fanfare composed by Hankinson programmatically

Figure 10.6 Excerpt from "Woza S'ambe," Prologue scene 1, no. 3, bars 7–12.

announces the arrival of Magogo's long-deceased father, King Dinuzulu, onto the scene. The music moves seamlessly into "Woza, Mntanami!", the king's call for Magogo to come with him. In the first of several recitative-style dialogues in the opera, the king tells Magogo that the ancestors are "pleased with your service to the nation."

He continues, "through your music, our youth have learnt our songs, through your devotion, you ensured the unity of the nation." She replies to him, "Wait, father! Wait a while. My work is incomplete." Here Khumalo employs natural

Figure 10.7 Excerpt from "Woza Mntanami! Woz'ekhaya," Prologue no. 4, bars 3–18.

isiZulu speech patterns in relatively free meter for the melodies that flow over Hankinson's sparse accompaniment.

With another brass fanfare and heavy emphasis on the drums, we are led into a brief moment of incidental scene change music by Hankinson, and then onto Act 1. Set in the king's Mahashini Royal Kraal, this scene pre-dates the birth of the princess and is centered on the celebrations surrounding the king's return from exile. "Umgwagwa Usehlomile" is sung by a chorus of warriors who perform the king's *ihubo*. *Amahubo* are ancient and important songs that are featured in all parts of Zulu cultural, political, and religious life.[19] In this operatic version of an *ihubo*, Khumalo gives us a spirited interaction between the warriors and Mankulumana, the king's chief minister, who leads them in a call and response. The warriors' line is a repetitive, descending melody that announces the arrival of the warriors and calls for them to congregate. Interjected between iterations of this refrain are the repeating, rousing calls from Mankulumana who comments on the fact that the Zulu nation will now be armed again as they face war against the British because King Dinuzulu has returned. Hankinson's accompaniment seems to march along with the characters on stage with emphasized beats at regular intervals, contributing to and reflecting on the atmosphere of celebration and war that the chorus establishes.

The warriors begin a war dance in response to Mankulumana's continued calls. While it makes sense for the warriors to perform a war dance in this moment of the narrative, the fact that it is and develops out of the operatic call and response that began the scene makes it feel vastly different compared to other truly traditional moments in the opera.

After this chorus, "Umgwagwa Usehlomile," we get the first of these many displays of wholly traditional Zulu war cries and dances found throughout the opera. The notated score stops, and the war dance takes over the soundscape of the opera, accompanied by a single drummer on stage. In a true call and response, Mankulumana calls "*Hebe!*" and the warriors respond with "*USuthu!*"

To the ululations and whistles of those surrounding them, the warriors exit for Mankulumana to take center stage for the following chorus, "Shayan' Ingungu MaZulu," an operatic continuation of the war cry that has just taken place. Here again, it is Mankulumana leading a call and response with the chorus in what amounts to modulations of functional harmonic progressions that build tension and excitement until the eventual arrival of the king. An example of this increase in dramatic tension is the set of rising melodic sequences Khumalo gives to Mankulumana.

Figure 10.8 Excerpt from "Shayan' Ingungu MaZulu," Act 1, scene 1, no. 8, bars 35–48.

The pattern of juxtaposing operatic choruses with their nonoperatic, traditional Zulu counterparts continues for the rest of the scene. For example, walking just ahead of the king when he finally arrives on stage is the clan's *imbongi* (praise poet) who recites the praises of Dinuzulu ("Umamonga Wosuthu"). Again, the offstage orchestral music stops entirely and the single drummer on stage resumes his role. The *imbongi's* onstage recitation is exemplary of this poetic, declamatory genre. *Izibongo* praise poems hold special significance in "naming, identifying, and therefore giving significance to the named person or object," in a specific, aesthetically acknowledged way.[20] They are considered the "highest of literary expression" in Zulu society and are characterized by complex language. Highly performative, the *imbongi* praise poet loudly recites the praises using complex language, repetitive assonances and alliteration, and metered

Figure 10.8 (Continued).

rhythms (dependent on when the *imbongi* needs to take a breath) all as fast as he can. According to Kai Kresse, the *imbongi* "tries to cast a spell on the audience with a sort of magical shower of words."[21]

The appearance of a traditional *izibongo* praise recitation in the opera is noteworthy not only because an operatic stage has never before hosted such an event but also because of what happens in the very next number. After the *izibongo* is completed and the king has arrived, the chorus of the royal court sings "Wena Wendlovu, Bayede." The primary melodic theme of this is a series of dominant-tonic progressions and is repeated throughout the opera, a leitmotif that signals the veneration of a king. In the first of many iterations, the primary theme alternates with an *a cappella recitativo* line performed by Mankulumana. In effect, Mankulumana's *recitativo* is particularly striking in how it recalls the patterns and sounds of the praise poet's recitation moments earlier. The audible similarities of the *recitativo* to the *izibongo* praise poetry, especially in terms of natural speech tones and rhythm, is a stark and surprising connection between European operatic conventions and Zulu musical culture.

Figure 10.9 Excerpt from "Wena Wendlovu, Bayede," Act 1, scene 1, no. 10, bars 10–16.

Unification and the Rainbow: Act 2, Scene 4

The celebratory nature of the music in Act 1 and the many appearances of traditional Zulu music associated with celebration, veneration, and military might reappear several times throughout the opera. Indeed, the specific veneration of royalty that we see upon his return from exile in Act 1 is replicated upon the ascension of Princess Magogo's brother, Solomon, in scene 4 of Act 2. The scene begins with the ceremonial *ihubo* "Uyamemez'okandaba!" which is a traditional choral piece in call and response form led by an older Mankulumana and sung in a completely un-operatic style. Repeated several times, the *a cappella* chorus announces Solomon as "King of the original succession." It is the only traditional piece notated within the score, and it appears in both standard notation and tonic solfa, an indication that it has not been changed or altered from its original form for the opera.

A traditional *hebe* and *isibongo* in honor of Solomon follows the chorus and accompanies the new king and his sister, the princess, onto the stage. The rest of the act is devoid of Zulu traditional interjections. Instead, Khumalo gives Solomon the opportunity to make his first speech as king through an operatic rendering. Like his father before him in Act 1 (see above), Solomon's speech ("Nanso Inkosi Yenu!") is introduced by Mankulumana, who announces the king using the same "Wena Wendlovu" motif from Act 1, although this time it is modulated to a different key, perhaps signaling the change in leadership.

For King Solomon, Khumalo provides a powerful and emotive melody that often borders on *recitativo* through which he delivers his monologue calling for unity among the Zulu people. In her 2015 article,[22] Innocentia Mhlambi argues that the opera's narrative surrounding the homogenization of the Zulu nation serves as an allegory for postapartheid calls for unity. The musical language employed at this point in the opera creates a symbolic encapsulation of this very idea, complementing and highlighting the allegorical references to unity in the libretto. At the climax of this aria, there is a notable shift in the texture where Khumalo introduces a musical sequence, a series of melodic repetitions that become higher and higher in pitch for each repetition, signaling to the audience the importance of the words:

> "Unity is love,
> Unity is power,
> Unity is success,
> Unity is victory."

At this crux, Hankinson simplifies the accompaniment down to just the strings, which establish a strong, repeating rhythmic pattern, and a lone trumpet, which contributes a dramatic flourish at the end of each repeated phrase. This minimalist approach manages to build a strong harmonic foundation while drawing more attention to the gravity of the message Solomon affirms here.

The final number of the scene continues along the thematic path of unity that Solomon begins in "Nanso Inkosi Yenu!" Solomon here signals for his sister, Princess Magogo, to join him in the center of the stage, symbolically elevating her status. Their duet, "Uthingo Lwenkosazana (The Rainbow)," is a vivid commentary

Figure 10.10 Excerpt from "Siyakhuleka, AmaZulu," Act 2, scene 4, no. 12, bars 41–53.

that announces: "Today the deluge has passed, and the rainbow has appeared." Khumalo's melodies for the brother and sister begin as wholly independent melodic lines. At first, Magogo's line is simply a response to her brother's call; however, her line quickly transitions into a polyphonic counterpart to Solomon's melody. The two melodies eventually evolve into the same melody, occasionally staggered by only a few beats. Soon, the princess, her brother, and a chorus of sopranos erupt with a unison repetition of Solomon's opening melody. The altos, tenors, and basses respond using the initial response Magogo gave Solomon at the beginning of the number. By the end of the "Uthingo Lwenkosazana," all independent melodies have melded into one for a powerful, climactic resolution. By setting up the vocal textures in this way, Khumalo performs the same unification that the metaphor of the rainbow expresses. What begins as a set of disparate musical lines ultimately transforms into one unified melody made up of multiple parts, just like a rainbow.

The Rainbow Nation and the Music of *Princess Magogo KaDinuzulu*

The symbolism of the rainbow taking center stage in "Uthingo Lwenkosazana" ought not to be lost on a South African audience. In the uncertainty surrounding the end of apartheid and the transition to majority rule, many South Africans found some level of reassurance after Nelson Mandela's inaugural speech in which he spoke of racial unity. Originally penned by Archbishop Desmond Tutu, the "rainbow nation" term and ideology centered on the promotion of multiculturalism and the coalescence of divergent traditions.[23] The rainbow nation undertaking celebrated distinct cultural markers like language, clothing, and food as unique and significant contributions toward a larger cultural umbrella that aimed to reflect all people instead of a select few.

This guiding principle took symbolic shape early on within two important emblems of the "new" South Africa, including the new, multicolored flag and new national anthem which is sung in an array of South African languages.[24] In fact, it was Khumalo who had an important hand in the creation of this musical symbol as the chairman of the committee tasked with overseeing the new national anthem (see Khumalo, Chapter 3). He also arranged the first half of the final composition. As emblems that occupied very public spaces, these two symbols represented the vision Mandela had for the "new" South Africa: a coming-together rather than the continued separation of races and cultures.

As exemplified by the powerful imagery of the new national anthem, music in the immediate postapartheid period served as a means of forging this new national consciousness and identity. The process of reconciliation that Mandela led and Tutu's rainbow nation ideology are reflected in *Princess Magogo KaDinuzulu*. Innocentia Mhlambi dissects the theme of reconciliation within Msimang's libretto in the sections of the opera I discuss above. She argues that the opera

> allows for the introduction of the themes of reclamation of human dignity and reconciliation—not only between South Africa's estranged races, but also between major political rivals; the African National Congress, the white sector whether (non)aligned to National Party and the once National Party-supported Inkatha Freedom Party. These themes are represented by the coronation of King Solomon in Act II, scene 4. The songs that offer this conversation speak of unity not only of the Zulu people but of the entire South African nation.[25]

She also discusses "Uthingo Lwenkosazana" and the symbol of the rainbow, drawn from the immediate postapartheid era political discourse, that it projects. She continues, "the drive of the music has echoes of Zulu folk music, but the expansive gaze that the opera allows plucks it out of the matrix of Zulu music and includes other forms such as the national choral tradition and other western musical forms which have since assumed a broader outlook."[26] In this chapter, I have attempted to contribute a musical analysis that complements Mhlambi's initial analysis.

George Mugovhani and Ayodamope Oluranti questioned in 2015 whether the European musical elements and Zulu musical elements in Khumalo's choral music exist as symbiosis or integration. I believe that both are true in the case of *Princess Magogo KaDinuzulu*. The symbiotic relationship between the operatic numbers which resulted from Hankinson and Khumalo's cooperation, as well as the nonoperatic appearances of onstage Zulu musical performances justified by the plot, reveals a mutually beneficial relationship where operatic conventions are employed to magnify and heighten the drama of the narrative. Khumalo's inclusions of staged Zulu musical renderings, whether they are war cries and dances, recitations of praise poetry, the princess accompanying herself on the *ugubu* bow in Act 2, ceremonial *amahubo*, or the extended *ijadu* celebration in Act 2, form a core and repeated presence on the operatic stage.

Even outside of the numerous onstage Zulu performances, however, defining principles of Zulu traditional music (and other pan-African musical elements) are woven into the fabric of each operatic number. Forms are often cyclic, the texture of the music is rarely homophonic without incorporating elements of call and response, or polyphony, and melodies are generally descending and adhere to the rules of isiZulu linguistic tones. In addition, melodies are rarely governed by predictable musical meter to the point where much of the opera can be termed *recitativo*. This is because Khumalo prioritizes natural isiZulu speech patterns. Paradoxically, recitative, one of the cornerstones of European operatic conventions, is a perfect medium through which this specific principle of Zulu music can be enacted.

The music of *Princess Magogo* presents the integration between traditional Zulu musical principles and customs associated with Western classical music. The opera highlights not only one of the heroes of Zulu traditional music, but Zulu music and Zulu culture through the lens of European operatic conventions, and is thus a perfect musical symbol of the postapartheid attempt at a multicultural state aware and proud of its many parts and fragments.

Conclusion

In 1998, Ingrid Byerly questioned existing theoretical templates for decolonization processes and power dynamic shifts,[27] like that of Frantz Fanon's 1961 theory (in which the colonized people's traditional art eventually sets into motion the demise of the "imitated" colonizer's art). She argued that these do not fully account for the unique complexity of the South African situation, noting that the often-used dualisms of Black culture versus white culture or African culture versus European culture are oversimplifications. Instead, she described a "coming together" of distinct cultural products, a series of collaborative and syncretic musical styles that began to spring up in the decade before apartheid ended, as an indication of South Africa's cultural trajectory out of apartheid toward the rainbow nation ideology. She argued that, in the transition between apartheid and postapartheid democracy, it was music that allowed for the peaceful diffusion of conflicts between separated peoples by providing the space for intercultural dialogue and intercultural collaborations. She describes a trajectory toward syncretism and hybridity, or what she calls the musical *indaba*. In her updated treatise on South Africa's musical *indaba* in 2008, Byerly describes how "musicians and their music challenged a society experiencing both doubt and fear in changing times. This was primarily achieved through the gradual collaborations between musicians of diverse genres: a concerted strategy resulting in what has come to be the 'collaborative' music of the era, and a harbinger of the social and political collaborations to come."[28] Interestingly, art music in South Africa was not, in Byerly's estimation, a contributor to the *indaba*, as it was seen more as an "official" art form instead of those "unofficial countercultures" that melded to form part of the resistance and, ultimately, the protest toward the end of the apartheid period, despite the fact that so many white South African composers had begun attempts to reflect Africanisms in their works in the 1980s. What made their efforts less legitimate in the fight for art to reflect the multicultural nature of South Africa? Perhaps it was the idea that these new Africanist works merely addressed a crisis within the field of South African art music itself brought on by the ending years of apartheid. Perhaps their works were seen too much as merely works of exoticism.[29]

Regardless, the case of *Princess Magogo* presents a stark antithesis to the trends of 1980s Africanist art music and an interesting dimension to continuing Byerly's idea of the indaba into the immediate postapartheid period. Byerly's musical indaba trajectory ends at 1994 because her study centered on the generation of protest music in the years leading up to the end of apartheid. We know from Mhlambi's work on the opera that *Princess Magogo*, with its focus on an actual historical figure who played a part in attempting to unify a fractured nation, taught South Africans about their history, the struggles of the past, and about how to overcome those struggles in the modern era. I contend that not only the syncretic nature of the music, but also the fact of Khumalo and Hankinson's compositional collaboration just eight years after the end of apartheid takes the didactic component of this opera further and establishes it as a natural progression of the trajectory that Byerly sets for us in the musical *indaba*.

It is an unfortunate fact that the postapartheid euphoria the country experienced in the late 1990s and early 2000s seems to have disappeared. With the wisdom of more than twenty years, it has become clear that the rainbow nation philosophy is better thought of as a sheen covering up the vast intercultural issues that continue to plague South Africa, manifesting as ongoing waves of xenophobia, tribalism, and persisting racial tensions between the white minority (who still enjoy a significant amount of privilege and control a vast majority of the economy) and the Black majority. These issues have been refocused in recent years as an entire generation of the so-called "born-frees" come of age and who actively question exactly what has changed in the years since their parents fought against apartheid in 1994. The vestiges and legacy of apartheid continue to afflict South Africa, and an ongoing economic apartheid maintains its oppression of most of the country. As a result, *Princess Magogo KaDinuzulu* is very much a product of its time. Nonetheless, its importance does not lie in whether or not it continues to reflect current discourse in the country. Its groundbreaking attributes and instructive elements will forever mark it as a cultural landmark in the history of music in South Africa.

11

"Walking in Thorns"

Nested Contexts in the Creation of *Princess Magogo KaDinuzulu*

Donato Somma

Introduction

There are at least two worlds relevant to the discussion of any opera: that of the fictionalized world presented on stage, and that of the society in which the opera is produced. The fiction on stage is conceived and driven by key artistic and production figures. These figures work to realize the fictional world of the opera, balancing words, music, and stagecraft, and negotiating a myriad of details to realize a story in music on stage. The artistic product of these deliberations meets social and political realities as the audience sits down to experience an opera, bringing with them the more unwieldy narratives of the outside world. Opera, in its bespoke house, with its stylized rituals, offers a time and space apart from reality. Though it can be a reflection or an escape, it is inevitably and intimately linked with the society that creates it.

The dialogue between what is on stage and a work's social context is an established way of reading opera, following, among others, the works of Rosselli and Parker in opera studies, under the broader umbrella of new musicology.[1] Throughout its history both dominant and, to a lesser extent, suppressed narratives in society have played out on the opera stages of Europe and the world.[2] These are not always in direct, obvious, or even conscious relationship with the reality outside of the opera house, as the opera theater is historically a privileged place and therefore most often in lockstep with dominant or aspirant powers and ideas through direct funding, censorship, or even general patronage.[3] In the postcolonial moment and through the present decolonizing turn in public consciousness, the medium and infrastructure of opera has survived in many places, in large part due to its resonance with a human drive for storytelling with and in music, but also because of opera's attractiveness to power that seeks to present itself writ large on stage.[4] The operatic syntax, its stage language and forms, is regularly deconstructed to serve as a container for local forms of theater-and-music combinations. A branch of contemporary opera in formerly colonized spaces addresses the colonial past by the inclusion of indigenous narratives, musical material, and performers.[5] These works operate at the fringe of the operatic world, and within that context form part of a repertoire still dominated by canonical Western works, the exception rather than the rule in commercial opera industries.

The creation of Opera Africa's *Princess Magogo KaDinuzulu* (2002) was unique for its time in South African history, bringing together the creative forces of a Black South African composer, poet, and singers into the hitherto exclusively white realm of opera. In this chapter, I explore how the work emerged from a complex set of nested cultural and political projects that spanned the personal, artistic, cultural, and national. I argue that Professor Mzilikazi Khumalo encountered opera as both he and South African opera sought their next challenge: his project was both intellectual and spiritual, the linguistic, musical, and historical project of presenting his culture. This was a continuing theme in his intellectual life attested to in other contributions to this volume. Opera's next challenge was a political and artistic one, to tell African stories in Africa. At this intersection, the music of Khumalo and opera found a common goal. Here, I discuss ways in which Khumalo was able to maintain his mission to articulate and disseminate a Zulu cultural patrimony, at times both facilitated and frustrated by the generic imperatives of opera. Though I will substantiate this claim further, my assignation of agency to "opera" per se is to indicate the momentum of the genre, reproducing itself across the colonized world and drawing indigenous artists deep into its received generic conventions, conventions packed with sedimented European aesthetic values.[6]

In *Princess Magogo*, the composer, avowedly not an opera composer until this commission,[7] has found ways to occupy the operatic stage in a culturally grounded way, to make Zulu history and culture speak in its own voice on an operatic stage. I argue that it is Khumalo's musical choices, making room for more than his own individual compositional voice, that steer the message of the narrative through the nested contexts of the opera's genesis. This is not to fix or even delimit authorial intention, but rather to hear and acknowledge, in the voices and words of the opera, particularly its heroine, a set of values that permeate the opera and align with what is already on record, in this work and others, as the primary drivers of Khumalo as a composer and linguist.[8]

In what follows, I present Khumalo and the heroine he creates as sharing a mission, and how this mission plays out in the opera in its historical context. I explore the central narrative of the opera as it emerges through concentric social and historical contexts: from the primary material of the historical character's life and works, through the refractions of her son and the IFP, from the creative collaborations of Msimang and Khumalo, into the generic imperatives of South African opera at the time, and briefly the heady national discourse of postapartheid South Africa.[9]

In the opera, Princess Magogo and others use the term "walking in thorns" to reference the pain of her life and times, a pricking of the vulnerable sole of the foot, making progress difficult and painful. We hear it in the prologue, from Dinuzulu: "Kunini uhambe emeveni . . ." ("For too long you have walked on thorns . . ." no. 4); again in Act 2, scene 2, she laments being pierced by the thorns of her misfortune. Finally, in the epilogue, her mother, Queen Silomo, offers to remove the thorns that pricked her each day of her life. This metaphor is apt also for the winding process of creation, a field filled with thorns, that all involved had to traverse to get the opera made. Notes of the music stave, thornlike in the huge

Figure 11.1 Sangomas and young Princess Magogo kaDinuzulu, Het Musiktheater, Amsterdam. Photo Credit: Opera Africa.

problems they present relative to their small size, offered endless challenges in the nested context of *Princess Magogo*. The route to production was also littered with thorns, as performers leveraged the labor of turning those little thorns on the stave back into music (Figure 11.1).

Synopsis and Music

Given the limited access to the complete opera on record, it is worth beginning with a brief synopsis and cursory comment on the sound world of the opera for the reader to get their mind and ear into the work's feel.

> The opera presents scenes from the life of Princess Magogo kaDinuzulu (listed as "alto" role in the libretto),[10] daughter of the Zulu royal house. The narrative of the opera unfolds as the main character recalls significant moments of her life from her deathbed. Visited by her illustrious ancestors (prologue), she is invited to take up her place among them in the afterlife. Before doing so, and as a way of assessing her own life and value, she reflects on her life.
>
> From her deathbed she revisits the tumultuous times of her father King Dinuzulu's (bass) return from exile on St Helena (Act 1, scene 1). As his people at the Mahashini royal residence celebrate, he receives news that his daughter has been born (scene 2), he rushes to Queen Silomo's (lyric soprano) hut, and they give thanks to the ancestors (scene 3). Five years later and the sickly young princess is cured with medicine made from the fat of the igogo buck; her brother gives her the name that she is most remembered by: Magogo (scene 4). The princess of the prologue reflects on her names and their meaning, most of which concern music. She then muses on the colonial threats, bad leadership, and the agitation of Bambatha as she prepares to reflect on his rebellion against the British and its effects on her life (Narrative Interlude). Scenes 5 and 6 deal with the decision to join Bambatha (bass-baritone) and the effects of it on the family respectively. The act ends with a confrontation with the British commander Duncan (tenor). In a climactic octet and choral scene (7), the king is taken away and charges his daughter to record the fall of the kingdom in song. In the second act the princess revisits the stress of the weight of her responsibilities, the loyalty between her and her brother Solomon (tenor) and their endurance of the torment of her foster mothers (Act 2, scenes 1-3). Their fortunes eventually turn, and Solomon is elevated to king (scene 4). The princess sings of the virtues of her lover Ndwandwe (baritone) in scene 5, but broader political alliances are planned in wedding her to Mathole Buthelezi, who skillfully mediates a sensitive

and important political peace (scene 6). She sacrifices her own happiness for the nation and bids farewell to Ndwandwe (scene 7). At the end of the opera, she is convinced that her life's work was worthy and there is an apotheosis. In a two-part epilogue, the princess is called home and ascends a stairway to heaven with her ancestors and relations.

As Princess Magogo moves through the successive moments of her past, the music associated with that time and cultural milieu is presented. Each of these historical moments already has a deeply embedded musical context, as the court ceremonial, rituals, and public life of the amaZulu engage music constantly. Even before treatment as operatic material, layers of musical meaning sediment in the work. Traditional song and praises are the bedrock from which arias, ensemble, and choral pieces emerge.

In this way, the opera is a catalog of the fine nuances at play in the broader Zulu musical world. Solo and ensemble arias and choral works composed by Khumalo present the overarching narrative of the princess as a sensitive observer and eventually player in the national history, but the opera is also replete with a huge range of traditional and tradition-derived musical moments—from interjections described as "war-cries" and acknowledgments of the king, to *amahubo*, dances, praises, and folksongs.[11] There are also the intimate compositions of the princess herself, both accompanied on the *ugubhu* and unaccompanied.

The process of creating the story in song was a collaboration between Msimang and Khumalo, working off the input of Dr. Mangosuthu Buthelezi, which was then translated into an operatic mold by Opera Africa, Venturas, Verster, and others. The decision to create a number opera was to allow the strengths of Khumalo free reign: creating choral set-pieces, solo and ensemble arias, and connective passages. These were then linked up by orchestral transitions and accompaniment by Michael Hankinson. Ballantine describes the opera as the result of "mutual acts of listening and response between Western musical genres and endogenous South African ones."[12] The choice of number opera and the large choral works set in public and often formal settings (royal court and household, church, etc.) create many static scenes in the opera, and at times, the temperament is closer to that of an oratorio. This oratorio quality is further emphasized by the sacred nature of the story that unfolds in the presence of the ancestors and which ends with the ascent of the main character to heaven. The static gravitas of much of the opera is balanced by moments of extrovert expression and kinetic storytelling provided by the explosive dance sequences and numerous praise poetry performances.[13] These draw on and often reproduce verbatim, performance practices that are ontologically extroverted, claiming and activating public space. This binary, the static/operatic and the kinetic/theatrical, creates both the interest and some of the cognitive dissonance experienced in the audience as performers switch codes. Live recordings of the opera reveal moments of distinct shift when the orchestral/operatic framework is replaced by the traditional performative framework: the code switch extends from the change in sound recording quality to timbral shift from pit orchestra to onstage drumming, to blend of voices (distinct between choral and traditional ensemble pieces), from audience response through the rupture of the fourth wall to the shift between the delivery style in the aria and semi-sung praises in the Narrative Interlude (discussed below). Largely uninformed reviews by foreign opera critics missed much of what was being presented by seeking an uninterrupted seam of linear operatic dramaturgy offered in canonical through-composed works.[14]

Musically, the opera has three interconnected sources: the composed arias and choral pieces; the traditional songs, dances, and pieces; and four songs by the princess herself. These sources should not be thought of as separate. They are intimately connected and draw from the same musical wellspring. Indeed, Mughovani's 2008 interview indicates clearly that the direction of travel of Khumalo as composer was to develop Zulu music in increasingly expanded forms, taking his knowledge of choral and traditional works with him into each successive project.[15]

A clear example of this is his use of *amahubo*, ur-form of Zulu music. The opera features several of them, the composed *ihubo* for Dinuzulu's return (Act 1, scene 1, "Umgwagwa Usehlomile" no. 6) and the traditional *ihubo* at Solomon's coronation (Act 2, scene 4 "Uyinkhosi Ohlanga" no. 8). In the former, one can hear, in the call and response between Mankulumane and the chorus, what Xulu identified in his exegesis of the musical principles of *amahubo*, as the defining "wavelike movement of the sound as the leader interacts with the chorus."[16] As Xulu notes, the *amahubo* speak to the very origins of the amaZulu, accompanying the nation's emergence from the reed beds.[17] They also form a musical network of significance in their cross-referencing of one another and their use in myriad social settings of varying significance.[18] Their presence in the opera is as material that cannot be separated from the fabric of identity, whether "traditional," arranged, or composed.

Traditional music forms the backbone of all three sources, where the *amahubo* and dances as well as folk melodies inform the compositional language of the historical Princess Magogo herself. Rycroft outlines her deep cumulative knowledge of Zulu royal, folk, and clan music, beginning with her upbringing with the widow queens of King Cetshwayo, her fostering with the Buthelezi clan, and religious instruction.[19] Khumalo's composition for voice draws on the same harmonic and melodic language, writ large for the public performance practice of choralism (see Magangane Chapter 5, and Mhlambi Chapter 8, this volume).

The Eponymous Princess Magogo

At the center of the opera is a telling of the life of Princess Constance Magogo kaDinuzulu. In this work, I will refer to the historical character by the honorific "uMntwana" (denoting a scion of the royal house) to distinguish her from the necessarily adapted Princess Magogo of the opera.[20] Her lineage provided a significant platform but was not the source of her renown, as she was a recognized composer, musician, *imbongi*, and historian in her own right. When Sandra de Villiers, CEO of Opera Africa, was looking for a subject for a new opera, an African opera, Professor Mazisi Kunene suggested the story of Princess Magogo. His own work and activism as a historian, poet, and pan-Africanist of international standing gave weight to his recommendation of the much-loved uMntwana as a figure of import. Chief Mangosuthu Buthelezi gave the project his blessing and contributed to rendering a version of the narrative of his late mother's life that would be crucial to the success of the project.[21] Professor Khabi Mngoma was able to make the necessary connections and bring the cultural capital of the Buthelezi family to bear on the work.[22]

In creating the storyline of the opera, the complex life of uMntwana was reduced to fit an operatic model. This is the case with all historical or quasi-historical figures that are treated operatically. Parallels with Mary Queen of Scots (*Maria Stuarda*, Donizetti, 1835), Salome (Richard Strauss, 1905), Francesca da Rimini (the subject of numerous operas in the nineteenth and early twentieth centuries) bear mention. In all cases, the complex woman is rendered understandable by creating an operatic version that is simple and contingent on relationships with men. Edits and changes were made, not to the content or chronology of the life of uMntwana, but to the focus of the events related in the opera, thus creating a narrative in which a heroine fulfills the marks to be hit by a lead female in an opera: a woman's life is disrupted (loss of father), she is tormented (at the hands of cruel elders), finds love, and must lose it. Appended to this in the case of *Princess Magogo* is the fulfillment of her role as a mother of the nation in alliance with Buthelezi. This is treated in detail in Mhlambi's analysis of the patriarchal national discourse in the opera (2015). In the mold of Clément's operatic heroine, with no possible escape from the genre's mores, "they suffer, they cry, they die."[23] A particular song by uMntwana used in the opera serves as a good illustration of this selective focus to create an operatic story. The song "Ngibambeni, Ngibambeni" (Act 2, scene 5, no. 14) that refers to the beauty of her lover, euphemistic but unmistakably erotic in its lyrics and delivery, is ascribed a place in the opera that implies its reference to Ndwandwe, her lover prior to marriage to Mathole Buthelezi. When Rycroft recorded her singing this song, it was presented to him as a love song to Mathole Buthelezi on the agreement of their betrothal.[24] The subplot of the love affair with Ndwandwe in the opera is central to building the sense of the personal sacrifice suffered by Princess Magogo, so it forms a key moment in her life for which there is no particular historical evidence. Mhlambi's reading of this as the crucial sacrifice to unify the nation[25] dovetails with the operatic imperative requiring an all-consuming love—its nineteenth-century works are unimaginable without it.

At the end of Act 1, Princess Magogo, a wide-eyed child observing the fallout of the Bambatha Rebellion, is charged by her father with telling the story, in song, of the dismantling of Zulu sovereignty by British aggression. In the beginning of Act 2, now a woman, she prays for guidance in living up to this task. Msimang and Khumalo render the historical uMntwana as an observer, drawing in the seminal events of modern Zulu identity and weaving them into song. In the heart of the opera, between the end of the first act and beginning of the second, these events become a duet across time and space with her mother, lamenting the sorrow Bambatha has brought them "Wangeza Bambatha?" ("What misery Bambatha?" Act 1, scene 6, no. 32) and uMntwana's favorite Psalm 91 "uJehova ungumlondolozi" (Act 2, scene 1, no. 4). UMntwana's life and work are the core of the nested contexts of the opera, and her work as a bearer of culture continues through the successive layers of the fictionalization of her life for the stage.

Mangosuthu Buthelezi: The Story

The opera ends with the celebration of the marriage alliance of Princess Magogo to a Buthelezi groom. Outside of the opera's narrative, their son produced a renewed impetus for a specific form of Zulu identity and would come to be identified with a key political expression of Zulu nationalism: the Inkatha Freedom Party (IFP).[26] Dr. Mangosuthu Buthelezi founded the party, and indeed credits his mother with forming the identity and cultural politics that ultimately found expression in the party.[27] It can be argued that the IFP as a cultural force witnessed the transition from the late anticolonial struggle to the antiapartheid struggle and the postapartheid Zulu polity. UMntwana's songs set ethical questions to leadership and steer the values of, if no one else, then at least the leadership of the IFP. Two key figures within the IFP were also driving forces in the primary creative triad of the opera and provided sanction for it.

Once the connection between Opera Africa's Sandra de Villiers and Dr. Buthelezi had been established, the next layer of the opera's creation could begin: a culturally legitimized conduit from the life of the historical uMntwana to the Princess Magogo that appeared on the stage in 2002 was established. In some ways, the role that Dr. Buthelezi had played earlier in the century, as interpreter of Zulu idiom on behalf of his mother, for Rycroft the ethnomusicologist, and as "avatar" of his grandfather in the film *Zulu*, was also continued. Sandra de Villiers relates the privileged access she had to Dr. Buthelezi, at the height of the demand for his time as an active member of parliament. She was able to gain approval for the finest details of historical narrative, costuming, cultural practice on a need-to-know basis as the production gained pace.[28]

Themba Msimang: The Poetry

Collectively, Themba Msimang and Dr. Buthelezi provided the deep-Zulu poetics and cultural sanction for the opera. As IFP leader and MP, respectively, they were placed to smooth the way for unprecedented depth of access to the cultural world of uMntwana: the aesthetic, poetic, and historical frames within which she existed and worked.

Msimang works tirelessly, as did Khumalo, for the promotion of indigenous languages as a primary root of South African self-knowledge in his ministerial capacity. He has created libretti since Princess Magogo, for Mnomiya's *Ziyankomo and the Forbidden Fruit* (2012), and text by Msimang was used in Ndodana-Breen's 2001 choral symphony, *Vela Zulu*. His poetic oeuvre, as analyzed by JJ Thwala, reflects an ongoing thematic concern with education both formal and informal, in conjunction with the religious and historical.[29] In the same work, Thwala relates the mutual inspiration in the close friendship between Khumalo and Msimang.³⁰ Msimang relates their shared history that prompted the two of them to collaborate on creating a King Shaka that they recognized, after their withdrawal from the 1986 made-for-television drama *Shaka Zulu*.³¹ The two shared roots in the Nkandla District, a heritage and an outlook on how to share that heritage through education. Their next collaboration would extend those interests. Khumalo was unable to set the prose version of the Princess Magogo story, initially drafted by Duma Ndlovu, to music. This prompted a scrapping of that first version of the story. Khumalo needed poetry, not just any poetry, but the idiomatic and lavish poetry of Msimang, that could transform the workaday world into one that wove the quotidian and fantastic into the same space. Here is part of his praise for the institution of Unisa, reflecting its origins in the Western Cape and final relocation in Tshwane:

> *Ukhoz' olubhul' amaphikw' eKapa,*
> *Lukhuphuka ngeziqongo zezintaba,*
> *Lwagoq' amaphikw' esigodlweni ePitoli.*³²

Khumalo requested him as the person whose words would unlock the music for his story. Together, they shared with uMntwana a love of words and historic idiom. Msimang gives this to the Princess Magogo character who processes politics through the long-range lens of praises, through the deference to tradition. The princess of the opera stands, as does the poet, outside of the action of her life and rearticulates the historic events. She is split in the opera between a first-person participant, in her adult years, and commentator in a state of vivid reverie. In both manifestations, her poet's eye observes and critiques the unfolding saga of Zulu history.

Mzilikazi Khumalo: A Clear Directive for a Shared Music

The "mutual acts of listening" suggested by Ballantine as a hallmark of the opera were not only across cultures separated by race but also, I suggest, a listening between the composer and the broader world of Zulu music.³³ Khumalo composed in his clear and recognizable voice for the opera, but also held the door open for countless traditional forms to enter the stage, carefully placing these in analogous spaces within the opera narrative.

As she reflects on her life, the fictionalized Princess Magogo realizes an overriding mission in her life: to convey the culture and history of the Zulu. She is explicitly charged with this task by her father at the end of Act 1. Her songs are a telling of history, personal reflection, and social commentary, as we hear from even the limited selection in the opera. The story of her people is intimately tied to language; the word and idiom are everything in her songs and retelling of her life. These are the concerns of a linguist, and Khumalo has invested in her musical representation his own deep love of isiZulu. This shared concern, between him and his opera's subject, is the sacred heart of *Princess Magogo* the opera. In the training and forming of the singers for the production is an enduring drive and message, the desire to catapult a musical understanding of isiZulu into the future.

Sandra de Villiers characterizes the production process as "around a table" both at her own home at the time and at the Buthelezi residence.[34] Though it was evidently not always the same figures, the core creative force of Khumalo and Msimang, with de Villiers completing the production side, sat with the bearer of the story, Dr. Mangosuthu Buthelezi, or the theater director Venturas and others, to negotiate the story of uMntwana into the opera *Princess Magogo KaDinuzulu*. Settling early on into routes for turning operatic forms into traditional ones, de Villiers offers the example of: "What is recitative? [. . .] They learnt how to do their first opera, but we . . . the Europeans learnt a lot from the culture. *Bonga* [*sic*] style is, in principle, recitative."[35]

This process can be read both ways, as the working of uMntwana's story and Zulu music into the operatic mold, or the operatic mold reforming around idiomatic musical and linguistic forms. Here, the transitional form of the tonic sol-fa notation in which Khumalo worked, the subsequent orchestration process, and the power dynamics at play "around the table" intersect. A zeitgeist underpinned the project for Buthelezi, Khumalo, Msimang, and de Villiers: that of reconciliation. Post the cynicism of the State Capture years, the narrative of reconciliation is exhausted, its foundational events of the Convention for a Democratic South Africa and later the Truth and Reconciliation Commission largely discredited as betrayals of Black South Africa in populist and many establishment polities. There was a time, however, when "around the table" work was the accepted mode of imperfect and labored transfer of the Black South African story into the public, formal domain.

Mzilikazi Khumalo's work sits at a juncture in South African musical history. It is telling a South African story, a heroic narrative that speaks to a complete subversion of apartheid power by presenting a Black South African woman as the central pillar of a nation. The will to tell such a story is there, as is the compositional ability and musical imagination required to communicate the story in song, but the long shadow of apartheid stretches well into the first decades of the new century, and for his artistic vision to be realized, Khumalo had to rely on substantial collaborative forces. While this is de rigueur for opera as a multidisciplinary endeavor, the core thorn for Khumalo was the frustration of loss of control between tonic sol-fa and staff notation.

Lucia has discussed the perception of sol-fa as never good enough to be welcomed into the realm of serious composition in many late apartheid institutions.[36] She has also spoken of the desire of Khumalo to be read as a composer in an African classical tradition.[37] The latter desire corners him in a staff notation episteme that he was in some ways excluded from at the time because of the second-class perception of tonic sol-fa. Today, the sacred cows of art music are all dismantled, an opera can eschew full orchestration (Neo Muyanga's *The Flower of Shembe*, 2012), can be disassembled in libretto and language (Brett Bailey's *Macbeth*, 2014). The conception of opera in South Africa had not moved sufficiently to reform itself around Khumalo with his particular musical approach in terms of the production of an opera of the scale he imagined and the practicalities of sounding out the music he had in mind. For the opera to be mounted as an opera, the traditional multidisciplinary team that typically put together such an endeavor had to be assembled. Once the transcription from Khumalo's tonic sol-fa to staff notation was completed by Ludumo Magangane, it was over to Michael Hankinson to develop the orchestration implied in the melodies transcribed. Conceding the orchestration and writing of transitional music to Hankinson was a cause of deep regret.[38] Here, then, is the postapartheid composer, with will and vision, a musical voice expressed in tonic sol-fa with ambitions to fill a traditionally conceived opera space.

The creation of *Princess Magogo* happens against the backdrop of some establishment composers seeking a "reconciliation aesthetics" between Black and white culture as entrenched under apartheid.[39] The question of tonic sol-fa as compositional technique belies deeper quests of how the transition from apartheid to democratic dispensation would play out in this corner of the performing arts. The juncture at which Khumalo's opera sits is between two crises of compositional authority: the early postapartheid scramble to represent the New South Africa in art music as received norm, and the decolonial moment of abandoning the forms altogether.

But the approach by Khumalo, to pack the stage with traditional Zulu musical expression and the authority of uMntwana's music itself, in many ways subverts the arguments about adaptation. The opera he wrote gives an enormous range of traditional music room to develop the narrative. Formally, the opera is organized into a prologue, two acts, and a two-scene epilogue. The prologue has five musical numbers, the first act has seven scenes and thirty-one musical numbers; the second act has seven scenes and twenty numbers. The epilogue has two scenes and five numbers. To divide the opera into its two halves, we have eight scenes in the first half and nine in the second. Another way of thinking about the material is that within these seventeen scenes, there are seventeen distinct instances of Zulu musical performance practice.

What follows is a description of some of the pieces drawing directly on traditions that intersperse the composed arias and ensembles, and the works of uMntwana. Taken together, they express a desire beyond the personal vision of a composer. They present a catalog of traditional forms stitched together with original compositions—the number opera becomes a map of traditional music.

The Prologue opens with Princess Magogo's mournful rendition of "Uyephi Na?" (no. 2). This *umlolozelo* (lullaby) sets a very intimate tone at the beginning of the opera; lilting and dreamy, it makes us consider the transitional state that the princess is in, drifting between this world and the next, nearing the completion of the cycle of life, in which childhood and old age, both so close to the otherworld, begin to merge. The piece itself may be attributed as traditional and, when discussing it with Rycroft, uMntwana attributed it to the Zulu clan in particular and ascribed great age to it.[40] She further specifies that this is a lullaby for a baby whose father is away.[41] In the opera, it is a prelude to the arrival of a vision of her own father, who has come to take her home. At the very beginning of the opera, the fictional Magogo is given dimension and backstory with this traditional piece, bringing with it the delicate intimacy of her music. Lullabies, like love songs accompanied on the ugubhu, are music expressed in, and concerning, the closest intimacy between people.

Soon after this moment, with the composed interactions between Magogo and her ancestors intervening, we hear the *ihubo* "Shayani ingungu maZulu" ("Beat the drums you Zulus," no. 8) led by Mankulumana, followed by the *inyosi* (royal praise singer) singing a shortened version of his praises (no. 9) in Act 1, scene 1.

The traditional call-and-response format, and the "roaring" character of the *ihubo*, is used here to express joy and a growing sense of strength among the uSuthu Brigade at the return of Dinuzulu from St. Helena. The opening line sets the tone for a military *ihubo* with the imprecation to beat the drum, called out in a high tenor by the Mankulumana character, and the line is given back to him in full male-chorus, thundering response. Later, the call "Let the soldiers sing their war chant loudly" builds intensity in the response through direct instruction, and the brigade sing of their style and panache, "white-spotted beshus" filling the stage with braggadocio so central to the art of self-praise. This is a grim joy, the flexing of returned vigor and readiness to take on a new fight, all underpinned by the roaring and thundering qualities inherent in *ihubo* as a song form. It is an example of the message and the form already aligned in an existing form, with little adaptation required to make a "fit" for the opera stage. *Inyosi* creates a shift from composed work in a traditional style to a traditional form in the truncated praises that follow. We get a sense of the density and depth of meaning in the metaphors, all of which speak of strength in comparison with forces and creatures of nature, themselves also euphemisms for other kings. Here the line "Who destroys completely, like the black bull from Ulundi" refers to his father, Cetshwayo, and his capital. The rapid delivery of the praises, rendered as surtitles in the performance, creates a fairly unique opportunity for non-Zulu speakers to simultaneously hear and read translations of the words. Richly idiomatic and not easily understood by cultural outsiders, a diverse audience at least begins to register the motifs of royal praises; the liturgical, ritualized tone; and intensity of their images. In scene 2, the Phefeni Regiment performs a traditional dance.

In the Narrative Interlude between scenes 4 and 5, Magogo performs one of uMntwana's own pieces "Sabulawa kwaZulu" ("We are Killed in kwaZulu" no. 23),[42] and this is followed directly by praises for the ancestors as part of the same number. This two-part number is a key character development moment that sees Magogo step out of her deathbed reverie and address the audience. She is in the liminal space between the recall of her past and the moment of her death, a lucid space into which the audience is invited. In front of a gauze traverse, signaling this new space of reflection, the simultaneously despairing, deferential, and chastising song of uMntwana is delivered. Each gliding phrase descends to a rumbling lower register, troping the destruction and ditches in the lyrics: "Every day we are killed by Dingane, every day we are thrown into dongas." Mbuso Khoza has described her as a philosopher,[43] and here we hear the discourse of a historicizing philosopher, reciting the names of those in the deep past whose actions shaped the tragedies of the present. The song, now an aria, lists these protagonists interspersed with the lamenting refrain "*Yehhe, baba, sabulawa kwaZulu!*" ("Oh, father, how we are killed in kwaZulu"), but also the critique of "*Senzeni na . . . ?*" ("What have we done?"). The aria ends with sung praises of ancestor figures ("*Musho, musho . . . !*" "Praise him, praise him . . . !"), which lead directly into recited praises, with the traditional metaphoric and euphemistic references, delivered in a traditional style. In this two-part piece, the character shifts from aria to praises as a vehicle for the message, driving home the root causes and original sins of the nation. Overwhelming in effect, the overloading of the audience is achieved by setting the brooding scene with the aria and increasing the tempo and quantity of information to create the climactic point of the interlude. All tragedy, all human and political failure is connected—the praises, distillations of the past, become prophecies of the future.

In scene 5, courtly protocol offers a view of call-and-response announcing of the king's arrival, a brief war song and war cries ("Bambani im'khonto," "Pick up your spears," no. 24 and "Hebe!" no. 265). Both brief moments are numbered in the opera, their performance, style, and narrative significance signaled in the libretto and carried over into the performance. What in canonical opera might be incidental is presented in *Princess Magogo* and named, significant in relating the aural space of the Mahashini Royal residence.

A similar use of court ceremonial occurs in Act 2, scene 4, where Solomon's coronation is heralded by the traditional "Uyinkosi Yohlanga" ("He is a national king" no. 8) followed by performances of war cries (no. 9) and Solomon's praises (no. 10).

In scene 5, two love songs, one with traditional origins improvised on by uMntwana, "Ngibambeni, Ngibambeni" ("Hold me, hold me" no. 14) and the traditional "Umqhubansuku" (no. 16) with *ugubhu*, present aspects of love, balancing direct report of the effect of love and offering rich metaphors. The first, learned from relatives in her younger days at the residence of Hamu kaMpande, and adapted to honor her husband, was recorded several times by Rycroft, each with variations in line with the practice of extemporizing on a musical form and narrative outline. It begs a mother to hold her daughter fast as she is wracked by love; the man in question is so fine on horseback ("Wagibel' amahhash' amfanela!") that it doesn't matter what color the horse: brown, bay, white, or speckled; she is blown along with the wind and needs her mother to anchor her. In the opera, this is taken to refer to her young love Ndwandwe, as he sneaks up on her while she sings it in a garden. Following their duet, the solo aria "Umqhubansuku," a traditional love song in the repertory of uMntwana and accompanied on the *ugubhu*, addresses father and sisters with the desperation and distraction of the singer in love. She threatens to set her hut alight with her in it on the day they part. Unable to cope with his beauty, she is tempted to set her dogs on him just to see him run.

These love songs initiate us into the unrestrained nature of traditional women's love songs as a genre. In contrast to the formal, coded ferocity of so much of the music, these direct portraits of desire present great vulnerability, asking for help and support in the face of overwhelming love. This works seamlessly with the love aria as a form and needs no adaptation for legibility on an opera stage. Furthermore, as arias, they crucially develop our sympathy for her impending sacrifice, giving up on this love for her duty to the nation. This is a key sacrifice in canonic opera, at least in the nineteenth-century operas that revolve around a love interest. Problematic as they are, this is precisely the kind of sacrifice on which the operatic narrative turns, a woman who "suffers, cries and dies."

Scene 6 presents what is won in exchange for the hand of Magogo. Apart from a brief choral piece that introduces what *ijadu* is, a celebration in dance and song, in this case to rejoice in a marriage with strong political implications, the entire scene is defined by arranged traditional pieces marked a–f of no. 17 in the libretto.

From the libretto listing:

17 Ijadu (Chorus, Warriors)

   a. Singamahemu (Buthelezi clan)
   b. Inkosi Mathole Praises (Imbongi)
   c. Siyajabule thinauSuthu (Usuthu clan)
   d. Inkomo kababa emnyama (Buthelezi clan reply)
   e. Wena Wendlovu & Dance (Imbongi, Chorus & Warriors)
   f. Shembe Dance

To give the stage over to the performance of a set of dance styles, praises as key storytelling moments that illustrate in performance the relationship between the clans and the Shembe is proof of the power of the traditional forms to exceed the operatic format. Instead of a duet between two houses, or a climactic choral scene, the movement of praises and responses and unique dance forms tells the audience who the characters are and how the marriage will draw them together. Clan songs are exchanged; praises of the groom are sung; the king is welcomed; and finally the Shembe, with their stately and hypnotic gestures and resounding horns, present something brand new right near the end of the opera.[44]

In significant quantity and quality, the audience is schooled in a wide variety of traditional forms. The work of the historical Magogo, as envisioned by Khumalo to communicate a tradition, is achieved in experiencing this opera.

Though recontextualized for the stage, they occur in an appropriate context within the diegesis of the opera. That is, praises happen in the story at a moment that they would occur in context, as do love songs and *amahubo*.

Conclusion

In many ways, Opera Africa could have appeared first in the nested contexts of this opera. In retrospect, it seems inevitable that Khumalo and Msimang would collaborate creatively again. But opera was an unlikely rallying banner, lacking the cultural continuity offered in the choral medium of the *UShaka* project. The opera was created out of a carefully negotiated collaboration. Deference was made to each contributor in an environment of mutual admiration: storyteller and final arbiter of matters of tradition in the person of Mangosuthu Buthelezi, composer Khumalo, librettist Msimang, transcriber Ludumo Magangane, and orchestrator Michael Hankinson. Specialists all, Sandra de Villiers chaired not only the company, but also the roundtable format of consultation between these august collaborators. Opera Africa was undoubtedly the incubator for the "mutual acts of listening" that Ballantine senses in the work. Building this careful trust was necessary, reflective of the reconciliatory tone of South African politics at the time, buoyant in its positive outlook on the potential of reconciliation.

Princess Magogo stands at a junction between the end of apartheid euphoria and the grinding realities of the new century. On the one hand, the world was receptive and applauding of good news stories from South Africa, and that recognizable "culture" flourishing was yet more evidence of normalizing stasis settling in at the tip of Africa.[45] Within the country, there was a brief attempt to go along with this, to set up the formerly white formal arts sector to tell the story of South Africa, with a new heroic arc and the burnishing of proto-struggle characters from the archives. Infrastructurally, enough remained of the audiences and expertise locked into the apartheid-era arts councils to muster large-scale opera. Cracks were beginning to show: Black talent in white production, appropriation of culture, and the postcolonial turn in public discourse would soon change the circumstances. Debates around cultural appropriation and opera today run in the direction of critique of appropriation of indigenous heritage by the global north, and rest on a reading of the history of settler-invaded lands pillaged for new material.[46] It is noteworthy that, at the time of the legal wranglings around *Princess Magogo*, the vision was of Africa appropriating opera. From the "Princess Magogo in Court" media release:

> The ironic part is that artists are excited and welcome the appropriation of the opera format to express South African classical music, genres and history as an art form, and are open and willing to collaborate with any artistic entity that shares this ideal.[47]

A shared musical and linguistic heritage forces its way through the nested contexts of producing an African opera in postapartheid South Africa. For both Khumalo and his operatic protagonist, there is an urgent and impassioned bid to present a musical and linguistic sound world for Zulu identity. Though this world already exists in the replete and multi-genre forms of traditional, neo-traditional, and contemporary Zulu music, a desire to expand the audience for this sound world may have been behind Princess Magogo allowing her songs and ideas to be recorded—quite aside from the hotly contested subsequent uses of those songs in decontextualized art music, uses that raised debates of cultural appropriation. It may also have been behind Khumalo's use of opera as a kind of Trojan Horse, to carry Zulu music history and language into new venues of expression and therefore to new audiences. This small selection of the traditional works and those composed by uMntwana in the opera argue for this reading of the opera *Princess Magogo KaDinuzulu*. The desire of born educators is to disseminate their subject as directly and widely as possible. *Princess Magogo KaDinuzulu* harnessed opera rather than providing simplified and linguistically denatured material to it but nevertheless succeeds as opera in the genre's own terms.

> "*Esexhamazela, bantu*
> *eselingis' ingan' icathula*"[48]

Tottering like the taunted lover in "Umqhubansuku," the opera hobbled through the thorns of staff notation and the thorns of legal challenge, into South African music history. When it is next staged, what two worlds will encounter each other as the curtain rises on a recumbent mezzo-soprano singing "Uyephi na?"

12

Representing Princess Magogo in the Opera *Princess Magogo KaDinuzulu*

Kholeka Shange

On May 4, 2002, the opera *Princess Magogo KaDinuzulu* (commissioned by Opera Africa) premiered in Durban's Playhouse. A month prior to the premiere, Opera Africa released a statement that framed this work as a "New Zulu opera."[1] Two days after the premiere, the narrative of this opera as a dramatic work that is inextricably tied to "Zuluness" was perpetuated by the journalist Margaret van Klemperer in the *Natal Witness* newspaper.[2] And interestingly, two years after the debut of this opera, the *New York Times* continued this motif wherein *Princess Magogo KaDinuzulu* (2002) was conceived of as a "South African Zulu opera."[3] In this regard, the opera was not only linked to the idea of a homogeneous "Zulu" identity, it was also located within a larger postapartheid national discourse. Moreover, on May 5, 2002, the *City Press*'s Mduduzi Dlamini related the premiere of the opera to Princess Magogo's posthumous awarding of the lifetime achievement award during the eighth South African Music Awards.[4] And in line with the master narrative of Princess Magogo as captured in Zulu historiography, Dlamini highlighted that Princess Magogo was "the mother of the Home Affairs Minister Dr Mangosuthu Buthelezi, who accepted the award on her behalf."[5]

I argue that Princess Magogo is continuously entangled with the "big" Zulu men that existed in her life. Often, Prince Mangosuthu Buthelezi is foregrounded as the foremost child of his mother. However, when he writes about his mother after her death in 1984, he captures the existence of the women that were in her life (i.e., Queen Silomo and Queen Zihlazile), and he also notes a sibling that is not commonly spoken of—Prince Arthur Edward Mshiyeni kaDinuzulu.[6] Furthermore, in the extended version of his mother's biography/obituary,[7] he acknowledges the fact that she had two daughters (i.e., Princess Morgina Phikabesho and Princess Admara Phokunani) and an unnamed son who passed away in infancy.

Prince Mangosuthu Buthelezi's overdetermined presence in the telling of Princess Magogo's narrative demonstrates the critical role that he has played in crafting a curated history of his mother and the royal family that she is tied to. And his contextualization of his mother's birth following King Dinuzulu's exile in St. Helena and the South African war (which he frames as the "Anglo-Boer" war) is partly the premise of the opera *Princess Magogo KaDinuzulu* (2002) (Figure 12.1).

Contrary to the suggested Zulu centricity of the opera, Innocentia Mhlambi asserts that this dramatic work transcends the confines of Zulu specificities and conventionalized Zulu history. Mhlambi submits that because the creators of this work (i.e., the composer Mzilikazi Khumalo, the librettist Themba Msimang, and the opera orchestrator Michael Hankinson in partnership with Opera Africa among state and corporate sponsors) produced it within the context of post-1994 South African rainbow nationalism, its narrative is connected to "a broader post-1994 national consciousness."[8] In addition, she proposes that the operatic story of Princess Magogo does not solely center on the politics of Zulu nationalism, but it is also co-opted into a Black Nationalist agenda—as captured through "the narratives of King Dinuzulu, the Bhambatha rebellion and the unification politics of King Solomon."[9]

Figure 12.1 Kelebogile Boikanyo, Thembisile Twala, and Zanele Gumede with Sibongile Khumalo in *Princess Magogo KaDinuzulu* (2002). Photo Credit: Opera Africa.

Interestingly, Mhlambi's reading of the opera suggests that this visual and sonic representation delinks Princess Magogo from a homogenized "Zuluness" that is inextricably tied to a tribalized and ethnic identity. In other words, it is through Khumalo and Msimang's operatic intervention wherein there is an exploration of a "national consciousness" that goes beyond what is constructed by the Zulu aristocracy, the Zulu intellectuals (i.e., *amakholwa*), and the British and Afrikaner colonizers that Princess Magogo is located within a broader "national" stage where she can become what Mhlambi refers to as a "'national woman' in history rather than a 'sacrificed' royal Zulu woman."[10]

Mhlambi's framing of the operatic Princess Magogo as a "'national woman' in history" who is tasked with the colossal duty of being a scribe/disseminator of the history of "her people" is important. However, I propose that it is equally vital to recognize the prior existence of a network of "*omama besizwe*" [women of *isizwe*] that generated a space where Princess Magogo as "*umama wesizwe*" [a woman of *isizwe*] could exist. And I emphasize the idea of a "network" because it constitutes a sisterly kinship that transcends biology. In this chapter, I maintain that it is through the interconnectedness of self-defining women in the Zulu monarchy that Princess Magogo as *umama wesizwe* is made.

My use of the term "*isizwe*" instead of "nation" is informed by the fact that the idea of a "nation" is not only Europeanized but is a point of robust contention in scholarship that explores the genesis of nationalism.[11] Furthermore, my choice of using "*isizwe*" is also influenced by the notion that it is through nationhood that space is demarcated into nation-states wherein institutionalized bureaucratic tools such as borders are created and maintained to exclude individuals or groups of people who do not fit neatly into ideas of citizenship and nationality. Although the term "*isizwe*" is typically reduced to only mean "nation,"[12] it may be used to refer to a "people"[13] that functions under a polity that is not necessarily informed by a European conception of nationhood.

The historian Nomathamsanqa Cynthia Tisani asserts that the interpretation of "*isizwe*" and "*izizwe*" (plural for *isizwe*) as "nation" and "nations" is a modern phenomenon.[14] Tisani claims that in the mid-nineteenth century these two terms (commonly used in isiNguni which predominantly comprises languages such as isiXhosa, isiZulu, siSwati, and isiNdebele) may have functioned to refer to any political entity that was independent. She suggests that J. B. Peires's idea that *isizwe* is used to mean clan and chiefdom is disputable. In her explanation of what constitutes *isizwe*, she states:

There is a difference in the use of the word *isizwe*. In the narrow sense the word is used to refer to a clan, an exogamous group that claims to descend from one ancestor. In such a context the word isizwe emphasizes the autonomy of a clan in relation to other clans. This is usually noted in religious contexts. Isizwe under inkosi is a politically independent unit that is separate from other izizwe, with different iinkosi.[15]

Although Tisani is speaking specifically about isiXhosa speakers, her observations are in line with similar assertions made by isiZulu-speaking writers Nyembezi and Nxumalo. They affirm that *isizwe* and *izizwe*[16] are "Abantu abaphethwe yinkosi eyodwa"[17] [People under the rulership of a particular inkosi]. Therefore, when I speak of *isizwe*, I am referring to the definitions of Tisani, Nyembezi, and Nxumalo.

The idea of *isizwe* is particularly important in the context of Khumalo and Msimang's operatic narrative. This is so because the opera highlights the British colonial state's continual refusal to formally recognize King Dinuzulu as the monarch of the "Zulu nation." This may be seen in Act 1, scene 7 where the colonial official Colonel Duncan refuses to accept King Dinuzulu's "kingship." In this scene, he insists "*Akunankosi yama Zulu lapha*" [There is no king of the "Zulu nation" here] while *isizwe* chants, "*Wena weNdlovu! Wena weNdlovu! Bayede/ Bayede, wena waphakathi!*" [You of the Elephant Hail/Hail to the one whose place is inside].[18] In other words, despite the colonial government's dismissal of King Dinuzulu, the *isizwe* collectively resists by acknowledging him as their *inkosi*. In this regard, the *isizwe* does not subscribe to the British colonial state's notion of nationhood and "kingship." As such, it is vital to note the distinctive relationship between a European conception of "kingship" and *ubukhosi*.

As suggested earlier, it is necessary to pay attention to Khumalo and Msimang's depictions of women to consider how the trope of Princess Magogo, the "big"[19] woman in the Zulu monarchy, may be disrupted as a way of valorizing the narratives of multiple women in the Zulu monarchy. And as Mhlambi has noted, the opera does the work of disentangling the operatic Princess Magogo from hegemonic "Zuluness" (which is masculinized). And I posit that through Mhlambi's conception of Princess Magogo as a "nation woman," it becomes possible to reflect upon the critical role that the women that came before her played in creating an environment wherein she could be *umama wesizwe*.

In the opera, even before the arrival of Princess Magogo, the women in this milieu are actively engaged with the politics of *isizwe*. In fact, before the appearance of King Dinuzulu, Queen Silomo, and their young sons Prince

Solomon and Prince Edward in Act 1, scene 1, the royal seat, a symbol of the power that a monarch occupies, is literally installed by a trio of Queen Silomo's "handmaidens" (an expression Msimang uses in the libretto) while an all-male regiment and Mankulumana the induna *enkulu* ["chief counselor"] await the arrival of the monarch(s). This fleeting but radical moment may be read as a metaphor for the visibilization of women's contributions in the making of the Zulu state. The ephemeral presence of the "handmaidens" is reminiscent of Zulu historiography's representation of isiZulu-speaking women. The scholar Jennifer Weir notes:

> Zulu historiography does not generally accord an important political place to Zulu women. There are few studies that focus on the role of *amakhosikazi* and *amakhosazana*. They have generally been treated as peripheral or insignificant in the politics of the state. The predominance of research on Zulu militarism and, therefore, men may not seem very remarkable because Zulu society is generally taken as a model of hierarchical patriarchy where men dominated both domestic and political affairs, and with the king at the apex.[20]

In consideration of Weir's observations, Khumalo and Msimang's choice to accord young Blackwomen[21] with the role of not only carrying the royal seat but also locating it within an environment that is devoid of it (an allegory for a "Zulu nation . . . in disarray")[22] is fundamental. Mindful of "hierarchical patriarchy" (as captured by Weir) and a hyper-masculinized Zulu identity, this Blackwomen-centred moment becomes significant in its subversion of androcentrism. And the youthfulness of the "handmaidens" is also worth noting because it not only suggests generational continuity between women in the Zulu monarchy, but it also situates young Blackwomen in the political affairs of the Zulu state. Although these women characters are not necessarily vocal in this moment, their act of installing the throne is the impetus for the King, Queen, and their sons to occupy their place as royals.

This scene also includes three older women who engage the royal seat before the arrival of the King, the Queen, and their sons. These women wave *amashoba* [bushy tails] around the royal seat and the royal kraal of *eMahashini*. Although *ishoba* [singular for *amashoba*] is usually used by *izangoma* ["traditional healers"] in their processes of divination, Khumalo and Msimang suggest that these women characters are participating in a ritual of cleansing the throne and the space that *isizwe* occupies. In this regard, their psychical work is consequential. In fact, when this trio of older women/*amakhosikazi* and the "handmaidens" enter the scene at different times, their presence is acknowledged by Mankulumana and the regiment. As this intergenerational network of women maneuvers around the royal court, the men respond by navigating around this nexus. This interaction between the men and the women in the Zulu monarchy challenges "the view of women in the Zulu state as a homogenous group marked by universal subordination."[23] In this scene, there is a consciousness (albeit limited) around the key role that women play in the formation of the Zulu state.

In this very same scene, Queen Silomo is characterized as a vocal royal woman. Although she is seated at the feet of her husband (a hierarchical positioning that alludes to women's submission in marriage) and her sons, she and her "handmaidens" lead the praise song "Wena Wendlovu!" which affirms King Dinuzulu's role as a monarch in the face of the colonial government's disdain for him. "*Wena wendlovu!*" [You of the elephant!], the queen and this network of women chant, while the rest of *isizwe* collectively retorts "*Wena wendlovu!*"

While Queen Silomo and the chorus of the women that accompany her refer to King Dinuzulu as the person of the elephant, it is crucial to remember that she too is of the elephant. As a Queen who is married to a King in the Zulu monarchy, her title is "*indlovukazi*" [the great elephant]. The academic Pamela Maseko warns against this narrow reading, despite the belief that this isiZulu word strictly denotes femaleness due to the addition of the suffix "-*kazi*." Maseko asserts, "When added to a noun as a suffix, this morpheme [meaning -*kazi*] adds a kind of superlative, a degree of greatness and awesomeness in the noun."[24] She notes that even though nouns that contain these suffixes are commonly used to refer to women, they do not exclusively apply to them. She explains:

> When the terms *indodakazi*, great man (sister-in-law),[25] *ubawokazi*,[26] great father (paternal uncle), *umhlekazi*, awesome/beautiful one (sir) and *umamakazi*, great mother (maternal aunt) are translated into English they do not begin to convey the meaning embedded in the root and suffix of the word. In isiXhosa, the responsibility of the carrier of the name and the connection in terms of social relation is, instead, of great worth.

Although Maseko is specifically writing about isiXhosa speakers, this suffix may also be found in isiZulu. As such, to frame Queen Silomo as *indlovukazi* is not only to recognize her as a royal woman, but it is to identify her greatness.

In addition, Khumalo and Msimang's representation of Queen Silomo as a singing royal woman is important because it is a reminder that she played a critical role in the making of Princess Magogo, the singing royal woman. As noted by Rycroft, Princess Magogo's "earliest musical education . . . was at the hands of her grandmothers, the widowed queens of King Cetshwayo, in whose huts she frequently slept as a child, as well as her mother and mother's co-wives."[27] Moreover, Gunner proposes that these royal women's transference of "cumulative knowledge of forms of song and dance from the different regions of Zulu territory" to Princess Magogo "represented a dense and rich cultural archive."[28] Significantly, Gunner conceives of royal women as carriers of archival knowledge(s). In fact, these royal women appear to have been walking archives themselves. Gunner's conception may be linked to the scholar Babalwa Magoqwana's idea that *ogogo* [grandmothers] may be understood as "institution[s] of knowledge that transfer . . . not only 'history' through *iintsomi* (folktales)" but they may also be seen as "bod[ies] of indigenous knowledge that store . . . , transfer . . . and disseminate . . . knowledge and values."[29] And even though Magoqwana particularly writes about *ogogo*, it is worth considering the idea that younger women (such as Queen Silomo) may be read as institutions of [indigenous] knowledge(s).

In this chapter, I postulate that by the time the operatic Princess Magogo is born in Act 1, scene 2, multiple women have paved the *indlela* [path] for her. In this context, these women may be framed as *ovulandlela*—as seen in the essayist, short story writer, and poet Makhosazana Xaba's anthology *Our Words, Our Worlds: Writing on Black South African Women Poets, 2000-2018*, in which she calls the early twentieth-century imbongi Notsizi Mgqwetho (arguably Princess Magogo's contemporary) the *vulandlela* of contemporary South African Black women poets. The writer and lexicographer Sibusiso Nyembezi defines *uvulandlela* as "Umuntu ohamba phambili ekuvuleni amathuba abekade engekho"[30] [A person who leads in creating opportunities where there were none]. Accordingly, Queen Silomo, who is also known to have been an imbongi who composed *izangelo* [praise poems for infancy] may be thought of as the *vulandlela* for her daughter Princess Magogo, whose birth takes place during Act 1, scene 2.

In this scene, in which King Dinuzulu is "enjoying the company of his councillors who are updating him on developments since he was banished to St Helena,"[31] Queen Silomo's "handmaidens" eagerly announce the birth of Princess Magogo. In the song "Ndabezitha nansi indaba,"[32] this trio proclaims:

Bek' indlebe wen' osenkundleni	Lend an ear, you who are in the courtyard
Ndabezitha nans' indaba	Your Majesty, here is the news
Kusindwe ngobethol' oSuthu	There is celebration at uSuthu village

USilomo useyisilomo	Silomo has become a favourite
Ngokubeleth' isithole	By bearing a daughter (heifer)
Eselam' amaguq' amabili.	Who comes after two boys (calves)

Once more, the role of the "handmaidens" is important. In this scene, they enter a royal court full of men and as Msimang states in his libretto, they "interrupt the proceedings with good news."[33] This disruption, which is directed to the men who are inside *enkundleni* [the royal court] and King Dinuzulu—who is referred to by his *isithakazelo* [clan name] and royal salute Ndabezitha—is momentous in that it becomes a catalyst for the King's eventual call for Princess Magogo to be "[*U*]*fakazi womlando wonke kaZulu*"[34] [the witness of the whole Zulu history] or an "oral historian" (as proposed by Mhlambi). In this operatic narrative, this juncture (i.e., the birth of Princess Magogo) may be seen as a turning point that ultimately catapults Princess Magogo into the politics of Zulu nationalism, Black Nationalism, and rainbow nationalism (as argued by Mhlambi).

Princess Magogo's birth is evidently met with excitement because she is a daughter among sons. In Act 1, scene 3, which takes place in the home of Queen Silomo, Princess Magogo's parents attribute the arrival of their daughter to the ancestors. In the song "Sibonga ogogo, sibonga izithutha," this duo suggests that Princess Magogo was conceived in St. Helena. Together they relate:

Queen:
Kunamhla lokhu sibong' ogogo	As for today we thank the ancestors

King:
Sibong' izithutha	We thank the ancestors

Queen:
Abafukamel' iqanda balilonda	Who sheltered and safeguarded the egg

King:
Ezasithutha eSentelina sez' ekhaya	Who transported us from St Helena back home

Queen:
Balonda ihlule esiqhingini	They safeguarded the foetus at the island

King:
Yasikelel' insindansinda yabelumbi	They secured the heavy white man's ship

Queen:
Balond' iqanda ladabul' amaza	They safeguarded the egg as it crossed the waves

King:
Ayiqhuzukanga ngonyaw' emadwaleni	Its feet did not trip against large, flat, exposed rocks

In this song, Princess Magogo's fragility and resilience are captured through her characterization as an egg that journeyed across the waters from the island of St. Helena. In addition, the idea that she was conceived on this island frames her as a transnational figure. This transnationalism is crucial because it destabilizes the fixity of Princess Magogo's geopolitics—which center on Zululand, Natal, and South Africa. Moreover, because Princess Magogo is the only daughter of her parents, her femaleness is emphasized. This may be seen in the songs "Ndabezitha nansi indaba" and "Imbali yawoMageba" (in scene 2 of the Epilogue). The former refers to Princess Magogo as *"isithole"* [a heifer] while the latter identifies her as *"Imbali yawoMageba"* [the flower of Mageba], *"[i]mbali yomculo"* [the flower of music], and *"[i]mbali yemilando"* [the flower of histories].

As stated earlier, the depiction of Princess Magogo as a child is crucial. This is so because she is widely portrayed as an adult woman who was a voiceless child with a troubled childhood. Her illness in Act 1, scene 4, represents one of the difficulties that she encountered in her childhood. In this scene, the ailing young Princess Magogo is lying on *icansi* [grass mat] as she is surrounded by her concerned mother and her equally distressed "handmaidens." Here, Princess Magogo is understood to be *ingane egulayo* [a sick child] and *inkosazana egulayo* [a sick Princess]. In the song "Iyagula lengane," the Queen and the "handmaidens" present this disease as *"impicabadala yelumbo"* [wizardry] and as such, they call for the intervention of *izangoma* ["traditional healers"] who cure her using fat from an antelope called *igogo*. Through this scene, Khumalo and Msimang suggest that the treatment of the young Princess' malady is the rationale behind her name Magogo.

Princess Magogo's naming is reminiscent of her great uncle King Shaka kaSenzangakhona's naming. The writer and poet Mazisi Kunene notes that when King Shaka's mother Queen Nandi (of the emaLangeni) was impregnated by King Senzangakhona, "The Langas had sent messengers to Jama of the Zulus, [. . .] But these messengers returned saying: "They have denied responsibility for the child, claiming her pregnancy was only an illness of intestinal beetles, a disease that invades the mind with madness."[35] And it is said that the beetle in question was called *ishaka*,[36] hence the name Shaka. In many ways, these somewhat overlapping narratives link Princess Magogo to histories that go beyond homogenized "Zuluness." As noted by Kunene, King Shaka was not only of the "Zulu" *isizwe*; he was also of the "Langa" *isizwe*. Similarly, Princess Magogo's genealogical histories center not only on the "Zulu" *isizwe*; she is also tied to her mother's *isizwe*, the Mdlaloses.

In this regard, it is contentious to identify Princess Magogo only as a child "*kaDinuzulu*" [of Dinuzulu] because she clearly belongs to both her parents. The song "Sibonga ogogo, sibonga izithutha" alludes to a partnership between Princess Magogo's mother and father. The prefix "si-" suggests a collective identity wherein both Queen Silomo and King Dinuzulu thank the ancestors for giving them a girl child that is Princess Magogo. And since Princess Magogo is commonly attached to her father, the scenes where she is connected to her mother become significant.

The relationship between mother and daughter is explored in Act 1, scene 6, in which Queen Silomo and Princess Magogo are lamenting the pending repercussions of the Bhambatha rebellion. In this context, they are not just reflecting on the imminent arrest of a monarch; they are bemoaning the loss of a husband and father. In this scene, a dying[37] Princess Magogo looks on as her mother sings to a younger version of her. In their duet "Wangenza Bambatha?" the Queen and the Princess (in her old age) express their regret about Bhambatha's actions. "Waze wangilaya ngoDlothovu!" [Oh! How you have done me in, regarding Dinuzulu], they grieve over King Dinuzulu's continuous detention.

Queen:

Waphum' esiqhingini;   He came from the island,

Princess:

Wambuyisel' esiqhingini!   And you have sent him back there

Queen:

Waphum' ekudingisweni;   He returned from exile,

Princess:

Wamfak' ekudingisweni!   And you are sending him back into exile

Queen:

Waphum' etilongweni;   He has just been released from jail

Princess:

Wambuyisel' etilongweni!   And you are sending him back to jail

Although the Queen and the Princess accord all responsibility to only one figure, Chief Bhambatha Zondi, it is vital to note that the Bhambatha rebellion (1906–8) was a collective protest (called "*impi yamakhanda*") against the poll tax that was imposed by the colonial British government. The Bhambatha rebellion was a critical moment in Zulu history and especially for the Zulu monarchy. As stated by Mhlambi, this rebellion "is considered, in anti-colonial history, as the epitome of 'Zulu nationalist consciousness.'"[38] She notes that even though this event results in the militarization of the colonial British government and a certain disintegration of the Usuthu Royal House, Chief Bhambatha's mobilization of *isizwe* in Zulu territory becomes the embodiment of Zulu nationalism and anticolonialism. Consequently, King Dinuzulu's ultimate call for the young Princess Magogo to be the scribe and disseminator of Zulu history is a sacrificial request that requires her to relinquish her childhood to serve the demands of the adult monarchs in her life. In the song "Manthithi qopha lo mlando" (in Act 1, scene 7), King Dinuzulu petitions:

Qopha lomlando	Record this history
Umpompoloze ngawo liphuma lishona	Shout it from dawn till dusk
Qopha lomlando	Record this history
Khona kuyokuzwa nezizukulwane	So that future generations may hear
Ngonya lweNkisimane	About the cruelty of the British Colonist
Ifuza indlu kaMageba!	Who is stripping the house of Mageba!

This appeal by King Dinuzulu happens in full view of *isizwe* and the colonial British government. As such, in this moment, Princess Magogo, the girl child, is crushed into her father's dreams for her and "eaten alive" (as seen in Lorde). And the leitmotif "Wangethwes' itshe ekhanda Dlothovu" [What a heavy load you have given me, Father] captures the weightiness of King Dinuzulu's call.

In Act 2, scene 1, Princess Magogo (the adult woman), who has become Christianized, agonizes over her father's wishes for her. In this scene, she enters a church where she contemplates the burden that her father has placed on her. And paradoxically, it is here that she seeks the counsel of her ancestors. Her assertion "Ngikhalakini mathongo amakhulu" [I (a)m appealing to the great ancestors] while occupying a Christian space reflects the idea that the historical Princess Magogo had "a strong devotion to the Anglican Church (though speaking no English) with a deep attachment to Zulu tradition."[39] As the operatic Princess Magogo pleads with her ancestors regarding how she should fulfill the colossal task of recording Zulu history, she simultaneously prays to God. In the hymn "UJehova ungumlondolozi," Princess Magogo draws upon Psalm 91, which is claimed to have been her beloved Psalm. In her rendition of this Psalm, she references early iterations of the isiZulu bible. According to the Bible Society of South Africa, the first isiZulu bible (which contains the dialect that is used by the operatic Princess) was published in 1893—that is seven years before the historical Princess Magogo was born. Therefore, Msimang's choice of this vernacular in the libretto is befitting as this edition of the isiZulu bible was a text that Princess Magogo was probably reading and reciting in her lifetime.

And as noted by her son Prince Mangosuthu Buthelezi, Princess Magogo "went through the Zulu bible thrice in her lifetime from cover to cover. She knew many of the Psalms of David by heart and often recited them when she conducted Prayers which she did twice every day apart from praying privately during the day."[40] In this regard, the church scene not only epitomizes the Christianization of Princess Magogo as a Zulu royal woman, but it also illustrates how language is a site of power.[41]

Princess Magogo's recitation of "UJehova ungumlondolozi" (named after a biblical subheading found in contemporary isiZulu bibles) is as follows:

Yena ohlezi ekusithekeni koPhezukonke	He who dwells in the shelter of the Most High
Wohlala ethunzini likaSomandla	Will rest in the shadow of the Almighty
Yena ohlezi ekusithekeni koPhezukonke	He who dwells in the shelter of the Most High
Wohlala ethunzini likaSomandla	Will rest in the shadow of the Almighty
Ngiya kuthi kuJehova	I will say of the Lord:
Uyisiphephelo sami nenqaba yami	You are my refuge and my fortress,
Uyisiphephelo sami nenqaba yami	You are my refuge and my fortress,
Ungu Thixo wami engimethembayo	You are my God in whom I trust
Ngokuba yena uyokhulula esihibeni somthiyi	Surely he will save you from the fowler's snare
Wokulula esihibeni somthiyi	Will free you from the fowler's snare
Nasobhadaneni olubhubhisayo.	And from the deadly pestilence.
Wokusibekela ngezimpaphe Zakhe	Will shelter you under his wings
Akufihle phansi kwamaphiko Akhe	And hide you underneath His wings
IqinisoLakhe libeyisihlangu nehawu	His truth will be your shield
Yena ohlezi ekusithekeni koPhezukonke	He who dwells in the shelter of the Most High
Wohlala ethunzini likaSomandla	Will rest in the shadow of the Almighty

Princess Magogo's psalmic expression "Ngokuba yena uyokhulula esihibeni somthiyi" is not found in contemporary isiZulu bibles. However, it may be found in a republished version of the late nineteenth-century isiZulu bible *IBhayibheli Elingcwele 1893 Isihumusho* (2018). In this text, the book of Psalms, which is commonly translated as "Amahubo" in current isiZulu bibles, is known as "Izihlabelelo." This is to say that in Izihlabelelo 91, verse 3, the psalmic words by Princess Magogo are captured as "Ngokuba yena wo ku kulula esihibeni somtiyi..."[42] And as demonstrated in this chapter, the hymnal that is sung by the operatic Princess Magogo closely resembles the words found in this late nineteenth-century isiZulu bible. As a result, Msimang's linguistic intervention in the opera may be interpreted as a commentary not only on the subjective nature of biblical transliterations but also on the malleability of the homogenized language (as seen in lexicographical practices of standardization) that is known as isiZulu.

In many ways, this particular scene exemplifies the complexities of Princess Magogo's identity: not only was the historical Princess Magogo a Zulu royal woman; she was a colonial subject who existed in a context in which there was a "struggl[e] to wield together a new cohesion around a Zulu nationalism that embraced both elements of tradition and modernity."[43]

In Act 2, scene 2, Msimang and Khumalo suggest that Prince Solomon (who was Queen Silomo and King Dinuzulu's heir) played a key role in the making of Princess Magogo as a monarchical figure. In the song "Ngiyakwethembisa Manthithi," the young Prince vows to ensure that his now orphaned young sister will one day become a prominent member of the Zulu monarchy. This pact is made in light of the strife and the displacement[44] that is experienced by the orphaned royal children at the hands of their mother's co-wives. Even though the opera confines the roles of these royal women to villains (as seen in Act 2, scene 3 in the song "UMagogo Nondlukulu"), they were part of a network of royal women who contributed to Princess Magogo's early music education.[45] In addition, Gunner asserts the following:

> Princess Magogo's troubled early life, and loss of her mother did not, ironically, isolate her from the company of other royal women, the mothers of her father Dinuzulu, and her many grandmothers, the widows of her grandfather, King Cetshwayo. It was in the company of these women—however difficult the proximity may have been at times—that Magogo absorbed the forms of cultural production that give such a deep insight into the complex subjectivities of Zulu women in the earlier precolonial and the colonial era.[46]

And this idea of a complex subjectivity is particularly important because Princess Magogo's eventual becoming as a notable Zulu royal woman demands her martyrization, which happens during and after her brother's coronation as King. During the coronation, the King espouses ideas of *ubunye* [oneness], *ubumbano* [unity], and *ukuhlangana* [assemblage]. He does this not just in relation to the sparring Buthelezi and Zulu *izizwe*; he communicates this appeal on behalf of "[*u*]*muzi ontsundu*" (as seen in the song "Nansi inkosi yenu!" in Act 2, scene 4). Mhlambi notes that this expression which she translates as "The brown House/brown-skinned people" is a "symbolic reference [...] [and] a referent that typified political discourse and songs leading up to the 1960s."[47] Furthermore, the use of the allegory of "[*u*]*muzi*" is interesting because it alludes to a marriage of sorts. In isiZulu, *umuzi* is commonly understood to mean a home that a wife builds with her husband (i.e., *ukwakha umuzi*). Unlike *ikhaya*, a concept that is tied to a place where one has been raised, *umuzi* is usually framed through the meeting of two families that then form *umuzi* that will become *ikhaya* for the children born in it. In other words, Msimang and Khumalo's reference to "[*u*]*muzi ontsundu*" suggests that it is necessary for divergent groups of brown-looking people to mobilize and unite to form an amalgamated nation.

Mhlambi explains that this leitmotif found in the song "draws on abstract but utopian ideals that are achieved by being united or a united nation: love, power, success and victory."[48] And it is against this backdrop of a collective call for unification and reconciliation that Princess Magogo is projected into the center of "the nationalism of sacrifice."[49] Act 2, scene 6 encapsulates this imposed act of renunciation. In this scene, *inkosi* uMathole Buthelezi is not only appointed as a prime minister—a position his grandfather *inkosi* uMnyamana Buthelezi held under King Cetshwayo's rule—in the Zulu *isizwe*; he is promised Princess Magogo as a wife. This agreement between King Solomon and *inkosi* uMathole happens despite the existence of a loving relationship between Princess Magogo and Khiphakonke Ndwandwe. Gunner claims that in a 1982 interview with Nicholas Cope and J. C. Dladla, Princess Magogo recounted the following:

> I had made my choice elsewhere. I was taken away from my fiancé by Solomon with his own hands. [She recounts how a number of the royal girls were called into the presence of Solomon and his councillors and asked to name their sweethearts. She does not name hers and instead is one of the group who agrees to "put up our top knots" and so make it clear that they were eligible for marriage. She continues:] We three agreed, not knowing whether we would be given men with head rings, going grey.[50]

Furthermore, Gunner indicates that the twenty-six-year-old Princess Magogo was married into *isithembu* [a polygamous marriage] with a man who was not only her brother's age group (i.e., in his mid-thirties); he was also in the same regiment. And while Princess Magogo was the tenth wife of *inkosi* uMathole, she was *undlunkulu* [the principal wife]. Gunner makes a critical observation about Princess Magogo's eminence and the peripheralization of "Zulu" royal women's narratives. She states

> It would have been quite possible for Princess Magogo to have slipped into the anonymity that has marked the (non)identity of other twentieth-century, and late-nineteenth-century royal Zulu women and the wives of key traditional leaders, such as Mathole Buthelezi. However, the sheer power of her performative eloquence plus, perhaps, the influence of her son, ensured that her profile was different.[51]

In consideration of Gunner's insightful assertions, it is clear how political Princess Magogo's marriage was. In the opera, the Princess hesitantly and distressingly gives up her relationship with Ndwandwe for the "marriage" of two *izizwe* that have a tumultuous history. In the song "Angivumanga, kuvume amathongo" (found in Act 2, scene 7), Princess Magogo agonizes:

Akuvumi mina kuvum' amathongo	It is not me who consents but it is my ancestors
Bathi ubunye yikusasa	They say unity is the future
Bathi ubunye yiphakade	They say unity is forever

In the above excerpt, it is evident that when the operatic Princess Magogo refers to her own subjectivity, she maintains her resistance. She states that it is not she who agrees but it is her ancestors who demand that she make this sacrifice. This is to say that the marriage to *inkosi* uMathole is not only a material exercise; it is a spiritual one. This framing of Princess Magogo's forebears as "national ancestors"[52] embodies the idea that in order for this Zulu royal woman to become, she has to take on the aspirations of those that came before her, those who are with her, and those who will come after her. Moreover, in the song "Sikhulekela ubunye" (in Act 2, scene 6), Mankulumana, King Solomon, and *inkosi* uMathole affirm the notion that even those who are no longer alive would advocate for a marital/political alliance between the Zulus and the Buthelezis. In this song, they declare:

Mankulumana:

Umxoshise ngesithole, Ndabezitha	Reward him with a heifer, your Majesty!
Umxoshise ngesithole sakwenu!	Reward him with a princess from your people!

King Solomon:

Bangavum' abaphansi	I'm sure the ancestors will give their approval

Inkosi Mathole:

Ilobolo liyokhokhwa yisizwe	Lobola will be paid by the nation
Uyoba ngunina wamaShenge	She will be the mother of the Buthelezi people

In this song, it is apparent that there is no consideration of Princess Magogo's viewpoint on a matter that involves her intimate life. It is also clear that Mankulumana, King Solomon, and *inkosi* uMathole are constructing an image of the woman they refer to as "[i]sithole" and "[u]nina wamaShenge." In this scene, they co-opt the ancestral into an imagined nationalistic future. In fact, Msimang and Khumalo insist on the permanence of the Zulu-Buthelezi marital union beyond the grave. In the epilogue in which Princess Magogo transitions into a world that is occupied by her ancestors, she makes a request which submits that her marriage to *inkosi* uMathole was driven by love from the beginning. In the song "Sengiyeza," she calls:

Ngihlangabeze, Sowalisa wami,	Meet me, my Sowalisa
Siphinde seluke intambo yothando,	So we may once again weave our thread of love
Eyagqashuka, Sowalisa wami,	Which had become unravelled, my Sowalisa
Eyagqashuka mhla sehlukana	Which had become unravelled the day we separated

In other words, even in her death, Princess Magogo continues to be a sacrificial figure. And the use of the pronoun "we" or the prefix "*si-*" in the second line of the above excerpt is an appropriation of her subjectivity into a collectivized subjectivity that is tied to Mhlambi's idea of a nationalism of sacrifice. And as the opera comes to an end, the Princess is eulogized for her singing voice and being an oral historian. Like a circle, this moment links back to the epilogue where Princess Magogo is called to "come home" by her ancestors. In his call (seen in the epilogue), King Dinuzulu acknowledges his daughter's sacrifices:

King Dinuzulu:

Ngivela kokhokho bakho	I am from your ancestors
abathe ngize ngibabongele,	who said I must come and say thank you
ngenkonzo yakho esizweni sawoJama	for your service to the nation of Jama
Ngomculo wakho	Through your music,
Intsha isifunde izingoma zomdabu,	our youth have learnt our indigenous songs
Ngokuzinikela kwakho	Through your devotion
isizwe sakithi sesi yimbokodo	our nation has become united

Once more, the motif of the martyrized "national woman" is cemented through the epilogue. Msimang's libretto insists on a celestial realm where "the Male

Royal Ancestors"[53] are the foremost figures "who commend [Princess Magogo] and call her home."[54] Even in death, the women that are represented in the epilogue maintain their status as "Women of the Nation."[55] And in many ways, this sequence and the opera as a whole "affirm [. . .] a normative nationalist vision regarding women's role in the nation."[56] As Princess Magogo witnesses "the heavens [. . .] revealed,"[57] the condition for her spiritual entry continues to center on her father. Msimang suggests that it is through Princess Magogo's act of keeping "her promise to her father intact"[58] that she is ushered into the next realm—one where the "big" men of Zulu history maintain their prominence.

* * *

The place of Princess Magogo in the Zulu monarchy is one that has been constructed by a number key of players, including her son Prince Mangosuthu Buthelezi and documentarians such as the composer Mzilikazi Khumalo and the librettist Themba Msimang. In this regard, Princess Magogo is not just a Zulu royal woman, but she is primarily represented as a "big" woman of a masculinist Zulu historical narrative. In this chapter, I focused on Khumalo and Msimang's operatic representation of Princess Magogo, and my central argument was that it is important to connect her to a network of women who influenced her artistic and cultural praxes in her formative years and beyond. I drew upon the scholar Innocentia Mhlambi's ideas about this opera's conception of nationalism to delink Princess Magogo from the conventional practice of inextricably tying her narrative to male-centric Zulu nationalism. Following Mhlambi, I proposed that in the opera, Princess Magogo is reimagined as a figure that transcends "Zuluness." However, as suggested by Mhlambi, the opera falls into the trap of confining her within the trope of the sacrificial "national woman."[59]

Worklist of James Steven Mzilikazi Khumalo (1932–2021)

Thomas M. Pooley[1]

The following worklist documents the information presently available for published and unpublished compositions and arrangements by Mzilikazi Khumalo. In some instances, only the titles of songs are available from the information recorded in Khumalo's personal archive. A comprehensive worklist will only be available once this archive has been properly ordered.

The following abbreviations are used for voice: Soprano (S), Alto (A), Tenor (T), and Bass (B).

COMPOSITIONS

1959   "Ma Ngificwa Ukufa" (When Death is Upon Me). Lyrics by Benedict Wallet Vilakazi. SATB ACLA (mixed choir). Shuter & Shooter, 2014.

1966   "Koze Kube Nini?" (Until When?) Lyrics by JSM Khumalo. SSA ACLA (female choir). Shuter & Shooter, 2014.

1969   "UGqozi" (Power of Inspiration). Lyrics by Benedict Wallet Vilakazi. SATB ACLA. Shuter & Shooter, 2014.

      "KwaDedangendlale" (Valley of a Thousand Hills). Lyrics by Benedict Wallet Vilakazi. SATB. Shuter & Shooter, 2014.

1981   "Lala Ngokuthula" (Little Girl--Rest in Peace). In loving memory of Naledi Mogoba, daughter of my late friend Stanley Mogoba. SATB and TTBB. Shuter & Shooter, 2014.

      "Imvukuzane" (A mole). Unpublished.

1983   "Halala Yunisa!" SATB. Shuter & Shooter, 2014.

      "Lala Mntwana Wami (Sleep My Baby)." SA. Unpublished.

      "S'khala Kini Makhosóhlanga!" (We are asking for help from you traditional kings). Lyrics by JSM Khumalo. SATB ACLA (mixed choir). Unpublished.

1981 "IZulu Elisha." Lyrics from Revelations 21:1-4. SATB ACLA. Shuter & Shooter, 2014.
1982 *UShaka KaSenzangakhona* (first tonic sol-fa version). Lyrics by Christian Themba Msimang. SAMRO Archive.
    "Halleluya Mdumiseni Nonke." Unpublished.
    "Kwaze Kwamnandekhaya." Unpublished.
1983 "Vukani Madoda" (Awake, Men). TTB ACLA (male choir). Unpublished.
1984 "Inhliziyo Kayideli." Lyrics by Otty Nxumalo. TTB ACLA. Unpublished.
    "Isibaya esiKhulu se Afrika." Lyrics by Christian Themba Msimang. Unpublished.
    "Inkondlo KaMnkabayi." (Mnkabayi's love song). Lyrics by Christian Themba Msimang. SSA. Shuter & Shooter, 2014.
1985 "Ibhange Lama-Afrika." African Bank Limited, 1975–1985. Lyrics by Christian Themba Msimang. Shuter & Shooter, 2014.
    Untitled. 10th Anniversary of the Founding of the Twelve Apostles Church in Christ, May. Unpublished.
    Untitled. 21st Anniversary of the Transkei Teachers' Association, June.
    Untitled. 60th Anniversary of the Swaziland National African Teachers Association, August.
1989 50th Anniversary of the establishment of the Freemantle Boys High School, Transkei, August.
1991 "Imbizo Yajubumjokwane." Tenor solo with ACLA.
1992 "Akhala Amaqhude Amabili." (Two Cocks Crowing). Composition based on two traditional songs. SATB. Shuter & Shooter, 2014.
    "Bantu Be Afrika Hlanganani." Traditional texts. Commissioned by the National Symphony Orchestra and orchestrated by Péter Louis van Dijk.
1995 "Ivukil Imvana kaThixo." SATB (mixed choir).
1996 (revised 1999)   *UShaka KaSenzangakhona*. Composed by J. S. Mzilikazi Khumalo on texts by Christian Themba Msimang.
    Orchestration by Christopher James; revised and enriched by Robert Maxym and with an overture.
Settings: I. Orchestra, soloists (SATB), choir (SATB), imbongi (praise poet); score available from SAMRO.
    II. Piano-vocal score published by Maxym Music, 1999.
    III. Chamber and IV. Band scores published by Maxym Music, 2003.

Preamble: "Ndabezitha!"
PART I *UKUZALWA KUKASHAKA* (The Birth of Shaka)
1. ILembe Labikezelwa Zinyandezulu (The Coming of ILembe was Foretold by the Great Ancestral Spirits)
2. Ikloba Lothando (A Blazing Furnace of Love)
3. Imbizo Yezinyandezulu (An Assembly of the Great Ancestral Spirits)
4. Imbizo Yajub'uMjokwane (The Assembly Chose Mjokwane)
5. Inkondlo kaNandi (Nandi's Love Song)
6. Langa Lami LaseLangeni (My Sun of Elangeni)
7. Laqhibuk'ikhow'eLangeni (A Mushroom Suddenly Burst Out at Elangeni)

PART II *UKUKHULA KUKASHAKA* (Shaka's Early Youth)
1. Beba Kumame Sigoduke (Get Onto Mother's Back, and Let Us Go)
1a. Narration and The Echoes
2. Nansi'Indaba Yempi (Here is the Story of the Warfare)
3. IhuboLika Mvelinqangi (The Hymn of the Creator)
4. Yith'omanqoba, Yith'ushikishi! (We are the Conquerors, We are the Invincible Ones!)

PART III *UMBUSO KASHAKA* (The Reign of Shaka)
1. Ladum'izulu! (The Thunder of the Heavens!)
1a. Narration and Echoes
2. Izibongo ZikaShaka (The Traditional Praises of King Shaka)

PART IV *UKUKHOTHAMA KUKASHAKA* (The Death of Shaka)
1. Ukungena Kwempethu (The Setting in of the Rot)
2. Esibayeni KwaNyakamubi (At the Cattle Kraal at Nyakamubi)
3. Isiphethu Sezinyembezi (A Well of Tears)
4. Isililo Esesabekayo (A Terrible Weaping and Wailing)

EPILOGUE
1. Uthi Mangithini? (What Can I Say?)
2. Siyashweleza Nodumehlezi (We Beg Your Pardon, Nodumehlezi)

1999 Insizwendala. In honor of Dr. Nelson Rolihlala Mandela. SATB (mixed choir).

2002 *Princess Magogo KaDinuzulu*
Opera in two acts with music by J. S. Mzilikazi Khumalo, Princess Magogo KaDinuzulu, and Michael Hankinson (with arrangements of traditional songs). Orchestrated by Michael Hankinson.
Libretto by Christian Themba Msimang.

Scoring: Orchestra, soloists, and choir. With traditional and Shembe dancers. Designs by Andrew Verster.

PROLOGUE—Scene 1. Princess Magogo's Bedroom
1. Orchestral Introduction
2. Uyephi Na? (Princess Magogo solo)
3. Woza Sambe (Male Chorus of Ancestors)
4. Woza Mntanami! Woz'Ekhaya—Recitativo 1 (Princess Magogo & King Dinuzulu)
5. Orchestral Scene Change Music

ACT 1. Scene 1: The Mahashini Royal Kraal
6. Umgwagwa Usehlomile (Mankhulumane & Chorus)
7. Hebe! (Warriors) Traditional Zulu War Cry
8. Shayani Ingungu MaZulu (Mankhulumane & Chorus)
9. Umamonga Wosuthu (Imbongi). Traditional Praises of King Dinuzulu
10. Wena Wendlovu, Bayede (Queen Silomo, Trio of Handmaidens, Chorus, Mankhulumane)
11. Ngiyanibingelela Zulu (King Dinuzulu & Chorus)
12. Kuhle Kwethu (Chorus)

Scene 2: The Mahashini Royal Kraal (Later)
13. Ndabezitha, Nansi Indaba (Trio of Handmaidens)
14. Zawuju Lezo Ndaba (King Dinuzulu)
15. Giyani 'Zinsizwa zoSuthu (King Dinuzulu, Trio of Handmaidens, Warriors)
16. Traditional War Dance (Warriors, Zulu Drummer)

Scene 3: Queen Silomo's Hut
17. Woza Ntandokazi (King Dinuzulu)
18. Sibonga Ogogo, Sibonga Izithutha (Queen Silomo & King Dinuzulu)

ACT 2. Scene 4: Queen Silomo's Hut (Five Years Later)
19. Iyagula Lengane (Queen Silomo & Trio of Handmaidens)
20. Inyanga Yegogo (Chorus of Villagers, Sangoma)
21. Hayan'Ingoma—Recitativo 2 (Princess Magogo)
22. Sabulawa KwaZulu (Princess Magogo)

Scene 5: The Mahashini Royal Kraal
23. Bambani Im'khonto (Warriors)—Zulu War Song
24. Hebe! (Warriors)—Zulu War Cry

25. Wena Wendlovu! (Bambatha, Male Chorus & Warriors)
26. Walishisizwe, Bambatha! (King Dinuzulu & Bambatha)
27. Basifunani? (Warriors)—Zulu War Cry
28. Koze Kube Nini! (King Dinuzulu)
29. Nangumlungu 'eshisizwe! (King Dinuzulu, Bambatha, Male Chorus and Warriors)

Scene 6: Somewhere in the Mahashini Royal Kraal
31. Wangenza Bambatha (Queen Silomo & Princess Magogo)

Scene 7: The Mahashini Royal Kraal
32. Ikhanda likaBambatha (Duncan)
33. Wenzen' Okandaba (Duncan, Silomo, King Dinuzulu, Trio of Handmaidens, Makhulumane & Chorus)
34. Manthithi Qophe lo Mlando (King Dinuzulu)

The following songs are undated:
Amahubo Esizwe Esimnyama (SATB ACLA, mixed choir)
Ngenze Njani (For Nomavenda Mathiane; MSOP|TEN(2)SOLI|SATB ACLA; traditional)
Sondela Enoch Mgijima (The Prophet of God)
Abanqobi Bahlodi (SATB ACLA, mixed choir)
Yithi'omanqoba, Yith'ushikishi. Lyrics by Christian Themba Msimang. SATB. Shuter & Shooter, 2014.
Xola, Hleziphi (Be Forgiving Hleziphi). Lyrics by Christian Themba Msimang. SATB. Shuter & Shooter, 2014.
Kuhle Kwethu! Lyrics by Christian Themba Msimang. SATB. Shuter & Shooter, 2014.
Sengiyenza Ntombi KaNtuzwa. Lyrics by Christian Themba Msimang. Soprano solo, TB. Shuter & Shooter, Msimang, 2014.
Isiphetho SikaShaka

ARRANGEMENTS

Note: Apart from the song cycle *Haya Mntwan' Omkhulu*, these arrangements are undated. Only the publication date is included here. Shuter & Shooter published a compilation of Khumalo's works in 2014, and so this information is included for reference purposes.

Abakwami	Traditional, arranged by SBP Mnomiya & JSM Khumalo. Shuter & Shooter, 2014.
Isalukazi Sami	Traditional, arranged by Ludumo Magangane & JSM Khumalo. Shuter & Shooter, 2014.
Isileyi Sam	Anonymous, arranged by JSM Khumalo. Shuter & Shooter, 2014.
Oonomathotholo	Xhosa Traditional, arranged by JSM Khumalo. Shuter & Shooter, 2014.
Ewe, Linamandla!	Traditional, arranged by JSM Khumalo. Shuter & Shooter, 2014.
eGalile	Anonymous, arranged by JSM Khumalo. Shuter & Shooter, 2014.
Ndikhokhele, Bawo!	Anonymous, arranged by JSM Khumalo. Shuter & Shooter, 2014.
Woza Mmeli Wami (Come my Redeemer)	Arranged by JSM Khumalo. Shuter & Shooter, 2014.
Noya Na?	Attributed to ET Marokana. Arranged by JSM Khumalo and Joseph Langa. Shuter & Shooter, 2014.
Ingoma KaNtsikana	Gaba Ntsikana, arranged by John Knox Bokwe & JSM Khumalo. Shuter & Shooter, 2014.
Uyeza, Uyeza Umgwebi Omkhulu	Anonymous, arranged by JSM Khumalo. Shuter & Shooter, 2014.
Sangena	Traditional, arranged by JSM Khumalo. Shuter & Shooter, 2014.
Iphíndlela	Traditional, arranged by JSM Khumalo. Shuter & Shooter, 2014.
Umahlalela	Traditional, arranged by JSM Khumalo and Joseph Langa. Shuter & Shooter, 2014.

Thula S'thandwa Sami	Traditional. Shuter & Shooter, 2014.
Shayelani Amabala	Traditional Children's song. Shuter & Shooter, 2014.
Hamba Lulu	Traditional Children's Song, arranged by JSM Khumalo. Shuter & Shooter, 2014.

Sizongena Laph'emzini! (We Shall Come into this Homestead)
Oalla Moholodi
Mankokotsane
One Nwele Bojoang Jwala

Haya Mntwan' Omkhulu
Composer: Mntwana Constance Magogo kaDinuzulu Buthelezi
Arranged by JSM Khumalo and Peter Klatzow
Commissioned by the SAMRO Foundation

1. Uyephi Na? (Where Has He Gone?)
2. Umuntu Ehlobile (A Man in All His Finery)
3. Ngibambeni, Ngibambeni! (Hold Me, Hold Me!)
4. Ngiyamazi uziBhebhu (I Know Zibhebhu)
5. Thambo Lenyoka (The Bone of a Snake)
6. Sabulawa KwaZulu (We Are Killed in KwaZulu)
7. Umqhubansuku (Something to While Away the Time)
8. Ubuhle Bensizwa Busentanyeni (A Young Man's Beauty is in the Shape of His Neck)

Arrangements for the Salvation Army (undated):
Umalusi NguJehova (The Lord's My Shepherd)
Uyeza uMgwebi Omkhulu

Score: "Ma Ngificwa Ukufa" (1959) by J. S. M. Khumalo

MA NGIFICWA UKUFA
(SATB)

B W Vilakazi   Mzilikazi Khumalo

Score: "Ma Ngificwa Ukufa"

Score: "Ma Ngificwa Ukufa"

Score: "Ma Ngificwa Ukufa"

Score: "Ma Ngificwa Ukufa"

Score: "Izibongo ZikaShaka" (1981) by J. S. M. Khumalo

IZIBONGO ZIKASHAKA

(SATB)

Traditional praises   Mzilikazi Khumalo

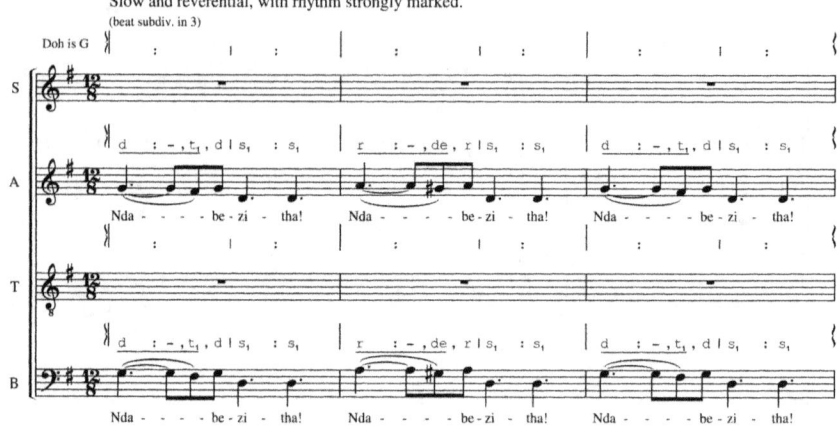

Score: "Izibongo ZikaShaka"

Score: "Izibongo ZikaShaka"

Score: "Izibongo ZikaShaka"

Score: "Izibongo ZikaShaka"

Score: "Izibongo ZikaShaka"

Score: "Izibongo ZikaShaka"

Tempo Primo
TTBB

Score: "Izibongo ZikaShaka"

Score: "Izibongo ZikaShaka"

Editor and Contributor Bios

Editors

Naomi André is the David G. Frey Distinguished Professor in the Department of Music at the University of North Carolina at Chapel Hill, USA, and Professor *Emerita* at the University of Michigan, USA. Her publications include the books *Black Opera: History, Power, Engagement* and *Voicing Gender: Castrati, Travesti, and the Second Woman in Early Nineteenth-Century Italian Opera* and coedited collections *African Performance Arts and Political Acts* and *Blackness in Opera*.

Innocentia Mhlambi is an associate professor of African Languages at the University of the Witwatersrand, South Africa. She teaches African-language literatures, Black film studies, oral literature and popular culture, and visual culture. She is the author of *African-language Literatures: Perspectives on isiZulu Fiction and Popular Black Television Series* and coeditor of *Mintiro ya Vulavula: Arts, National Identities and Democracy*. She has published extensively on aesthetics, literature, Black opera, popular culture, broadcast, and print media in South Africa. She is currently researching Black opera in post-1994 South Africa.

Thomas M. Pooley is a professor of musicology and chair of the Department of Art and Music at the University of South Africa. He holds a PhD in musicology from the University of Pennsylvania, USA, and degrees from the University of KwaZulu-Natal, South Africa, and Wits University, South Africa. He is the author of *The Land Is Sung: Zulu Performances and the Politics of Place* (2023) and is Editor-in-Chief of *Muziki: Journal of Music Research in Africa*, and founding managing editor of the open-access journal, *Analytical Approaches to African Music*.

Donato Somma is a senior lecturer in Music in the Wits School of Arts, University of the Witwatersrand, Johannesburg, South Africa. His research areas include the persistence of opera in Africa, from its forms and functions in the larger politics to the spaces and infrastructures that house it. Underpinning this is an interest in memory and narration and their relation to the fractured histories of South Africa.

Contributors

Richard Cock is well known in South Africa as a choral music director and conductor. He studied at the University of Cape Town, Cape Town, South Africa, and later at the Royal School of Church Music in the United Kingdom. After eight years of experience in the UK, he returned to South Africa where he has made a notable contribution in several fields, focusing on the upliftment of music in all communities. He formed a close relationship with Mzilikazi Khumalo, which was cemented by their cooperation in the Sowetan Nation Building Massed Choir Festival which they directed together for eighteen years.

Diliza Khumalo studied music and African languages at the University of Zululand, Empangeni, South Africa, before pursuing a career in education and as a motivational speaker. He is an experienced singer and choral conductor who worked closely with his late father, Professor Mzilikazi Khumalo, training choirs for the Nation Building Massed Choir Festivals.

Ludumo Magangane studied music at the University of Zululand, Empangeni, South Africa, under Professor Khabi Mngoma, and holds a Secondary Teachers' Diploma and a Bachelor of Education degree. He became a teacher in Mathematics and Music and taught at Kenneth Masekela Senior Secondary School in Kwa Thema. In 1993, he was promoted to deputy Chief Education Specialist for School Guidance and Counselling. He conducted the Kwa Thema Youth Choir and was cofounder of the Bonisudumo Choristers which was involved in the Nation Building Massed Choir Festivals from 1989 to 2009. He coordinated the East Rand choirs and was later a music director of the festival.

Robert Maxym received musical training at the Manhattan School of Music in New York, USA, the Institute des Hautes Etudes Musicales in Montreux, Switzerland (conducting with Rudolf Kempe), and the Musikhochschule in Munich, Germany. A conducting fellow at Tanglewood in 1980, he received masterclass instruction from Bernstein, Ozawa, Previn, Davis, and Tennstedt. As a conductor, Maxym has held numerous positions, including Musikalischer Oberleiter of the Essen Opera. He has conducted orchestras in over twenty countries during his fifty-year career. Founder/Chairman of the International Wolf-Ferrari Society in Düsseldorf, Germany (1983). As an orchestrator and composer, he collaborated with Khumalo and Msimang on the orchestration of "UShaka" and the publication of the piano-vocal score in dual notation (1994–99).

Megan Quilliam is an ethnomusicologist and arts administrator based in Colorado. She was born in South Africa and immigrated to the United States as a teenager. She completed a BM in Musicology from the University of Sydney's (Australia) Conservatorium of Music in 2011 and received her PhD in Ethnomusicology from the University of Colorado at Boulder in 2023. Her dissertation is entitled "Musical Theater and Opera in Postapartheid South Africa." Dr. Quilliam began her career in arts administration in 2019 and currently serves as Development Associate for Central City Opera, the United States' fifth oldest professional opera company.

Kholeka Shange is a lecturer in the Anthropology department at the University of the Witwatersrand, Johannesburg, South Africa, and she is a curator of the Wits Anthropology Museum. She holds a PhD in the History of Art, an MA in Film and Television Studies, and a BA in Dramatic Arts from the same institution. Previously, she worked as a Director for the Upstart Youth Development Project (in Makhanda, Eastern Cape), and she also held the role of Book Review Editor for the *Journal of Contemporary African Studies*.

David Smith obtained his BMus from the University of Cape Town, Cape Town, South Africa, in 1974. His PhD (UCT, 1992) was awarded for his dissertation "Historic case studies reflecting sources of change in the theory of scales and modes in the West." Apart from a period of school music teaching, he taught music theory at the former University of Natal (now the University of KwaZulu-Natal), Durban, South Africa, and was appointed its first Professor of Opera and Choral Studies in 2002. He pursues research into South African music and is an experienced choral trainer working mainly with Black choirs in the Durban area.

Sandra de Villiers studied at the Conservatorium of Music, Stellenbosch University, South Africa, and at the Mozarteum, Salzburg, Austria, where she obtained Masters degrees in Opera, and in Lieder, Oratorio, and Church Music (performance). She served as a senior lecturer and Head of Opera at the Technikon Natal Music Department. In 1994, she founded the Opera Africa Company and the Opera Africa Educational Trust with the objective of building representative opera audiences and to empower gifted and previously disadvantaged soloists and choristers. Productions toured in South Africa, the United Kingdom, the United States, Netherlands, and Norway, including the first African opera, *Princess Magogo KaDinuzulu*, commissioned by Opera Africa.

Notes

Acknowledgements

1 *African Performance Arts and Political Acts*, ed. Naomi André, Yolanda Covington-Ward and Jendele Hungbo (Ann Arbor, MI: University of Michigan Press, 2021). The coeditors for this volume on Mzilikazi Khumalo were involved with the 2017 conference and that collection of essays has contributions by Naomi André, Innocentia Mhlambi, and Thomas Pooley.

Introduction

1 Deborah Posel, "The Apartheid Project, 1948–1970," in *The Cambridge History of South Africa, Volume 2: 1885–1994*, ed. Robert Ross, Anne Kelk Mager and Bill Nasson (Cambridge: Cambridge University Press, 2011), 319–68.
2 E. Jefferson Murphy, "Schooling for Servitude: Some Aspects of South Africa's Bantu Education System," World Education Project of the Curriculum Center (Storrs: University of Connecticut, 1972).
3 William Beinart, *Twentieth Century South Africa* (New York: Oxford University Press, 2000).
4 Vivienne Pieters, "Music and Presbyterianism at the Lovedale Missionary Institute, 1841–1955" (PhD diss., University of South Africa, 2022).
5 Thomas Pooley, "Singing in South African Schools," in *The Routledge Companion to Interdisciplinary Studies in Singing, Volume 2: Education,* ed. Helga Gudmundsdottir, Carol Beynon, Karen Ludke, and Annabel Cohen (New York: Routledge, 2020), 123–33.
6 Starting with the ANC in 1959 and gaining wider formal backing from the United Nations in 1968, the academic and cultural boycott of Apartheid South Africa was an effective tool in focusing public attention on the racial segregation of the Apartheid state. It is credited, in part, with the final demise of the system by using sporting, academic and cultural isolation to establish the Apartheid state as pariah. (South African History Online, "South Africa's Academic and Cultural Boycott," https://www.sahistory.org.za/article/south-africas-academic-and-cultural-boycott (accessed September 21, 2023).
7 David Coplan, *In Township Tonight! South Africa's Black City Music and Theatre*, 2nd edn (Chicago: University of Chicago Press, 2008).

8   "The power of the white community made acculturation, in practice anglicization, attractive (as culture always speaks to power), and churches and schools became centers of elite African cultural development. Yet despite urbanization, continuity with rural cultural traditions continued to provide a resource for African adaptation to the caste system of color. Educated Africans drew on their pre-colonial past for elements of moral community, social control, and cultural coherence, combining them with similar elements from the dominant society" (Coplan, *In Township Tonight!* 136).

9   Yvonne Huskisson, *The Bantu Composers of Southern Africa* (Braamfontein: SABC, 1969). The second edition was published as *Black Composers of Southern Africa: An Expanded Supplement to The Bantu Composers of Southern Africa*, ed. Sarita Hauptfleisch (Pretoria: Human Sciences Research Council, 1992).

10 Veit Erlmann, *African Stars: Studies in Black South African Performance* (Chicago: University of Chicago Press, 1991). The album *Reuben T. Caluza, The B-Side* is available from SAMRO and reinterprets Caluza's Double Quartet recordings made in London in 1930.

11 Veit Erlmann, "Symbols of Inclusion and Exclusion: Nationalism, Colonial Consciousness, and the 'Great Hymn,'" in *Music, Modernity, and the Global Imagination* (New York: Oxford University Press, 1999), 129.

12 Grant Olwage, "John Knox Bokwe, Colonial Composer: Tales about Race and Music," *Journal of the Royal Musical Association* 131, no. 1 (2006): 1–37. For a discussion of Sontonga's hymn see David Coplan and Bennetta Jules-Rosette, "Nkosi Sikelel' iAfrika and the Liberation of the Spirit of South Africa," *African Studies* 64, no. 2 (2005): 285–308.

13 Pieters, "Music and Presbyterianism."

14 Grant Olwage, "The Class and Colour of Tone," *Ethnomusicology Forum* 13, no. 2 (2004): 203–26.

15 See Richard Cock's chapter (this volume) for more detail on this project of reconciliation through choralism.

16 Discussions on decoloniality in music studies are still embryonic. For a recent exchange of ideas, see Carina Venter, William Fourie, Juliana Pistorius and Neo Muyanga, "Decolonising Musicology: A Response and Three Positions," *SAMUS* 36/37 (2017): 129–54.

17 George Mugovhani, "*Muzika wa Dzikhwairi*: An Essay on the History of Venda Choral Music," *Muziki* 10, no. 2 (2013): 75–89; Christine Lucia, "Travesty or Prophecy? Views of South African Black Choral Composition," in *Music and Identity: Transformation and Negotiation*, ed. Eric Akrofi, Maria Smit and Stig-Magnus Thorsén (Stellenbosch: SUN Press, 2007); Christine Lucia, ed., *The World of South African Music: A Reader* (Cambridge: Cambridge Scholars Press, 2005); Grant Olwage, "Music and (Post) Colonialism: The Dialectics of Choral Culture on

a South African Frontier" (PhD diss., Rhodes University, 2003); Markus Detterbeck, "South African Choral Music (Amakwaya): Song, Contest and the Formation of Identity" (PhD diss., University of Natal, Durban, 2002).

18 Naomi André, Karen Bryan and Eric Saylor, eds., *Blackness in Opera* (Urbana: University of Illinois Press, 2012); Naomi André, *Black Opera: History, Power, Engagement* (Urbana: University of Illinois Press, 2018). For work on South African opera, see Hilde Roos, *The La Traviata Affair: Opera in the Age of Apartheid* (Oakland: University of California Press, 2018); Juliana Pistorius, "Predicaments of Coloniality, or, Opera Studies Goes Ethno," *Music and Letters* 100, no. 3 (2019): 529–39.

19 Coplan, *In Township Tonight!*.

20 Erlmann, *African Stars*; Erlmann, *Music, Modernity and the Global Imagination* .

21 The work of Christine Lucia in establishing a critical edition for the choral composer Joshua Mohapeloa is an important development, though his music was mostly written in the mid-twentieth century.

22 For more about the fallacy of race being biologically based, see Dorothy Roberts, *Fatal Invention: How Science, Politics, and Big Business Re-create Race in the Twenty-First Century* (New York: New Press, 2011). An important intervention in the analysis of race in South Africa is a recent monograph by Zmitri Erasmus, *Race Otherwise: Forging a New Humanism for South Africa* (Johannesburg: Wits University Press, 2017).

23 This segregation of a racialized tradition to 'ethnomusicology' was recognized by Houston Baker when he wrote: "Music for musicology is Europe and European of an inventively bounded cast, caste, and cask" (p. xi). "Foreword," in *Music and the Racial Imagination*, ed. Ronald Radano and Philip V. Bohlman (Chicago: University of Chicago Press, 2000).

24 One such figure is the composer Michael Moseu Moerane (1904-1980). Christine Lucia's publications on Moerane, and her Michael Moerane Critical Edition Project (https://aoinstitute.ac.za/moerane/ accessed December 6, 2020), offer important insights into a Black choral composer of the earlier generation who possessed a bachelor's degree in music, and whose compositions include orchestral work.

25 Ndwamato George Mughovani, "The Manifestations of the 'African Style' in the Works of Mzilikazi Khumalo" (M.Mus Dissertation, University of the Witwatersrand, 1998); The role of indigenous African choral music in the search for identity: With special reference to Mzilikazi Khumalo's music, *Muziki* 7, no. 1 (2010): 60–75.

26 Christine Lucia, "Back to the Future?: Idioms of 'Displaced Time' in South African Composition," in *Composing Apartheid: Music for and Against Apartheid*, ed. Grant Olwage (Johannesburg: Wits University Press, 2008), 11. See also Lucia's

introduction to *The World of South African Music*; Olwage, "John Knox Bokwe, Colonial Composer," 1–37.

27 James Steven Mzilikazi Khumalo, ed., *South Africa Sings: Volumes 1–3* (Braamfontein: SAMRO, 1998 [2nd edn, 2010], 2008, 2012).

28 Peter Klatzow, ed., *Composers in South Africa Today* (Cape Town: Oxford University Press, 1987). Another important work that mostly documented white composers was *South African Music Encyclopedia* published in four volumes and edited by Jacques P. Malan (Cape Town: Oxford University Press, 1979 to 1986).

29 Christine Lucia, "Celebrating Composer Kevin Charles Volans, b. 1949," *Musicus* 37, no. 1 (2009): 3–18.

30 Christine Lucia, "'The Times Do Not Permit': Moerane, South Africa, Lesotho, and *Fatše La Heso*," *Muziki* 16, no. 2 (2019): 89.

31 Christine Lucia, "Mapping the Field: A Preliminary Survey of South African Composition and Performance as Research," *SAMUS: South African Journal of Musicology* 25, no. 1 (2005): 83–108.

32 Lindelwa Dalamba, "Beyond King Kong: Literary, Historical and Musicological Perspectives on Todd Matshikiza," *South African Music Studies* 38, no. 1 (2019): 258–60 (but see entire issue); Salim Washington, "Exiles / Inxiles: Differing Axes of South African Jazz During Late Apartheid," *South African Music Studies* 32, no. 1 (2012): 91–111.

33 Mhlambi has offered a critical reading of the themes of Zulu nationalism and its relations to the emerging post-apartheid polity (Innocentia Mhlambi, "The Question of Nationalism in Mzilikazi Khumalo's Princess Magogo KaDinuzulu (2002)," *Journal of African Cultural Studies* 27, no. 3 (2015): 294–310, https://doi.org/10.1080/13696815.2015.1049245.)

34 The change that took place in his works from the 1980s onward is discussed in more detail in this volume by his son, Diliza Khumalo (Chapter 2), and by Thomas Pooley (Chapter 1).

35 Ndwamato George Mugovhani, "An Interview with Mzilikazi Khumalo," *SAMUS: South African Music Studies* 28, no. 1 (2008): 155–68; "The Role of Indigenous African Choral Music in the Search for Identity: With Special Reference to Mzilikazi Khumalo's Music," *Muziki* 7, no. 1 (2010): 60–75.

36 David Rycroft, "The Zulu Bow Songs of Princess Magogo," *International Library of African Music* 5, no. 4 (1976): 41–97. Mhlambi, "The Question of Nationalism," 294–310.

37 Walter Mignolo, *The Darker Side of Western Modernity: Global Futures, Decolonial Options* (Durham, NC: Duke University Press, 2011), 17.

38 Jean Comaroff and John Comaroff, *Theory from the South* (New York: Routledge, 2013).

39 Achille Mbembe, *Critique of Black Reason* (Durham: Duke University Press, 2017); Sabelo Ndlovu-Gatsheni, "Decoloniality as the Future of Africa," *History Compass* 13, no. 10 (2015): 485–96, and *Epistemic Freedom in Africa: Deprovincialization and Decolonization* (New York: Routledge, 2018).
40 Mignolo, *Darker Side*.

Chapter 1

1 *UGqozi* (Power of Inspiration) is the title of a poem by Benedict Wallet Vilakazi that Khumalo set to music. It is one of Khumalo's most widely performed songs and speaks to the role that he played in many spheres of African arts and letters through his career. See Benedict Wallet Vilakazi, *Amal'ezulu*, African Treasury Series No. 8 (Wits University Press, 2021).
2 Andrew Eason, "'All Things to All People to Save Some': Salvation Army Missionary Work among the Zulus of Victorian Natal," *Journal of Southern African Studies* 35, no. 1 (2009): 7–27, https://doi.org/10.1080/03057070802685502, p. 15.
3 James Steven Mzilikazi Khumalo, "In His Own Words," Unpublished manuscript (1989), p. 2.
4 The nine siblings are: Albertinah, John, Stanford, Catherine, Mzilikazi, Thandi, Beatrice, Nomsa, and Nomavenda. See Nomavenda Mathiane, *Eyes in the Night: An Untold Zulu Story* (Northcliff: Bookstorm, 2016).
5 Diliza Khumalo, Zoom interview, June 25, 2020.
6 Ludumo Magangane, chapter 5.
7 Khumalo, "In His Own Words," 3.
8 Khumalo, "In His Own Words," 4.
9 Ndwamato George Mugovhani, "An Interview with Mzilikazi Khumalo," *South African Music Studies* 28, no. 1 (2008): 166.
10 Saul Dubow, *Apartheid, 1948 to 1994* (Oxford: Oxford University Press, 2014).
11 Mpume Zondi, "Introduction," in *Amal'ezulu*, ed. Benedict Wallet Vilakazi (Braamfontein: Wits University Press, 2021), xxi–xxxiii and xxvi–xxvii.
12 James Steven Mzilikazi Khumalo, "Plot and Character in Vilakazi's Novels" (Unpublished honours article: University of South Africa, Pretoria, 1972).
13 William Beinart, *Twentieth Century South Africa* (Oxford: Oxford University Press, 2000).
14 Diliza Khumalo, Zoom interview with the author, June 25, 2020.
15 James Steven Mzilikazi Khumalo, "Zulu Tonology, Part 1," *African Studies* 40, no. 2 (1981): 53–130, https://doi-org.oasis.unisa.ac.za/10.1080/00020188108707573;

James Steven Mzilikazi Khumalo, "Zulu Tonology, Part 2," *African Studies* 41, no. 1 (1982): 3–125, https://doi.org/10.1080/00020188208707579.

16 Anthony Traill, James Steven Mzilikazi Khumalo and Paul Fridjhon, "Depressing Facts About Zulu," *African Studies* 46, no. 2 (1987): 255–74.

17 Diliza Khumalo, Zoom interview with the author, June 25, 2020.

18 Deuteronomy Bhekinkosi Zeblon Ntuli, *Citation to the Degree of Doctor of Musicology* (Honoris Causa) (Pretoria: UNISA, 2003).

19 James Steven Mzilikazi Khumalo, "Preface," in *English-Zulu, Zulu-English Dictionary*, ed. Clement Doke and Benedict Vilakazi (Braamfontein: Wits University Press, 2008).

20 Mary Bill, unpublished manuscript, 1997.

21 Ntuli, *Citation*.

22 Quoted in Yvonne Huskisson, *The Black Composers of Southern Africa: An Expanded Supplement to The Bantu Composers of Southern Africa*, ed. Sarita Hauptfleisch (Pretoria: Human Sciences Research Council, 1992), 10.

23 Translation from *Zulu Horizons* by Benedict Wallet Vilakazi rendered into English verse by Florence Louie Friedman (Johannesburg: Witwatersrand University Press, 1973).

24 Mugovhani, "Interview," 166–7.

25 See Richard Cock, chapter 4.

26 Mugovhani, "Interview," 155.

27 Khumalo was famous for revising his songs and arrangements over and over again, a practice he explained as follows: "I must also say that I do not really 'change my original compositions': what I do is change a few sections which I am unhappy with and this, I think is my right as a composer. [. . .] If you don't know sufficient music and you write, you do make mistakes. And if you see a mistake you have to correct it, unless you are a fool" (Mugovhani, "Interview," 167).

28 Mngoma established the Ionian Orchestra and Choir in Orlando West, Soweto. These ensembles were to nurture generations of black musicians performing works by Handel, Mozart, Beethoven, Mendelssohn, and other composers. This fascination with Western art music was characteristic of the times (Inge Mari Burger, "The Life and Work of Khabi Mngoma" (PhD diss., University of Cape Town, 1992). For a reflection on the striving of the black elite and its relationship to Western high culture, see Bloke Modisane, *Blame Me on History* (New York: Penguin, 1990).

29 Mngoma published an influential chapter on composition: "The Correlation of Folk and Art Music among African Composers," Proceedings of the Seventh Symposium on Ethnomusicology, ed. Andrew Tracey (Grahamstown: Rhodes University, 1988).

30 Black Orpheus was comprised of Abiah Mahlase, Tommy Matome, Bushy Mabece, Aitken Morare, Jabulani Mazibuko (assistant leader), Solly Zulu, Mayo Miza, and Khumalo himself as leader. Cyril Khumalo used a horn to keep them in tune.
31 Khumalo, "In His Own Words," 5.
32 Mugovhani, "Interview," 166.
33 Ndwamato George Mugovhani, "The Role of Indigenous African Choral Music in the Search for Identity: With Special Reference to Mzilikazi Khumalo's Music," *Muziki* 7 (2010): 27.
34 Ngũgĩ wa Thiong'o, *Decolonising the Mind: The Politics of Language in African Literature* (Oxford: James Currey, 2005), 15.
35 Khumalo, "In His Own Words," 2.
36 Christian Themba Msimang's spent much of his career as an academic lecturer at Unisa, where he was professor of African languages and acting registrar before turning to politics as a member of parliament and national chairperson of the Inkatha Freedom Party.
37 Khumalo, "In His Own Words," 6.
38 Mugovhani, "Interview," 158.
39 The Soweto Songsters were conducted by Mzilikazi Khumalo, Bonisudumo Choristers by Themba Madlopha, the Daveyton Adult Choir by Abiah Mahlase, and the Cenestra Male Choir by Ludumo Magangane.
40 Paul Boekkooi, "Musical Epic in Praise of Shaka," *The Star*, May 22, 1996.
41 Perhaps the only precedent is Michael Moerane. See Christine Lucia, "'The Times Do Not Permit': Moerane, South Africa, Lesotho, and *Fatše La Heso*," *Muziki* 16, no. 2 (2019): 87–112.
42 Controversy over the orchestrations by James and Maxym have been discussed at length in Anthoni Schonken's MMus dissertation, "Authorship and Ownership of uShaka kaSenzangakhona" (Stellenbosch: Stellenbosch University, 2013).
43 Annemarie van der Walt, "Mzilikazi Khumalo: A Choral Legend in His Own Time," in *Composer's Corner* (Braamfontein: SAMRO, n.d.), 37–9.
44 Mzilikazi Khumalo, Themba Msimang, Robert Maxym and Christopher James, *UShaka KaSenzangakhona: Piano-vocal Score* (Centurion: Maxym Music, 2005), xlviii.
45 Mzilikazi Khumalo, "Serious Music in an African Context," *NewMusicSA Bulletin* 3–4 (2004/2005): 13–15.
46 Thomas Pooley, "'Never the Twain Shall Meet': Africanist Art Music and the End of Apartheid," *South African Music Studies* 30/31, no. 1 (2010): 45–69.
47 The success of this new direction for art and traditional musics in South Africa is evident in the efforts of other composers like Michael Blake and Nofinishi Dywili who collaborated on The Bow Project organized through NewMusicSA beginning in 1999.

48 Martin Scherzinger, "'Art' Music in a Cross-Cultural Context: The Case of Africa," in *The Cambridge History of Twentieth Century Music*, ed. Nicholas Cook and Anthony Pople (Cambridge: Cambridge University Press, 2004).
49 *South Africa Sings*, Volume 1; *South Africa Sings*, Volume 2; *South Africa Sings*, Volume 3 (Braamfontein: SAMRO).
50 James Stewart Mzilikazi Khumalo, *South Africa Sings, Volume 1*, 1st edn (Johannesburg: SAMRO, 1998), 3.
51 See Innocentia Mhlambi and Kholeka Shange (chapters 8 and 12). Liz Gunner, "A Royal Woman, an Artist, and the Ambiguities of National Belonging: The Case of Princess Constance Magogo," *Kunapipi* 24, no. 1 (2002), https://ro.uow.edu.au/kunapipi/vol24/iss1/18.
52 Some were recorded commercially by Gallo, but there were also recordings made by the International Library of African Music, and by West German Radio. See SAMRO Booklet on Princess Magogo.
53 David Rycroft, "The Zulu Bow Songs of Princess Magogo," *African Music* 5, no. 4 (1975/1976): 41–97.
54 Peter Klatzow, "The Composer's Dilemma: Writing for Time or Place," *South African Journal of Musicology* 24, no. 1 (2004): 135–41.
55 Anthony Tommasini, "Opera Review: Varied Cultures Entwine Around a Zulu Princess," *New York Times*, June 7, 2004. This was a review of a performance by African Renaissance Opera company supported by the Chicago Chamber Orchestra at the Ravinia Festival.
56 Christopher Ballantine, "On Being Undone by Music: Thoughts Toward a South African Future Worth Having," *South African Music Studies* 34–35 (2015): 501–20.
57 Naomi André, "Winnie, Opera, and South African Artistic Nationhood," *African Studies* 75 (2016): 10–31.

Chapter 5

1 Christine Lucia, *Music Notation: A South African Guide* (Pretoria: Unisa Press, 2012).
2 www.johnkersey.org (accessed September 30, 2022).
3 Lucia, *Music Notation*.
4 Andrew Lewis and Johann Steyn, "A Critique of Mission Education in South Africa According to Bosch's Mission Paradigm Theory," *South African Journal of Education* 23, no. 2 (2003): 101–6.
5 Yvonne Huskisson, *The Bantu Composers of Southern Africa* (Auckland Park: South African Broadcasting Corporation, 1969).

6 Grant Olwage, "Singing in the Victorian World: Tonic sol-fa and discourses of religion, science and Empire in the Cape Colony," *Muziki* 7, no. 2 (2010): 193–215.
7 Markus Detterbeck, "South African Choral Music (Amakwaya): Song, Contest and the Formation of Identity" (PhD diss., University of Natal, 2002).
8 Lucia, *Music Notation*.

Chapter 6

1 Khumalo's two large works involving solo singers, chorus and orchestra – *UShaka KaSenzangakhona* and *Princess Magogo KaDinuzulu* have attracted the most published comment, both within South Africa and outside. The latter was presented in the USA in 2004, the former in 2006, both at the Ravinia Festival. See Anthony Tommasini, "Opera Review: Varied Cultures Entwine Around a Zulu Princess," *New York Times*, June 7, 2004; Michael Cameron, "Life of the Legendary Zulu King is the Subject of 'UShaka,'" *Chicago Tribune*, June 10, 2006. His corpus of a cappella choral songs lags in formal recognition.
2 For a wide-ranging reflection, see Thomas Pooley, "Obituary: James Steven Mzilikazi Khumalo, 1932–2021," *Muziki: Journal of Music Research in Africa* 19, no. 2 (2022): 86–91.
3 Christine Lucia's editions of their works are available online: https://african-composers-edition.co.za/composers/joshua-mohapeloa/ and here: https://african-composers-edition.co.za/composers/michael-moerane/ (accessed October 25, 2023).
4 M.S. De Jongh, *Directory of South African Music Collections*. See the directory webpage here: https://libguides.sun.ac.za/SAMusicCollections (accessed October 25, 2023).
5 Mzilikazi Khumalo, *Izingoma zikaMzilikazi Khumalo* (Pietermaritzburg: Shuter & Shooter, 2014).
6 James Steven Mzilikazi Khumalo, ed., *South Africa Sings: Volumes 1–3* (Braamfontein: SAMRO, 1998 [2nd edn 2010], 2008, 2012).
7 "Wi, wi, sizongena" (side A, track 1) is clearly related to the more elaborate version published in *Izingoma* (pp. 200–10). The album may be streamed online: https://www.regalzonophone.com/Albums/Soweto-Songsters (accessed October 25, 2023).
8 "Ungifanise Nawe" (Make me like You) goes beyond the usual sense of 'arrangement', combining as it does the music of a Salvation Army chorus (sung in Zulu) "with added music in traditional African style and words in Zulu" (booklet notes, p. 6).

9 The compact disc (Marco Polo 8223832) featuring 'Five African Songs' under Khumalo's name is simply a pendant to the recording just mentioned. It contains four of his nation-building arrangements (printed in either the *SAS* series or in *Izingoma*, or in both), and 'Bantu Be-Afrika Hlanganani', but in orchestral versions by Peter-Louis van Dijk.

10 See Markus Detterbeck, "South African Choral Music (Amakwaya): Song, Contest and the Formation of Identity" (PhD diss., University of Natal, Durban, 2002), 213. It may be that the details of the 'oral history' of such a work can be traced in sources like YouTube comments: for example, Vernon Ndimeni notes that "at Ohlange High School (KZN, South Africa), this song would be sung as part of the repertoire of the annual classical music competition which was [held] among the school's four Houses (Ntsihlele, Mdima, Luthuli, Charles). This was during the Mafukuzela Week commemorative event ... during the [tenure] of principal Mr S. D. Ngcobo." Accessed online: www.youtube.com/watch?v=3--4QQooh24.

11 Published in Vilakazi's collection *Amal'ezulu* (1945) and set by Khumalo in 1969.

12 It is surely no surprise that Khumalo uses Mascagni's key and marks his sections with Italian terms exclusively, including unusual usages like *spianato* and *affetuosamente* (in addition to *affetuoso*).

13 Duncan Brown, *Voicing the Text: South African Oral Poetry and Performance* (Cape Town: Oxford University Press, 1998), 80.

14 Vilakazi suggested that such poems unfold according to "the rhythmical structures of izibongo ... the 'breath-group', the verbal units defined by the performer's regular pauses for breath" (Brown, *Voicing the Text*, 78). Some such performative division may be reflected in the work's sections.

15 Ndwamato George Mugovhani and Ayo Oluranti, "Symbiosis or Integration: A Study of the Tonal Elements in the Choral Works of Mzilikazi Khumalo and Phelelani Mnomiya," *Muziki: Journal of Music Research in Africa*, Vol. 2, no. 2 (2015), 3.

16 "Multi-part organization of voices is common in the traditional music of all the Nguni peoples. In any choral song there are at least two voice-parts, singing non-identical texts. The temporal relationship between these parts observes the principle of non-simultaneous entry." (David Rycroft, quoted in Mugovhani and Oluranti [2015], 10). Some of Khumalo's treatments pair non-simultaneous entry with differing texts, others do not.

17 The arrangement "Akhala Amaqhude Amabili" seems resolutely 'gendered', and exploits tenors as a 'high voice', before essaying a *fugato* for four solo voices, surely the most gender-neutral style in the composer's quiver. He then runs the process in a textural reversal, but with increasing division of parts. It is a tour de force perfectly written for a large choir.

18 James Stewart Mzilikazi Khumalo, *South Africa Sings, Volume 1*, 1st edn (Johannesburg: SAMRO, 1998), 5. His interest and insights in this area are gathered in his doctoral dissertation, "An Autosegmental Account of Zulu Phonology" (University of the Witwatersrand, 1987). He makes clear in his editorial notes that this gliding phenomenon is a feature of Nguni languages generally: it is found in Ndebele, Swati, Xhosa and Zulu speakers.

19 It is not only the spirituals: sober hymns and folk-like carols are also held hostage by the 'catchy' and often overblown orchestral treatments that accompany armies of choristers.

Chapter 7

1 Derryck Cooke, *Gustav Mahler: A Performing Version of the Draft for the Tenth Symphony* (London: Faber, 1989).
2 Pavel Lamm, *Boris Godunov* by Modest Musorgsky Orchestration by Dmitri Shostakovich, Libretto by Moussorgsky (Vienna: Universal Edition, 1928).
3 Raymond Leppard, *L'incoronazione di Poppea* by Claudio Monteverdi (London: Faber, 1962).

Chapter 8

1 "Sigiya Ngengoma" is a colloquial phrase, meaning people are dancing to music popularized by a local kwaito music group, Trompies in the mid-1990s. The song is from their album *Sigiya Ngengoma* (Gallo, 1995) produced by Dangerous Crew Combination (DCC).

2 The SABC's *Shaka Zulu* was problematic on many fronts. Some of the problems had to do with the construction of blackness in filmic media globally and locally; historical contingences steeped in racial histories of colonialism and later apartheid found their way into this film; and a racially biased cultural economy of media production in South Africa excluded an African visual voice. However, when Khumalo's epic premiered in 1996, the version, which invariably drew from similar historical sources as the film, had a different effect. It was embraced and confirmed to be a convincing testament of Zulu military history and their heroic king. Conflicting interpretations of *officialese* and *non-officialese* (in a Bakhtinian sense) renditions of Zulu history through the span of time were constituted by multivalent articulations embedded deeply within cultural and political memories of South Africa's national consciousness, and signaled punctures in the hegemony of the colonial and apartheid regimes' propaganda.

3 Christine Lucia, "Mapping the Field: A Preliminary Survey of South African Composition and Performance as Research," *SAMUS* 25 (2005): 83–108.
4 Pierre Bourdieu, trans. Richard Nice, "The Field of Cultural Production or The Economic World Reversed," in *The Field of Cultural Production: Essays on Art and Literature*, ed. Randal Johnson (Cambridge: Polity Press [Amsterdam: Elsevier], 1983), 29–73.
5 Thomas Pooley, "'Never the twain Shall Meet': Africanist Art Music and the End of Apartheid," *South African Music Studies* 30, no. 1 (2010): 45–69.
6 Mantoa Motinyane, Ndebele Mpho and Christine Lucia, "Translating Mohapeloa: Perspectives from Mantoa Motinyane and Mpho Ndebele with an Introduction by Christine Lucia," *South African Music Studies* 36–37 (2018): 246–64.
7 Richard Schechner, "From Ritual to Theatre and Back: The Structure/Process of the Efficacy/Entertainment Dyad," *Educational Theatre Journal* 26, no. 4 (1974): 455–81; Victor Turner, *From Ritual to Theatre: The Human Seriousness of Play* (New York: Performing Arts Journal Publications, 1982); Michael David McNally, "The Indian Passion Play: Contesting the Real Indian in 'Song of Hiawatha' Pageants 1901–1965," *American Quarterly* 58, no. 1 (2006): 106–36; Louise Meintjies, "Shoot the Sergeant, Shatter the Mountain: The Production of Masculinity in Zulu Ngoma Song and Dance in Post-Apartheid South Africa," *Ethnomusicology Forum* 12, no. 2 (2005): 173–201; Achille Mbembe, "Variations on the Beautiful in the Congolese World of Sounds," *Politique Africaine* 100 (2006): 71–91; Liz Gunner, "Jacob Zuma, the Social Body and the Unruly Power of Song," *African Affairs* 108, no. 430 (2009): 27–48.
8 Lara Allen, "Music and Politics," *Social Dynamics: A Journal of African Studies* 30 (2004): 1–19; Gunner, "Jacob Zuma, the Social Body and the Unruly Power of Song," 27–48; and Paolo Israel, *In Step with the Times: Mapiko Masquerades of Mozambique* (Athena, OH: Ohio University Press, 2014).
9 Philip Antoni Schonken, "Authorship and Ownership of UShaka KaSenzangakhona" (MMus Thesis, Stellenbosch University, 2013); George Mugovhani Ndwamato, "The Role of Indigenous African Choral Music in the Search for Identity: With Special Reference to Mzilikazi Khumalo's Music," *Muziki* 7 (2010): 60–75; George Mugovhani Ndwamato, "Muzika wa Dzikhwairi: An Essay on the History of Venda Choral Music," *Muziki* 10 (2013): 75–89.
10 Ndwamato George Mugovhani and Ayodamope Oluranti, "Symbiosis or Integration: A Study of the Tonal Elements in the Choral Works of Mzilikazi Khumalo and Phelelani Mnomiya," *Muziki* 12, no. 2 (2015): 1–21.
11 I have elected to use the original autograph copy of the tonic sol-fa arrangement that Khumalo worked on as he proceeded with composition, elaboration, and amendments to the work. This copy was procured from Constance Nhlapho from Kwa-Thema, a chorister in the Bonisudumo Choir which was under

the directorship of Mr Ludumo Magangane. Magangane was instrumental in reversioning this tonic solfa rendition into staff notation.

12 See Innocentia Mhlambi, "A Literary Reflection of the Bhambatha Rebellion," in B. W. Vilakazi's *Nje Nempela* and E. Zondi's *Insumansumane* (Master's Dissertation, University of the Witwatersrand, 2002).

13 Veit Erlmann, *African Stars: Studies in Black South African Performance* (Chicago: University of Chicago Press, 1991); Veit Erlmann, *Music, Modernity and the Global Imagination: South Africa and the West* (New York: Oxford University Press, 1999).

14 Jean Comaroff and John Comaroff, *Of Revelation and Revolution Vol 2: The Dialectics of Modernity on a South African Frontier* (Chicago: University of Chicago Press, 1997).

15 Hlonipha Mokoena, "The Black House, or How the Zulus Became Jews," *Journal of Southern African Studies* 44, no. 3 (2018): 401–11.

16 The naming of dances is in accordance with the names from where they originate within the KwaZulu-Natal region (Vusabantu Ngema, "Symbolism and Implication in the Zulu Dance Forms: Notions of Composition, Performance and Appreciation of Dance Among the Zulu" (MA Thesis, University of KwaZulu-Natal, 2007), 37.

17 Veit Erlmann, "Horses in the Race Course: The Domestication of Ingoma Dancing in South Africa, 1929–39," *Popular Music* 8, no. 3 (1989): 259–73.

18 Ngema, "Symbolism and Implication in the Zulu Dance Forms," 2.

19 At the J. S. M. Khumalo symposium, in August 2018, I was alerted to these clapping routines and their variations by the rendition of this section of the oratorio ('*Izibongo ZikaShaka*', bar 9-138, 44–50) by the Khumalo family during the dinner. When guests clapped randomly to beats of the melody, the family taught them how the falling beats were synchronized with the imagined falling accent of the dancer's foot. It is in the variations of the clapping that I cognitively listened for both forms of dance genres: *indlamu* with its gaze to the heroic past of the Zulu people, and *ingoma*, a dance routine which registers connections to the past, but with emphasis on capturing transformations which have since befallen the Zulu people.

20 Meintjes, "Shoot the Sergeant, Shatter the Mountain," 174.

Chapter 9

1 Hein de Villiers was inspector of music in the province of Natal and later played a key role in the production staged by Opera Africa.

2 I grew up in the Cape and studied music at Stellenbosch University. A Wilcocks Bursary enabled me to further my studies at the Mozarteum in Salzburg, Austria, before I returned to Pietermaritzburg and Durban in 1980.

3 This chapter is based in part on interviews with Thomas Pooley, Naomi André, and Innocentia Mhlambi.
4 Professor Mazisi Kunene (1930–2006) was poet laureate of South Africa and an anti-apartheid activist in exile (leaving in 1959). He taught at the University of California, Los Angeles, before returning to teach at the University of Natal.
5 Mangosuthu Gatsha Buthelezi (1994-2023)served for decades as Prime Minister of the Zulu kingdom and was a Member of Parliament and former President of the Inkatha Freedom Party. He was the leader of the KwaZulu Bantustan during the apartheid era.
6 Mahlabathini town, also spelt 'Mhlabathini', is in the Ugu District Municipality, KwaZulu-Natal. It was the family home of Mathole Buthelezi and Princess Magogo and is still the Buthelezi seat.
7 Professor Msimang was at that time a professor of African languages at the University of South Africa. He served as Head of Department and later as the acting Registrar of the university before becoming a Member of Parliament for the Inkatha Freedom Party.
8 The late Themistocles Venturas (1958-2017) was a theater producer and practitioner in KwaZulu-Natal.
9 Gerhard Geist was the former conductor of the Frankfurt Opera House. He conducted Opera Africa's Faust in 1998/99. Venturas and Verster had also been involved with that production.

Chapter 10

1 Liz Gunner, "A Royal Woman, an Artist, and the Ambiguities of National Belonging: The Case of Princess Constance Magogo," *Kunapipi Journal of Post-Colonial Writing* 24, no. 1 & 2 (2002): 221.
2 Pamela Karantonis and Dylan Robinson, eds., *Opera Indigene: Re/Presenting First Nations and Indigenous Cultures* (Surrey: Ashgate Publishing Limited, 2011), 84 & 89.
3 David Rycroft, "The Zulu Bow Songs of Princess Magogo," *African Music* 5, no. 4 (1975/1976): 41.
4 Innocentia Mhlambi, "The Question of Nationalism in Mzilikazi Khumalo's *Princess Magogo kaDinuzulu* (2002)," *Journal of African Cultural Studies* 27, no. 3 (2015): 294–310.
5 Mhlambi, "The Question of Nationalism."
6 Christine Lucia, "Back to the Future? Idioms of 'Displaced Time' in South African Composition," in *Composing Apartheid: Music for and Against Apartheid*, ed. Grant Olwage (Johannesburg: Wits University Press, 2008).

7. George Mugovhani Ndwamato and Ayodamope Oluranti, "Symbiosis or Integration: A Study of the Tonal Elements in the Choral Works of Mzilikazi Khumalo and Phelelani Mnomiya," *Muziki* 12, no. 2 (2015): 1–21.
8. Rycroft, "Zulu Bow Songs"; and Dave Dargie, "Umakhweyane: A Musical Bow and its Contribution to Zulu Music," *African Music* 8, no. 1 (2007): 60–81.
9. David Coplan, *In Township Tonight! South Africa's Black City Music and Theatre*, 2nd edn (Chicago: University of Chicago Press, 2008); David Graver and Loren Kruger, "South Africa's National Theatre: The Market or The Street?" *New Theatre Quarterly* 5, no. 19 (1989).
10. *Mail & Guardian Staff Reporter*, "Opera's Long Road to Bullhoek," December 9, 1994.
11. Hankinson, email correspondence with author, July 2018.
12. Hankinson, email correspondence with author, July 2018.
13. Rycroft, "Zulu Bow Songs," 76.
14. Rycroft, "Zulu Bow Songs."
15. Rycroft, "Zulu Bow Songs."
16. Rycroft, "Zulu Bow Songs," 54.
17. Mhlambi, "Question of Nationalism."
18. Hankinson, personal communication with author, July 2018.
19. Musa Khulekani Xulu, "The Re-Emergence of Amahubo Song Styles and Ideas in Some Modern Zulu Musical Styles" (Thesis, University of KwaZulu Natal, 2013).
20. Liz Gunner and Mafika Gwala, *Musho!: Zulu Popular Praises* (East Lansing: Michigan State University Press, 1991), 2.
21. Kai Kresse, "Izibongo – The Political Art of Praising: Poetical Socio-Regulative Discourse in Zulu Society," *Journal of African Cultural Studies* (2007): 175.
22. Mhlambi, "Question of Nationalism."
23. Saul Dubow, "South Africa and South Africans: Nationality, Belonging, Citizenship," in *The Cambridge History of South Africa, Volume 2: 1885–1994*, ed. Robert Ross, Anne Kelk Mager and Bill Nasson (New York: Cambridge University Press, 2016), 58 & 63.
24. Nigel Worden, *The Making of Modern South Africa: Conquest, Apartheid, Democracy*, 5th edn (Wiley Blackwell, 2012), 156.
25. Mhlambi, "Question of Nationalism," 304.
26. Mhlambi, "Question of Nationalism," 306.
27. Ingrid Byerly, "Mirror, Mediator and Prophet: The Musical Indaba of Late-Apartheid South Africa," *Ethnomusicology* 42, no. 1 (1998): 1–44.
28. Ingrid Byerly, "Decomposing Apartheid: Things Come Together. The Anatomy of a Musical Revolution," in *Composing Apartheid: Music for and Against Apartheid*, ed. Grant Olwage (Johannesburg: Wits University Press, 2008), 259.
29. Thomas Pooley, "'Never the Twain Shall Meet': Africanist Art Music and the End of Apartheid," *South African Music Studies* 30–31, no. 1 (2010): 45–69.

Chapter 11

1 John Rosselli, *The Opera Industry in Italy from Cimarosa to Verdi: The Role of the Impresario* (Cambridge: Cambridge University Press, 1984); Roger Parker, *Leonora's Last Act: Essays in Verdian Discourse* (Princeton: Princeton University Press, 1997).
2 A recent example of this excess in opera is *St Kilda – A European Opera* (Maclean 2007). For African resonance see *The Head and The Load* (Kentridge, Sibisi and Miller 2018). Mia Pistorius, "Review: The Head and the Load, dir. William Kentridge," *South African Music Studies* 38 (2018): 86–7.
3 The commissioning of *Aida* (Verdi, 1871) as a reflection of the fantastical ambitions of Khedivial Egypt serves as a prominent example of this. Adam Mestyan, "Arabic Theatre in Early Khedivial Culture, 1868–72: James Sanua Revisited," *International Journal of Middle Eastern Studies* 46 (2014): 120, https://doi.org/10.1017/S002074381311.
4 Ruth Bereson, *The Operatic State: Cultural Policy and the Opera House* (London: Routledge, 2002).
5 Canadian opera-trained tenor Jeremy Dutcher created a multimedia performance and album *Wolastoqiyik Lintuwakonawa* (2018) with archival recordings of songs in the Wolostoq language. "How a Canadian Opera Singer is Honouring his Indigenous Roots," *The National CBC* (podcast audio), https://www.cbc.ca/news/thenational/how-a-canadian-opera-singer-is-honouring-his-indigenous-roots-1.4825432; Shirley Thompson's 2019 work, *Memories in Mind: Women of the Windrush*, uses the soprano operatic voice as a central pillar to tell the story of migrant women from the Caribbean's arrival and experience in Britain in the 1960s and 1970s. "Memories in Mind: Women of the Windrush Tell Their Stories," *Tete-A-Tete*, https://www.tete-a-tete.org.uk/event/memories-in-mind-women-of-the-windrush-tell-their-stories/.
6 Dickinson has carved a space for non-Western modernity in the introduction to *The Arab Avant-Garde*, re-centering the art music world in Arab musical cultures. Kay Dickinson, "Introduction: 'Arab' + 'Avant-Garde,'" in *The Arab Avant-Garde: Music, Politics, Modernity*, ed. Thomas Burkhalter, Kay Dickinson and Benjamin Harbert (Connecticut: Wesleyan University Press, 2013), 1–36. In opera studies, Karantonis and Robinson engage with the representation of indigenous peoples in various settler-invaded nations, and the continuing use of indigenous forms, musics, and voices to nation-build. Pamela Karantonis and Dylan Robinson, *Opera Indigene: Re/presenting First Nations and Indigenous Cultures* (Surrey: Ashgate, 2011).
7 George Mughovani, "An Interview with Mzilikazi Khumalo," *South African Music Studies* 28, no. 1 (2008): 160.
8 Mughovani, "An Interview with Mzilikazi Khumalo," 157.

9. The opera toured internationally in Europe and the United States. This forms another context for the opera, in the wider sphere of international opera. After its 2002 premiere at the Durban Playhouse, it was staged at the South African State Theatre, with a national tour in 2006. It featured prominently at 2004 Ravinia Festival and was also broadcast by WFMT Radio in Chicago. Amsterdam (2005) and Oslo (2007) also hosted the opera.
10. This synopsis is generated from the Synopsis and Libretto of the opera that correspond with the filmed Oslo performance version (2007), courtesy of Opera Africa. The libretto offers corresponding English translations and the surtitle cues. I've followed the orthography used in the libretto for both number titles and names, hence "Bambatha" as opposed to the more common "Bhambatha."
11. A glossary of terms was developed for copy related to the opera. These terms are taken from the glossary, provided by Opera Africa.
12. Christopher Ballantine, "On Being Undone by Music: Thoughts Towards a South African Future Worth Having," *South African Music Studies* 34–35, no. 1 (2015): 513.
13. See Innocentia Mhlambi in this book, Chapter 8.
14. Tommasini's review of the Ravinia performance for the *New York Times* would clearly have preferred a more flamboyant, less polished performance on the one hand, but also measures dance, aria and orchestration by rather narrow criteria. Anthony Tommasini, "Opera Review: Varied Cultures Entwine Around a Zulu Princess," *New York Times*, June 7, 2004, https://www.nytimes.com/2004/06/07/arts/opera-review-varied-cultures-entwine-around-a-zulu-princess.html. Sandra de Villiers has also spoken of the inherent bias behind some European conductors in their approach to the work, judging it exclusively by canonical western opera standards and norms (personal communication, 2018).
15. Mughovani, "An Interview with Mzilikazi Khumalo," 167.
16. Musa Xulu, "The Re-Emergence of amaHubo Song Styles and Ideas in Some Modern Zulu Musical Styles" (PhD diss., University of Natal, 1992), 171.
17. Xulu, "The Re-Emergence," 3.
18. Xulu, "The Re-Emergence," 78–9.
19. David Rycroft, "The Zulu Bow Songs of Princess Magogo," *African Music: Journal of the African Music Society* 5, no. 4 (1975): 42.
20. Here I am indebted to the work of Kholeka Shange (see Chapter 12), whose enquiry into the status and reading of uMntwana recovers her from political and patriarchal objectification and historicization of her and her work. "uMntwana" redirects attention from western "princess" to an African royalty discourse, at the same time eliding her individuality, so prized in normalized western readings. It serves here as a restorative gesture highlighting the fictionalization that happens of necessity in theatrical representations of history.

21 Sandra de Villiers, author's co-interview with Naomi André and Innocentia Mhlambi, Strand, Western Cape, 5 July 2019.
22 De Villiers, author's co-interview, July 5, 2019.
23 Catherine Clément, "Opera, or the Undoing of Women" (Thesis, Minneapolis, University of Minnesota, 1999 [1988]), 11.
24 Rycroft, "The Zulu Bow," 49.
25 Mhlambi, "The Question of Nationalism," 307.
26 In the opening of Mhlambi's treatise of Khumalo's opera (2002), she problematises the assumed convention of speaking about a homogenous Zulu identity throughout the history of the Zulu Empire.
27 Her name features in numerous documents on the official website, most often in relation to the forming of Dr Mangosuthu Buthelezi's own sense of cultural identity and historical destiny. Mangosuthu Buthelezi, "Building on a Strong Legacy in a New Season of Struggle for Economic and Social Justice Structured on Democratic Ideals." Address at National Elective Conference, August 24, 2019. http://www.ifp.org.za/national-elective-conference-of-the-inkatha-freedom-party-address-by-prince-mangosuthu-buthelezi-mp/. Also in relation to women in the culture see Mangosuthu Buthelezi, "Message from Prince Mangosuthu Buthelezi," Press Release. Zulu Royal Women Series: Princess Magogo Seminar, August 30, 2019. http://www.ifp.org.za/uzulu-arts-and-heritage-npo-presents-the-princess-magogo-seminar-the-first-of-the-zulu-royal-women-series/.
28 De Villiers, author's co-interview, July 5, 2019.
29 Themba Msimang referenced this in his address to the symposium on the intellectual legacy of J. S. M. Khumalo held at Unisa. See also Joseph Thwala, "An Explication of Some Aspects of Christian Themba Msimang's Poetry" (PhD diss., University of Zululand, 2000).
30 Thwala, "An Explication of Some Aspects," 44–6.
31 William Faure, dir., *Shaka Zulu* (Johannesburg: South African Broadcasting Corporation, 1986).
32 "The hawk that claps its wings in Cape Town, Ascends with the mountains, peaks, Fold the wings in the capital city Pretoria." From *Nge-Unisa Eminyakeni Elikhulu*, quoted in Thwala, "An Explication of Some Aspects of Christian Themba Msimang's Poetry," 41.
33 Ballantine, "On Being Undone By Music," 513.
34 De Villiers, author's co-interview, July 5, 2019.
35 De Villiers, author's co-interview, July 5, 2019.
36 Christine Lucia, "Travesty or Prophecy? Views of South African Black Choral Composition," in *Music and Identity: Transformation and negotiation*, ed. Eric Akrofi et al. (Stellenbosch: African Sun Media, 2007), 165.

37 Christine Lucia and Grant Olwage, "The Joshua Pulumo Mohapeloa Critical Edition," *South African Music Studies* 36–37, no. 1 (2018): 160.
38 De Villiers, author's co-interview, July 5, 2019.
39 Thomas Pooley, "'Never the Twain Shall Meet': Africanist Art Music and the End of Apartheid," *South African Music Studies* 30–31, no. 1 (2010): 45–69.
40 Rycroft, "The Zulu Bow Songs," 45.
41 Rycroft, "The Zulu Bow Songs," 45.
42 Rycroft recorded a version with similar sentences and expression, noting that other recordings of it were made previously. Rycroft, "The Zulu Bow Songs," 54–5. Khumalo himself made recordings of uMntwana from which he worked in composing *Princess Magogo*. Mughovani, "An Interview with Mzilikazi Khumalo," 159.
43 Kwanele Sosibo, "Musician Mbuso Khoza on Princess Magogo and Neutered Patriarchy," *Mail & Guardian*, May 4, 2018, https://mg.co.za/article/2018-05-04-princess-magogo-and-neutered-patriarchy.
44 Aside from these moments of material from the cultural parent tradition there is the choral music of Khumalo and the solo arias that are conceived in a style derived from traditional musics. Mughovani has explored the deep imbrication of tradition and original musical material in relation to Khumalo's *Izibongo ZikaShaka*. George Mughovani, "The Role of Indigenous African Choral Music in the Search for Identity: With Special Reference to Mzilikazi Khumalo's Music," *Muziki* 7, no. 1 (2010): 60–75.
45 Von Rhein's *Chicago Tribune* article (2004), in anticipation of the performance at Ravinia, expresses this moment in international enthusiasm. John von Rhein, "Ravinia Kicks off Centennial with Story of Zulu Princess," *Chicago Tribune*, May 30, 2004, https://www.chicagotribune.com/news/ct-xpm-2004-05-30-0405300405-story.html.
46 Karantonis and Robinson, *Opera Indigene*.
47 KZN Philharmonic Orchestra, "Princess Magogo in Court," *Artslink*, 2003, https://www.artlink.co.za/news_article.htm?contentID=18401.
48 "Stumbles, dear people, like a baby toddling, learning to walk!"

Chapter 12

1 Liz Gunner, "A Royal Woman, an Artist, and the Ambiguities of National Belonging: The Case of Princess Constance Magogo," *Kunapipi* 24, no. 1 (2002): 205, https://ro.uow.edu.au/kunapipi/vol24/iss1/18.
2 Gunner, "A Royal Woman," 205.

3   Anthony Tommasini, "Opera Review; Varied Cultures Entwine Around a Zulu Princess," *New York Times*, June 7, 2004, https://www.nytimes.com/2004/06/07/arts/opera-review-varied-cultures-entwine-around-a-zulu-princess.html.
4   Gunner, "A Royal Woman," 205.
5   Gunner, "A Royal Woman," 205.
6   Mangosuthu Buthelezi, "Princess Constance Magogo," in *Petticoat Pioneers: Women of Distinction*, ed. Ruth Gordon (Pietermaritzburg: Shuter and Shooter (Pty) Ltd, 1988), 236.
7   Buthelezi, "Princess Constance Magogo," 236.
8   Innocentia Mhlambi, "The Question of Nationalism in Mzilikazi Khumalo's Princess Magogo kaDinuzulu," *Journal of African Cultural Studies* 27, no. 3 (2015): 295.
9   Mhlambi, "The Question of Nationalism," 295.
10 Mhlambi, "The Question of Nationalism," 295.
11 Benedict Anderson, *Imagined Communities: Reflections on the Origin and Spread of Nationalism* (London: Verso Books, 1983). Homi K. Bhabha, *Nation and Narration* (London; New York: Routledge, 1990).
12 George Robinson Dent and Cyril Lincoln Sibusiso Nyembezi, *Scholar's Zulu Dictionary* (Pietermaritzburg: Shuter & Shooter Publishers (Pty) Ltd, 2009), 583.
13 Dent and Nyembezi, *Scholar's Zulu Dictionary*, 583.
14 Cynthia Nomathamsanqa Tisani, "Continuity and Change in Xhosa Historiography During the Nineteenth Century: An Exploration Through Textual Analysis" (PhD diss., University of Cape Town, 2002), 156.
15 J. B. Peires, "Traditional Leaders in Purgatory: Local Government in Tsolo, Qumbu, and Port St. Johns, 1990–2000," *African Studies* 59, no. 1 (2000): 90.
16 Nyembezi and Nxumalo also note that the term 'izizwe' not only refers to "Abantu abaphethwe yinkosi eyodwa", but can also mean "ufufunyane," which is a form of mental illness (2018, 307). However, Dent and Nyembezi define 'izizwe' as "insanity; evil spirits" (2009, 583).
17 Cyril Lincoln Sibusiso Nyembezi and Otty E. H. Mandla Nxumalo, *Inqolobane YeSizwe* (Pietermaritzburg: Shuter & Shooter (Pty) Ltd, 2018), 307.
18 Mhlambi, "The Question of Nationalism," 305.
19 I use the term 'big' to signal the esteem allotted to the historic Princess Magogo due to her lineage, artistic and cultural praxis, and marital status.
20 Jennifer Weir, "'I Shall Need to Use Her to Rule': The Power of 'Royal' Zulu Women in Pre-Colonial Zululand," *South African Historical Journal* 43 (November 2000): 4, http://dx.doi.org/10.1080/02582470008671905.
21 Kholeka Shange, "Malibongwe: Poems from the Struggle by ANC Women," *Journal of Contemporary African Studies* 39, no. 4 (2021): 651, https://doi.org/10.1080/02589001.2021.1938978.
22 Mhlambi, "The Question of Nationalism," 299.

23 Jennifer Weir, "Chiefly Women and Women's Leadership in Pre-colonial Southern Africa," in *Women in South African History: Basus'iimbokodo, Bawel'imilambo/They Remove Boulders and Cross Rivers*, ed. Nomboniso Gasa (Cape Town: HSRC Press, 2007).

24 Pamela Maseko, "Language as Source of Revitalisation and Reclamation of Indigenous Epistemologies: Contesting Assumptions and Re-imagining Women Identities in (African) Xhosa Society," in *Whose History Counts: Decolonising African Pre-colonial Historiography*, ed. June Bam, Lungisile Ntsebeza and Allan Zinn (Stellenbosch: African Sun Media, 2018), 50.

25 It is important to note that even though the term "indodakazi" means "sister-in-law" in isiXhosa, in isiZulu, this expression is used to refer to a "daughter" (Doke et al., 1996: 165) or "daughter in law" (*ibid*).

26 In isiZulu, the term "ubabekazi" refers to a "paternal aunt" (Doke et al., 1996: 58). In addition, "ubabekazi" may also be "applied to cross-cousin (female) of my father [i.e. *umzala kababa*]" (*ibid*).

27 David K. Rycroft, "The Zulu Bow Songs of Princess Magogo," *African Music* 5, no. 4 (1975/76): 42, http://www.jstor.org/stable/30249726.

28 Gunner, "A Royal Woman," 216.

29 Babalwa Magoqwana, "Repositioning uMakhulu as an Institution of Knowledge: Beyond 'Biologism' Towards the Body of Indigenous Knowledge," in *Whose History Counts: Decolonising African Pre-colonial Historiography*, ed. June Bam, Lungisile Ntsebeza and Allan Zinn (Stellenbosch: African Sun Media, 2018), 78.

30 Sibusiso Nyembezi, *Isichazimazwi Sanamuhlula Nangomuso* (Pietermaritzburg: Reach Out Publishers, 1996).

31 See Msimang's libretto.

32 Although most of the song translations in this chapter are by Msimang, I have made alterations where necessary as a way to bring further clarity to the meaning of Msimang's isiZulu words. A word of gratitude to my grandfather Bhekinsizwa Mathe and my mother Nomfundo Shange for guiding me through the translation process. Ngiyabonga!

33 See Msimang's libretto.

34 See Act 1, scene 7.

35 Mazisi Kunene, *Emperor Shaka the Great: A Zulu Epic* (Pietermaritzburg: University of KwaZulu-Natal Press, 2017), 9.

36 South African History Online, "Shaka Zulu", undated, https://www.sahistory.org.za/people/shaka-zulu.

37 In the book *Opera, or the Undoing of Women*, the writer Catherine Clément notes that the opera genre is one that normalizes the figure of the dying woman. Clément asserts "The emotion is never more poignant than at the moment when the voice

is lifted to die. Look at these heroines. With their voices they flap their wings, their arms writhe, and then they are, dead, on the ground" (1979, 5).

38 Mhlambi, "The Question of Nationalism," 302.
39 Buthelezi, "Princess Constance Magogo," 236.
40 Buthelezi, "Princess Constance Magogo," 236.
41 Frantz Fanon, ed., "The Negro and Language," in *Black Skin, White Masks* (London: Pluto Press, 2008), 8–27.
42 Bible Society of South Africa, *IBhayibheli Elingcwele 1893 Isihumusho* (Belville: Bible Society of South Africa, 2018), 581.
43 Gunner, "A Royal Woman," 209.
44 Mhlambi, "The Question of Nationalism," 300.
45 Rycroft, "The Zulu Bow Songs," 1975/76.
46 Gunner, "A Royal Woman," 210.
47 Mhlambi, "The Question of Nationalism," 305.
48 Mhlambi, "The Question of Nationalism," 305.
49 Mhlambi, "The Question of Nationalism," 306.
50 Gunner, "A Royal Woman," 209.
51 Gunner, "A Royal Woman," 209.
52 Mhlambi, "The Question of Nationalism," 307.
53 See Msimang's libretto.
54 See Msimang's libretto.
55 See Msimang's libretto.
56 Mhlambi, "The Question of Nationalism," 307.
57 See Msimang's libretto.
58 See Msimang's libretto.
59 Mhlambi, "The Question of Nationalism," 295.

Worklist of James Steven Mzilikazi Khumalo (1932–2021)

1 Thank you to Diliza Khumalo, Ludumo Magangane, and Nandipha Mnyani (SAMRO) for assistance compiling the worklist.

Bibliography

Allen, Lara. "Music and Politics." *Social Dynamics: A Journal of African Studies* 30, no. 2 (2004): 1–19. https://doi.org/10.1080/02533950408628682.
Anderson, Benedict. *Imagined Communities: Reflections on the Origin and Spread of Nationalism*. London: Verso Books, 1983.
André, Naomi. *Black Opera: History, Power, Engagement*. Champaign: University of Illinois Press, 2018.
André, Naomi, Jabulisile Mhlambi, and Donato Somma. "Special Cluster: New Voices in Black South African Opera." *African Studies* 75, no. 1 (2016). https://doi.org/10.1080/00020184.2015.1129137.
André, Naomi, Karen Bryan, and Eric Saylor, eds. *Blackness in Opera*. Champaign: University of Illinois Press, 2012.
André, Naomi, Yolanda Covington-Ward, and Jendele Hungbo, eds. *African Performance Arts and Political Acts*. Ann Arbor: University of Michigan Press, 2021.
Baker, Houston. "Foreword." In *Music and the Racial Imagination*, edited by Ronald Radano and Philip V. Bohlman. Chicago: University of Chicago Press, 2000.
Ballantine, Christopher. "On Being Undone by Music: Thoughts towards a South African Future Worth Having." *South African Music Studies* 34–35, no. 1 (2015): 501–20.
Beinart, William. *Twentieth Century South Africa*. New York: Oxford University Press, 2000.
Bereson, Ruth. *The Operatic State: Cultural Policy and the Opera House*. London: Routledge, 2002.
Bhabha, Homi K. *Nation and Narration*. London/New York: Routledge, 1990.
Bible Society of South Africa. *IBhayibheli Elingcwele 1893 Isihumusho*. Belville: Bible Society of South Africa, 2018.
Bill, Mary. "Farewell to James Mzilikazi Khumalo." Wits University Department of African Languages, Monday, December 1, 1997.
Boekkooi, Paul. "Musical Epic in Praise of Shaka." *The Star*, May 22, 1996.
Bourdieu, Pierre, trans. Richard Nice. "The Field of Cultural Production or The Economic World Reversed." In *The Field of Cultural Production: Essays on Art and Literature*, edited and introduced by Randal Johnson, 29–73 [*Poetics* 12, no. 4: 311–56]. Cambridge: Polity Press, 1993 [1983] [Amsterdam: Elsevier Science Publishers].
Brown, Duncan. *Voicing the Text: South African Oral Poetry and Performance*. Cape Town: Oxford University Press, 1998.

Buthelezi, Mangosuthu. "Building on a Strong Legacy in a New Season of Struggle for Economic and Social Justice Structured on Democratic Ideals." Address at National Elective Conference, August 24, 2019. http://www.ifp.org.za/national-elective-conference-of-the-inkatha-freedom-party-address-by-prince-mangosuthu-buthelezi-mp/.

Buthelezi, Mangosuthu. "Message from Prince Mangosuthu Buthelezi." Press Release. Zulu Royal Women Series: Princess Magogo Seminar, August 30, 2019. http://www.ifp.org.za/uzulu-arts-and-heritage-npo-presents-the-princess-magogo-seminar-the-first-of-the-zulu-royal-women-series/.

Buthelezi, Mangosuthu. "Princess Constance Magogo." In *Petticoat Pioneers: Women of Distinction*, edited by Ruth Gordon. Pietermaritzburg: Shuter and Shooter (Pty) Ltd, 1988.

Byerly, Ingrid. "Mirror, Mediator and Prophet: The Musical Indaba of Late-Apartheid South Africa." *Ethnomusicology* 42, no. 1 (1998): 1–44.

Byerly, Ingrid. "Decomposing Apartheid: Things Come Together. The Anatomy of a Musical Revolution." In *Composing Apartheid: Music For and Against Apartheid*, edited by Grant Olwage, 255–80. Johannesburg: Wits University Press, 2008.

Cameron, Michael. "Life of the Legendary Zulu King is the Subject of 'UShaka.'" *Chicago Tribune*, June 10, 2006.

Clément, Catherine. *Opera, Or, The Undoing of Women*. Minneapolis: University of Minnesota Press, 1988.

Cock, Richard and James Steven Mzilikazi Khumalo, eds. *National Building Massed Choir Festival Prescribed Music*. Johannesburg: Sowetan, 1990–2003.

Comaroff, Jean and John Comaroff. *Of Revelation and Revolution: Christianity, Colonialism, and Consciousness in South Africa*. Chicago: University of Chicago Press, 1991.

Comaroff, Jean and John Comaroff. *Theory from the South*. London: Routledge, 2013.

Cooke, Derryck. *Gustav Mahler: A Performing Version of the Draft for the Tenth Symphony*. London: Faber, 1989.

Coplan, David. *In Township Tonight! South Africa's Black City Music and Theatre*. 1st edn. Johannesburg: Ravan Press, 1985.

Coplan, David. *In Township Tonight! South Africa's Black City Music and Theatre*. 2nd edn. Chicago: University of Chicago Press, 2008.

Coplan, David and Bennetta Jules-Rosette. "Nkosi Sikelel' iAfrika and the Liberation of the Spirit of South Africa." *African Studies* 64, no. 2 (2005): 285–308.

Dargie, Dave. "'Umakhweyane': A Musical Bow and Its Contribution to Zulu Music." *African Music* 8, no. 1 (2007): 60–81.

Dent, George Robinson and Cyril Lincoln Sibusiso Nyembezi. *Scholar's Zulu Dictionary*. Pietermaritzburg: Shuter & Shooter Publishers (Pty) Ltd, 2009.

Detterbeck, Markus. "South African Choral Music (Amakwaya): Song, Contest and The Formation of Identity." PhD diss., University of Natal, 2002.

De Villiers, Sandra. Donato Somma Co-interview with Naomi André and Innocentia Mhlambi, Strand, Western Cape, July 5, 2019.

Dhlomo, Rolfes Robert Reginald. *UShaka KaSenzangakhona*. Pietermarizburg: Shuter & Shooter Publishers (Pty) Ltd, 1937.

Dickinson, Kay. "Introduction: 'Arab' + 'Avant-Garde.'" In *The Arab Avant-Garde: Music, Politics, Modernity*, edited by Thomas Burkhalter, Kay Dickinson, and Benjamin Harbert, 1–36. Connecticut: Wesleyan University Press, 2013.

Dubow, Saul. *Apartheid, 1948–1994*. Oxford: Oxford University Press, 2014.

Dubow, Saul. "South Africa and South Africans: Nationality, Belonging, Citizenship." In *The Cambridge History of South Africa: Volume 2 1885: 1994*, edited by Robert Ross, Anne Kelk Mager, and Bill Nasson, 17–65. New York: Cambridge University Press, 2016.

Dutcher, Jeremy. "How a Canadian Opera Singer is Honouring his Indigenous Roots." *CBC News* [podcast audio], 2018. https://www.cbc.ca/player/play/1320988227851.

Eason, Andrew. "'All Things to All People to Save Some': Salvation Army Missionary Work among the Zulus of Victorian Natal." *Journal of Southern African Studies* 35, no. 1 (2009): 7–27. https://doi.org/10.1080/03057070802685502.

Endfield, Cy, dir. *Zulu*. West Hollywood, CA: Paramount Pictures, 1964.

Erlmann, Veit. "'Horses in the Race Course': The Domestication of Ingoma Dancing in South Africa, 1929-39." *Popular Music* 8, no. 3 (1989): 259–73. https://doi.org/10.1017/S026114300000355X.

Erlmann, Veit. *African Stars: Studies in Black South African Performance*. Chicago: University of Chicago Press, 1991.

Erlmann, Veit. *Music Modernity and the Global Imagination*. New York: Oxford University Press, 1999.

Fanon, Frantz. "The Negro and Language." In *Black Skin, White Masks*, edited by Frantz Fanon, translated by Charles Lam Markmann, 10–17. London: Pluto Press, 2008.

Faure, William, dir. *Shaka Zulu*. Johannesburg: South African Broadcasting Corporation, 1986.

Gunner, Liz. "A Royal Woman, an Artist, and the Ambiguities of National Belonging: The Case of Princess Constance Magogo." *Kunapipi: Journal of Post-Colonial Writing* 24, no. 1 & 2 (2002): 205–23. https://ro.uow.edu.au/kunapipi/vol24/iss1/18.

Gunner, Liz. "Jacob Zuma, the Social Body and the Unruly Power of Song." *African Affairs* 108, no. 430 (2009): 27–48. https://dx.doi.org/adn064.

Graver, David and Loren Kruger. "South Africa's National Theatre: The Market or The Street?" *New Theatre Quarterly* 5, no. 19 (1989): 272–81. https://doi.org/10.1017/S0266464X00003341.

Harris, Clement Anntrobus. "The War Between the Fixed and Movable Doh." *Musical Quarterly* 4, no. 2 (1918): 184–95. https://www.jstor.org/stable/738052.

Huskisson, Yvonne. *The Bantu Composers of Southern Africa*. Johannesburg: South African Broadcasting Corporation, 1969.

Huskisson, Yvonne. *Black Composers of Southern Africa: An Expanded Supplement to The Bantu Composers of Southern Africa*, edited by Sarita Hauptfleisch. Pretoria: Human Sciences Research Council, 1992.

Israel, Paolo. *In Step with the Times: Mapiko Masquerades of Mozambique*. Athena: Ohio University Press, 2014.

Karantonis, Pamela and Dylan Robinson, eds. *Opera Indigene: Re/presenting First Nations and Indigenous Cultures*. Surrey: Ashgate Publishing Limited, 2011.

Khumalo, James Stewart Mzilikazi. "Plot and Character in Vilakazi's Novels." Honours article. University of South Africa, 1972.

Khumalo, James Stewart Mzilikazi. "Zulu Tonology, Part 1." *African Studies* 40, no. 2 (1981): 53–130. https://0-doi-org.oasis.unisa.ac.za/10.1080/00020188108707573.

Khumalo, James Stewart Mzilikazi. "Zulu Tonology, Part 2." *African Studies* 41, no. 1 (1982): 3–125. https//doi.org/10.1080/00020188208707579.

Khumalo, James Stewart Mzilikazi. "An Autosegmental Account of Zulu Phonology." PhD diss., Wits University, 1987.

Khumalo, James Stewart Mzilikazi. "'Leftward ho!' in Zulu Tonology." *South African Journal of African Languages* 9, no. 2 (1989): 59–69. https://doi.org/10.1080/02572117.1989.10586780.

Khumalo, James Stewart Mzilikazi. "Mzilikazi Khumalo: In His Own Words." Unpublished manuscript, 1989.

Khumalo, James Stewart Mzilikazi. "Preface." In *English-Zulu, Zulu-English Dictionary*, edited by Clement Doke and Benedict Vilakazi. Braamfontein: Wits University Press, 2008.

Khumalo, James Stewart Mzilikazi. *South Africa Sings, Volume 1*. 1st edn. Johannesburg: SAMRO, 1998.

Khumalo, James Stewart Mzilikazi. *South Africa Sings, Volume 1*. 2nd edn. Johannesburg: SAMRO, 2010.

Khumalo, James Stewart Mzilikazi. *South Africa Sings, Volume 2*. Johannesburg: SAMRO, 2008.

Khumalo, James Stewart Mzilikazi. *South Africa Sings, Volume 3*. Johannesburg: SAMRO, 2012.

Khumalo, James Stewart Mzilikazi. *Izingoma zikaMzilikazi Khumalo*. Pietermaritzburg: Shuter and Shooter, 2014.

Khumalo, James Stewart Mzilikazi. "Curriculum Vitae." Unpublished manuscript. SAMRO, Undated.

Khumalo, James Steven Mzilikazi and Christian Themba Msimang. "Orchestration and Enhancement by Robert Maxym and Christopher James." *UShaka KaSenzangakhona: An Epic in Praise-Poetry*. Johannesburg: SAMRO, 1996.

Khumalo, James Steven Mzilikazi, Christian Themba Msimang, Princess Constance Magogo kaDinuzulu and Michael Hankinson. *Princess Magogo KaDinuzulu*. Durban: Opera Africa, 2002.

Khumalo, Sibongile. *Haya, mntwan' omkhulu! Sing, Princess! Songs of Princess Magogo KaDinuzulu*, accompanied by Jill Richards and arranged by Mzilikazi Khumalo and Peter Klatzow. Johannesburg: SAMRO, 2003.

Klaaste, Aggrey. "Programme Note." National Building Mass Choir Festival Programme. Johannesburg: Sowetan, 1989.

Klatzow, Peter, ed. *Composers in South Africa Today*. Cape Town: Oxford University Press, 1987.

Kresse, Kai. "Izibongo – The Political Art of Praising: Poetical Socio-Regulative Discourse in Zulu Society." *Journal of African Cultural Studies* 11, no. 2 (2007): 171–96.

Kunene, Mazisi. *Emperor Shaka the Great: A Zulu Epic*. Pietermaritzburg: University of KwaZulu-Natal Press, 2017.

KZN Philharmonic Orchestra. "Princess Magogo in Court." Media release. *Artslink*, 2003. https://www.artlink.co.za/news_article.htm?contentID=18401.

Lamm, Pavel. *Musorgsky: Boris Godunov* (Orchestration by Dmitri Shostakovich, Libretto by Moussorgsky). Vienna: Universal Edition, 1928.

Leppard, Raymond. *L'incoronazione di Poppea* by Claudio Monteverdi. London: Faber, 1962.

Levy, Michael, ed. *Princess Magogo – A Portrait*. Braamfontein: SAMRO, 2003.

Lewis, Andrew and Johann Steyn. "A Critique of Mission Education in South Africa According to Bosch's Mission Paradigm Theory." *South African Journal of Education* 23, no. 2 (2003): 101–6.

Lucia, Christine. "Mapping the Field: A Preliminary Survey of South African Composition and Performance as Research." *South African Music Studies* 25, no. 1 (2005): 83–108. https://hdl.handle.net/10520/EJC97748.

Lucia, Christine, ed. *The World of South African Music: A Reader*. Cambridge: Cambridge Scholars Press, 2005.

Lucia, Christine. "Back to the Future?: Idioms of 'Displaced Time' in South African Composition." In *Composing Apartheid: Music for and Against Apartheid*, edited by Grant Olwage, 11–34. Johannesburg: Wits University Press, 2008.

Lucia, Christine. "Travesty or Prophecy? Views of South African Black Choral Composition." In *Music and Identity: Transformation and Negotiation*, edited by Eric Akrofi, Maria Smit, and Stig-Magnus Thorsén, 161–80. Stellenbosch: African Sun Media, 2009.

Lucia, Christine. *Music Notation: A South African Guide*. Pretoria: UNISA Press, 2011.

Lucia, Christine. "'The Times Do Not Permit': Moerane, South Africa, Lesotho, and *Fatše La Heso*." *Muziki* 16, no. 2 (2020): 87–112. https://doi.org/10.1080/18125980.2020.1787860.

Lucia, Christine. *Michael Moerane: Critical Edition Project*. Undated. https://aoinstitute.ac.za/moerane/.

Lucia, Christine and Grant Olwage. "The Joshua Pulumo Mohapeloa Critical Edition: An interview with Christine Lucia." *South African Music Studies* 36–37, no. 1 (2018): 157–77. https://hdl.handle.net/10520/EJC-f185ffc2c.

Magangane, Ludumo. *The National Anthem of South Africa*. Johannesburg: Partridge, 2016.

Magoqwana, Babalwa. "Repositioning uMakhulu as an Institution of Knowledge: Beyond 'Biologism' Towards the Body of Indigenous Knowledge." In *Whose History Counts: Decolonising African Pre-colonial Historiography*, edited by June Bam, Lungisile Ntsebeza, and Allan Zinn, 75–90. South Africa: African Sun MeDIA, 2018.

Maseko, Pamela. "Language as Source of Revitalisation and Reclamation of Indigenous Epistemologies: Contesting Assumptions and Re-imagining Women Identities in (African) Xhosa Society." In *Whose History Counts: Decolonising African Pre-colonial Historiography*, edited by June Bam, Lungisile Ntsebeza, and Allan Zinn, 35–56. South Africa: African Sun MeDIA, 2018.

Mathiane, Nomavenda. *Eyes in the Night: An Untold Zulu Story*. Northcliff: Bookstorm, 2016.

Mbembe, Achille. "Variations on The Beautiful in The Congolese World of Sounds." *Politique Africaine* 10, no. 4 (2006): 69–91. https://polaf.hypotheses.org/_wp_link_placeholder.

McKenzie, Steven. "Opera Celebrates St Kilda History." *BBC News Scotland*, June 23, 2007. http://news.bbc.co.uk/2/hi/uk_news/scotland/highlands_and_islands/6763371.stm.

McNally, Michael David. "The Indian Passion Play: Contesting the Real Indian in 'Song of Hiawatha' Pageants, 1901–1965." *American Quarterly* 58, no. 1 (2006): 106–36. https://www.jstor.org/stable/40068350.

Meintjes, Louise. "Shoot the Sergeant, Shatter the Mountain: The Production of Masculinity in Zulu Ngoma Song and Dance in Post-Apartheid South Africa." *Ethnomusicology Forum* 12, no. 2 (2005): 173–201. https://www.jstor.org/stable/20184480.

"Memories in Mind: Women of the Windrush Tell Their Stories." *Tete-A-Tete*, July 28, 2019. https://www.tete-a-tete.org.uk/event/memories-in-mind-women-of-the-windrush-tell-their-stories/.

Mestyan, Adam. "Arabic Theatre in Early Khedivial Culture, 1868–72: James Sanua Revisited." *International Journal of Middle Eastern Studies* 46, no. 1 (2014): 117–37. https://doi.org/10.1017/S0020743813011.

Mhlambi, Innocentia Jabulisile. "A Literary Reflection of the Bhambatha Rebellion." In Benedict Vilakazi's *Nje Nempela* and E. Zondi's *Insumansumane*. Master's diss., University of the Witwatersrand, 2002.

Mhlambi, Innocentia Jabulisile. "The Question of Nationalism in Mzilikazi Khumalo's Princess Magogo kaDinuzulu (2002)." *Journal of African Cultural Studies* 27, no. 3 (2015): 294–310. https://doi.org/10.1080/13696815.2015.1049245.

Mhlongo, Donnie. *Ilanga LaseLangeni*. Durban: Palm, 1991.

Mignolo, Walter. *The Darker Side of Western Modernity: Global Futures, Decolonial Options*. Durham, NC: Duke University Press, 2011.

Mngoma, Khabi. "The Correlation of Folk and Art Music Among African Composers." In *Proceedings of the Seventh Symposium on Ethnomusicology*, edited by Andrew Tracey. Grahamstown: Rhodes University, 1988.

Modisane, Bloke. *Blame Me on History*. New York: Penguin, 1990.

Mokoena, Hlonipha. "The Black House, or How the Zulus Became Jews." *Journal of Southern African Studies* 44, no. 3 (2018): 401–11. https://doi.org/10.1080/03057070.2018.1461457.

Motinyane, Mantoa, Ndebele Mpho, and Christine Lucia. "Translating Mohapeloa: Perspectives from Mantoa Matinyane and Mpho Ndebele with an Introduction by Christine Lucia." *South African Music Studies* 36–37, no. 1 (2018): 246–64. https://hdl.handle.net/10520/EJC-f186d979e.

Mugovhani, Ndwamato George. "The Manifestations of the 'African Style' in the Works of Mzilikazi Khumalo." MMus diss., University of the Witwatersrand, 1998.

Mugovhani, Ndwamato George. "An Interview with Mzilikazi Khumalo." *South African Music Studies* 28, no. 1 (2008): 155–68. https://hdl.handle.net/10520/EJC133270.

Mugovhani, Ndwamato George. "The Role of Indigenous African Choral Music in the Search for Identity: With Special Reference to Mzilikazi Khumalo's Music." *Muziki* 7, no. 1 (2010): 60–75. https://doi.org/10.1080/18125980.2010.483861.

Mugovhani, Ndwamato George. "Muzika wa Dzikhwairi: An Essay on the History of Venda Choral Music." *Muziki* 10, no. 2 (2013): 75–89. https://doi.org/10.1080/18125980.2013.844984.

Mugovhani, Ndwamato George and Ayodamope Oluranti. "Symbiosis or Integration: A Study of the Tonal Elements in the Choral Works of Mzilikazi Khumalo and Phelelani Mnomiya." *Muziki* 12, no. 2 (2015): 1–21. https://doi.org/10.1080/18125980.2015.1127619.

Murphy, E. Jefferson. "Schooling for Servitude: Some Aspects of South Africa's Bantu Education System." World Education Project of the Curriculum Center. Storrs, CT: University of Connecticut, 1972.

Ndodana-Breen, Bongani, Warren Wilensky, and Mfundi Vundla. *Winnie the Opera*. Pretoria: Vundowil, 2011.

Ngema, Vusabantu. "Symbolism and Implication in the Zulu Dance Forms: Notions of Composition, Performance and Appreciation of Dance Among the Zulu." MA diss., University of KwaZulu-Natal, 2007.

Ntuli, Deuteronomy Bhekinkosi Zeblon. *The Degree of Doctor of Musicology (Honoris Causa): James Steven Mzilikazi Khumalo – Citation*. Pretoria: University of South Africa, 2003.

Nyembezi, Cyril Lincoln Sibusiso. *Isichazimazwi Sanamuhlula Nangomuso*. Pietermaritzburg: Reach Out Publishers, 1996.

Nyembezi, Cyril Lincoln Sibusiso and Otty E. H. Mandla Nxumalo. *Inqolobane YeSizwe*. Pietermaritzburg: Shuter & Shooter (Pty) Ltd, 2018.

Olwage, Grant. "Music and (Post) Colonialism: The Dialectics of Choral Culture on a South African Frontier." PhD diss., Rhodes University, 2003.

Olwage, Grant. "The Class and Colour of Tone: An Essay on the Social History of Vocal Timbre." *Ethnomusicology Forum* 13, no. 2 (2004): 203–26. https://www.jstor.org/stable/20184481.

Olwage, Grant. "John Knox Bokwe, Colonial Composer: Tales about Race and Music." *Journal of the Royal Musical Association* 131, no. 1 (2006): 1–37. https://doi.org/10.1093/jrma/fki010.

Olwage, Grant. "Singing in the Victorian World: Tonic Sol-Fa and Discourses of Religion, Science and Empire in the Cape Colony." *Muziki* 7, no. 2 (2010): 193–215. https://doi.org/10.1080/18125980.2010.526801.

Parker, Roger. *Leonora's Last Act: Essays in Verdian Discourse*. Princeton: Princeton University Press, 1997.

Peires, Jeff B. "Traditional Leaders in Purgatory: Local Government in Tsolo, Qumbu and Port St. Johns." *African Studies* 59, no. 1 (2000): 97–114.

Pieters, Vivienne. "Music and Presbyterianism at the Lovedale Missionary Institute." PhD diss., University of South Africa, 2022.

Pistorius, Juliana. "Predicaments of Coloniality, or, Opera Studies Goes Ethno." *Music and Letters* 100, no. 3 (2019): 529–39. https://doi.org/10.1093/ml/gcz046.

Pistorius, Juliana. "Review: The Head and the Load, dir. William Kentridge." *South African Music Studies* 38 (2018): 82–9. https://www.ajol.info/index.php/samus/article/view/195578.

Pooley, Thomas. "'Never the Twain Shall Meet': Africanist Art Music and the End of Apartheid." *South African Music Studies* 30/31, no. 1 (2010): 45–69. https://hdl.handle.net/10520/EJC133298.

Pooley, Thomas. "Singing in South African Schools." In *The Routledge Companion to Interdisciplinary Studies in Singing, Volume 2: Education*, edited by Helga R. Gudmundsdottir, Carol Beynon, Karen M. Ludke and Annabel J. Cohen, 123–33. New York: Routledge, 2020.

Pooley, Thomas. "Obituary: James Steven Mzilikazi Khumalo, 1932–2021." *Muziki: Journal of Music Research in Africa* 19, no. 2 (2022): 86–91.

Posel, Deborah. "The Apartheid Project, 1948–1970." In *The Cambridge History of South Africa, Volume 2: 1885–1994*, edited by Robert Ross, Anne Kelk Mager, and Bill Nasson, 319–68. Cambridge: Cambridge University Press, 2011.

Randel, Don Michael, ed. *The New Harvard Dictionary of Music*. Cambridge, MA: Harvard University Press, 1986.

Roos, Hilde. *The La Traviata Affair: Opera in the Age of Apartheid*. Oakland: University of California Press, 2018.

Rosselli, John. *The Opera Industry in Italy from Cimarosa to Verdi: The Role of the Impresario*. Cambridge: Cambridge University Press, 1984.

Rycroft, David. "The Zulu Bow Songs of Princess Magogo." *African Music: Journal of the African Music Society* 5, no. 4 (1975): 41–97. https://doi.org/10.21504/amj.v5i4.1617.

SAMRO. *Princess Magogo: A Portrait*. Braamfontein: Southern African Music Rights Organisation Ltd, 2003.

SAMRO. *Khumalo, Mzilikazi (1932-)*. Braamfontein: SAMRO Biographical Notes, 2005.

Schechner, Richard. "From Ritual to Theatre and Back: The Structure/Process of the Efficacy/Entertainment Dyad." *Educational Theatre Journal* 26, no. 4 (1974): 455–81. https://doi.org/10.2307/3206608.

Schonken, Philip Antoni. "Authorship and Ownership of UShaka KaSenzangakhona." MMus diss., Stellenbosch University, 2013.

Shamase, Maxwell Z. "The Royal Women of the Zulu Monarchy – Through the Keyhole of Oral History: Princess Mkabayi Kajama (c.1750–c.1843)." *Inkanyiso, Journal of Humanities and Social Sciences* 6, no. 1 (2014): 15–22. https://hdl.handle.net/10520/EJC155748.

Shamase, Maxwell Z. "The Royal Women of the Zulu Monarchy through the Keyhole of Oral History: Queens Nandi (c.1764 –c.1827) and Monase (c.1797–c.1880)." *Inkanyiso, Journal of Humanities and Social Sciences* 6, no. 1 (2014): 1–14. https://hdl.handle.net/10520/EJC155749.

Shange, Kholeka. "Malibongwe: Poems from the Struggle by ANC Women." *Journal of Contemporary African Studies* 39, no. 4 (2021): 647–52. https://doi.org/10.1080/02589001.2021.1938978.

Smith, David. "Review of Hans Roosenchoon, Timbila and other African-Inspired Works." *South African Music Studies* 15 (1995): 95–61.

Sony. *UShaka Press Release*. Johannesburg: Song Music South Africa, 1997.

Sosibo, Kwanele. "Musician Mbuso Khoza on Princess Magogo and Neutered Patriarchy." *Mail & Guardian*, May 4, 2018. https://mg.co.za/article/2018-05-04-princess-magogo-and-neutered-patriarchy.

South African History Online. "South Africa's Academic and Cultural Boycott." n.d. https://www.sahistory.org.za/article/south-africas-academic-and-cultural-boycott (accessed September 21, 2023).

South African History Online. "Shaka Zulu." n.d. https://www.sahistory.org.za/people/shaka-zulu (accessed October 4, 2020).

Soyinka, Wole. *Opera Wonyosi*. Bloomington: Indiana University Press, 1981.

Staff Reporter. "Opera's Long Road to Bullhoek." *Mail & Guardian*, December 9, 1994.

Stellenbosch University. *Directory of South African Music Collections*. 2022. https://libguides.sun.ac.za/SAMusicCollections.

Stevens, Robin. "Tonic Sol-Fa: An Exogenous Aspect of South African Musical Identity." In *Music and Identity: Transformation and Negotiation*, edited by Eric Akrofi, Maria Smit, and Stig-Magnus Thors, 37–51. Stellenbosch: African Sun Press, 2007.

Thwala, Joseph. "An Explication of Some Aspects of Christian Themba Msimang's Poetry." PhD diss., University of Zululand, 2000.

Tisani, Nomathamsanqa Cynthia. "Continuity and Change in Xhosa Historiography During the Nineteenth Century: An Exploration Through Textual Analysis." PhD diss., University of Cape Town, 2002.

Tommasini, Anthony. "OPERA REVIEW; Varied Cultures Entwine Around a Zulu Princess." *New York Times*, June 7, 2004. https://www.nytimes.com/2004/06/07/arts/opera-review-varied-cultures-entwine-around-a-zulu-princess.html.

Traill, Anthony, James Steven Mzilikazi Khumalo, and Peter Fridjhon. "Depressing Facts About Zulu." *African Studies* 46, no. 2 (1987): 255–74. https://doi.org/10.1080/00020188708707678.

Turner, Victor. *From Ritual to Theatre: The Human Seriousness of Play*. New York: Performing Arts Journal Publications, 1982.

van der Walt, Annemarie. "Mzilikazi Khumalo: A Choral Legend in His Own Time." In *Composer's Corner*, 37–9. Braamfontein: SAMRO, n.d.

Venter, Carina, William Fourie, Juliana Pistorius, and Neo Muyanga. "Decolonising Musicology: A Response and Three Positions." *South African Music Studies* 36/37, no. 1 (2017): 129–56. https://journals.co.za/content/journal/10520/EJC-f185862a3.

Vilakazi, Benedict. "*Amal'ezulu*." African Treasury Series No. 8. Johannesburg: Wits University Press, 2021.

Von Rhein, John. "Ravinia Kicks Off Centennial With Story of Zulu Princess." *Chicago Tribune*, May 30, 2004. https://www.chicagotribune.com/news/ct-xpm-2004-05-30-0405300405-story.html.

Weir, Jennifer. "'I Shall Need to Use Her to Rule': The Power of 'Royal' Zulu Women in Pre-Colonial Zululand." *South African Historical Journal* 43, no. 1 (2000): 3–23. https://doi.org/10.1080/02582470008671905.

Weir, Jennifer. "Chiefly Women and Women's Leadership in Pre-colonial Southern Africa." In *Women in South African History: Basus'iimbokodo, Bawel'imilambo/They Remove Boulders and Cross Rivers*, edited by Nomboniso Gasa, 3–20. Cape Town: HSRC Press, 2007.

Worden, Nigel. *The Making of Modern South Africa: Conquest, Apartheid, Democracy*. 5th edn. Oxford: Wiley-Blackwell, 2012.

Xulu, Musa Khulekani. "The Re-Emergence of amaHubo Song Styles and Ideas in Some Modern Zulu Musical Styles." PhD diss., University of Natal, 1992.

Xulu, Musa Khulekani. "The Re-Emergence of Amahubo Song Styles and Ideas in Some Modern Zulu Musical Styles." PhD diss., University of KwaZulu-Natal, 2013.

Zondi, Eliot. *Insumansumane*. Pietermaritzburg: Shuter and Shooter, 1986.

Zondi, Mpume. "Introduction." In *Amal'ezulu*, edited by Benedict Vilakazi, xxi–xxxiii. Braamfontein: Wits University Press, 2021.

Discography

Khumalo, Mzilikazi. *UShaka KaSenzangakhona*. Sibongile Mngoma, Sibongile Khumalo, Themba Mkhwani, and Peter Mcebi (Soloists); with the Soweto Songsters, Bonisudumo Choristers, Daveyton Adult Choir, and Cenestra Male Choir; and the National Symphony Orchestra of the S.A.B.C. conducted by Robert Maxym. Johannesburg: Sony, 1999.

Khumalo, Mzilikazi and Péter Louis Van Dijk. *Khumalo: 5 African Songs / Van Dijk: San Gloria / San Chronicle*. National Symphony Orchestra of the S.A.B.C conducted by Richard Cock. Cape Town: Marco-Polo, 1995.

Khumalo, Sibongile. *Sibongile Khumalo*. 2005. With Arjan Tien and the Chamber Orchestra of South Africa. Works: *Haya Mntwana' Mkhulu!* (Sing, Princess, Sing!). Songs by Princess Constance Magogo kaDinuzulu arranged by Mzilikazi Khumalo with Orchestration by Peter Klatzow.

Miller, Philip and Tshegofatso Moeng. *Reuben T. Caluza, The B-Side*. Arrangements of songs by Reuben T. Caluza by Philip Miller and Tshegofatso Moeng. 2021. https://philipmiller.bandcamp.com/album/reuben-t-caluza-the-b-side.

Nation Building: Celebrating 10 Years in Music. 1998. With the Bonisudumo Choristers, Soweto Songsters, and the National Symphony Orchestra of the S.A.B.C. conducted by Richard Cock and Mzilikazi Khumalo.

Soweto Songsters. *Presenting the Salvation Army Soweto Songsters*. Audio-cassette recording. Atlanta: The Salvation Army, 1993. Re-released on The Regal Zonophone, CRC019, as *Soweto Songsters*. https://www.regalzonophone.com/albums/soweto-songsters.

Soweto Songsters. *Lwandle Losindiso*. Compact disc recording CDVM (WLM) 010. South Africa: Ukhozi FM, 1999.

Tracey, Hugh. *The Zulu Bow Songs of Princess Magogo kaDinuzulu*. International Library of African Music. Music of Africa Series: 37, 1973.

Trompies. *Sigiya Ngengoma*. Johannesburg: Gallo, 1995.

* No recording of the opera *Princess Magogo KaDinuzulu* (2002) has been released to date.

Index

Note: Page locator followed by 'n' refer to notes.

a cappella choir, music for   14, 87–98
   Khumalo's arrangements   94
   "Woza, Mmeli Wami!"   95–8
Africana womanism   15, 124, 136–7, 139–40, 177–8, 181, 186, 191–7, 200–5
African Footprint   75
Africanization   2, 5, 10, 38, 148, 179, 190–1, 196, 199, 201–2, 204–5
African Paraphrases (Volans)   33
African Stars (Erlmann)   7
African Teachers Association of South Africa (ATASA)   20
Aggrey Klaaste Trust   75
amahubo (anthems)   48, 116–18, 160, 166, 175–7
"Amahubo Esizwe Esimnyama" song   83–4
amakholwa (Zulu intellectuals)   191
amakhosikazi (mature women)   193
amaZulu   175–6
ancestors   46–7, 64, 99, 102, 118, 125, 158–9, 174–5, 183–5, 192, 196
André, Naomi   6, 12
Anglo-Zulu war   2
anti-colonialism   179
apartheid   1–8, 64–5, 67, 101, 145, 150–1, 167–9, 181–2, 187
   Black choral community during   26
   policy of   19
   South African politics during   155
   theatrical works during   149–50
   tribulations of   149
   under Verwoerd   21
art music   2, 6–9, 16, 32–5, 37–8, 45, 112–15, 132–3, 147–8, 168, 182, 188
ATASA; *see* African Teachers Association of South Africa (ATASA)

Bach, Johann Sebastian   8, 44
Ballantine, Christopher   37
Ballet, Joffrey   141
Bantu Composers of Southern Africa, The (Huskisson)   5
Bantu Education Act (1953)   2–3
Bender, Anna   57
Bhambatha rebellion   155, 190, 198
Bhengu, John   5
Bill, Mary   24
biography   13, 17–38
Black choralism   5–10, 147–8
Black Lives Matter movement   6
Black nationalism, politics of   10, 196
Black opera in South Africa   2, 6, 14–15, 34–8
Black Orpheus Folk Singers   27
Blacks   3; *see also* Africana womanism; Africanization
Bokwe, John Knox (1855–1922)   6–7, 10, 80
Bonisudumo Adult Choir   27
Bonisudumo Choristers   63, 73
Botha, Elize   57
Boulanger, Nadia   8
Brahms, Johannes   8
Buskaid Soweto String Ensemble   68–9, 71
Buthelezi, Mangosuthu   10, 35–6, 45, 48, 117, 137–43, 175, 177–9, 181, 189
Buthelezi, Mathole   10
Byerly, Ingrid   167–8

Caltex   66
Caluza, Reuben Tholakele (1895–1969)   5–7, 81
Cantata Chorale   136
Cape Argus   73
Cavalleria Rusticana (Mascagni)   90
CD; *see* compact disc (CD)

Cenestra Male Choir 27
choral music in South Africa 5–10,
    50–1, 147–8
  composers 5–6
  hermeneutics of 6
Choristers, Gauteng 52
classical 32–3
Clément, Catherine 178
Cock, Richard 4, 13, 26–8, 30, 52, 57,
    77, 107
Comaroff, Jean 10–11
Comaroff, John 10–11
Commission on National Symbols 57
composers 5–6, 8, 80–1
Composers in South Africa Today
    (Klatzow) 8–9
Constitution of the Republic of South
    Africa, 1993 (Act 200 of 1993) 57
Cooke, Derryck 108
Coplan, David 5–7
Council of Muslim Theologians 58
culture 28
  music 1–2, 5
  Zulu 24–5
Curwen, John 77, 78

Dargie, Dave 148–9
Daveyton Adult Choir 27
decolonial thinking 10–12
decolonization 6, 10–12, 15, 182
*Decolonizing the Mind: The Politics of
    Language in African Literature*
    (Ngũgĩ wa Thiong'o) 28
Detterbeck, Markus 6
de Villiers, Hein 36, 135, 137–8, 140
de Villiers, Johan 57
de Villiers, Sandra 15, 36, 177, 179, 181
"Die Stem van Suid Afrika" (de
    Villiers) 57, 59–61
Die Zauberflöte (The Magic Flute)
    (Mozart) 135
Dingane, Michael 155, 184
Dlamini, J. C. 21
Dlamini, Mduduzi 189
Doke, Clement M. 21
dual notation system 4, 13, 14, 26, 34,
    69, 74, 77, 80, 86, 87, 109, 244
du Plessis, Hubert (1922–2011) 8

eisteddfod 97
Elijah (Mendelssohn) 135
Enoch, Prophet of God (Temmingh) 150
Erlmann, Veit 5–7
eSikhawini 136
ethnicity 21

Faust (Gounod) 135–6
feminism 15, 84, 94, 124, 177–8, 194, 197
Fort Hare University 19–20

Gaba, Ntsikana 5–7
Gay Gaieties 19
Geist, Gerhard 36, 138
gendered quality 94
Glover, Sarah Ann 77
"Great Hymn" (Gaba) 5–6
Group Areas Act (1950) 21, 44
Grové, Stefans (1922–2014) 8
Gunner, Liz 145

"Hamba Kahle" (Fare thee well)
    (Matshikiza) 81
Handel, George Frideric 8, 18–19, 44
Hankinson, Michael 15, 36–7, 137–41,
    145–7, 151–60, 164, 166, 168, 175,
    182, 187, 190, 209
harmonic progression 152
Havemann, Dolph 57
Haya Mntwan' Omkhulu (Khumalo) 77
"Haya" style 89
Haydn, Josef 8, 135
Hoeksma, E. M. 61
Huskisson, Yvonne 5

igogo 197
ihubo "Uyamemez'okandaba!" (traditional
    anthem) 163, 176
ijadu 186
Ikloba Lothando (A Fiery Love)
    (Khumalo) 118–19, 125
"Imbali yawoMageba" (Khumalo) 197
"Imbizo Yezinyandezulu"
    (Khumalo) 104–6, 124–5
imbongi 29–30, 161–2
Imilonji kaNtu 68
Impempe Yomlingo (Magic Flute) 150
"Imvukuzane" song (Khumalo) 82

Index

indigenous knowledge 11–12, 195
indlamu (dance style) 116–17, 126–32
ingoma dance 116–17, 126, 129–32
Inkatha Freedom Party (IFP) 179
"Inkondlo kaMnkabayi"
 (Khumalo) 82, 90
"Inkondlo kaNandi" (Nandi's Love Song)
 (Khumalo) 32
Inkondlo kaZulu (Vilakazi poem) 89
inkosi 192, 202–3
"Insizw'endala" song (Khumalo) 82, 90
International Library of African
 Music 27, 33, 48
In Township Tonight! (Coplan) 5–7
inyosi (royal praise singer) 184
iSandlwana 43
isishameni (dance style) 126
"Isitandwa sam" (My love) 80–1
isiZulu idioms 82–4
isiZulu linguistic tones 167
isizwe (nation) 191–2, 197
"Ixhegwana" song (Caluza) 81
izangelo (praise poems for infancy) 195
izangoma (traditional healers) 193
izibongo (praise poetry) 161–2
"Izibongo ZikaShaka" 14, 16, 28–9, 43,
 81, 84–5, 88, 224–41
Izingoma zikaMzilikazi Khumalo 87
izithakazelo (the honorific names) 126
izithopho (personal praises and
 attributes) 126
izizwe (nations) 191–2, 202–3
"IZulu Elisha" song (Khumalo) 90–1

James, Christopher 14, 30, 70,
 100, 102–4
jazz 9
Johanna, Ntombizodwa 17–18
Johannesburg Youth Orchestra 68–9

kaCetshwayo, Dinuzulu 10, 176
kaDinuzulu, Solomon 10
kaDinuzulu, uMntwana Constance
 Magogo (1900–1984) 33, 35, 145,
 152–65, 174–8, 189–205
Kagel, Mauricio 8
kaNtu, Imilonji 63
kaSenzangakhona, uShaka 43, 47

Kaufman, Welz 141
Khosa, S. J. 52–3, 69
Khoza, Mbuso 184
Khumalo, Andreas 17–18
Khumalo, Diliza 13, 27
 interview with 39–55
 Mngoma's influence on 27, 43–4
 overview 39
Khumalo, James Steven Mzilikazi
 (1932-2021) 1, 7–17, 57, 64–5,
 87, 137, 138
 academia 21–4
 a cappella choral legacy 88
 achievements in musical
  culture 1–2, 5
 as adjudicator 25–6
 Africanizing opera 34–8
 appointment at Wits 21
 arrangements 211–13
 biography 13, 17–38
 career 2–4, 11, 19, 21–4, 30, 44–6, 48,
  88, 100
 as choir master 24–8
 choral writing 13
 Cock working with 13–14, 63–75
 compositions 15, 42, 172, 207–11
 as curator of South African song 34
 early choral works (1959–80) 7, 147–8
 family history 13
 as figure of national importance 26
 as figure in African Linguistics in
  Southern Africa 24, 41–2, 173
 Hankinson collaboration with 15,
  137–41
 intellectual legacy 12
 "Izibongo ZikaShaka" 14, 16, 28–9,
  43, 81, 84–5, 88, 224–41
 Khumalo, Diliza's interview on 39–55
 Koapeng worked with 30
 last years of 38
 life, perspectives on 2–5, 16
 "Ma Ngificwa Ukufa" song 20, 28, 81,
  215–23
 Masters on isiZulu tonology 22, 53
 Maxym collaboration 14, 30–1
 member of TUATA 20
 Msimang collaboration with 110–11,
  173, 175–8

Mugovhani's interviews
with 10, 92–3
on National Anthem
Committee 13, 57–61
phonology, work on 22–3
Princess Magogo KaDinuzulu 4, 7,
9–10, 14–15, 24–5, 35–7, 48, 77, 88,
135–43, 145–69
retirement 32–4
at SAMRO 4, 32–4, 48–9
shared music, directive for 180–7
South Africa Sings 8, 14, 34, 74, 87–8
Soweto 21–4
studies and teaching of 19–21
as teacher and principal 44–5
tonic sol-fa notation, innovations
to 14, 30, 52, 80–5
tonology, work on 23, 53
as transcriber and arranger 35
at Unisa 11–12, 20–4, 28, 30, 46, 100
UShaka KaSenzangakhona 4, 7, 9–10,
14, 24–5, 28–31, 43, 47, 77, 84, 88,
99–110
Via Afrika Prize 23
at Wits University 2–4, 11, 19, 21–4,
30, 44–6, 48, 88, 100
works/works for choir 14, 45–
6, 87–98
youth of 17–19
Khumalo, Litlhare Rose 19
Khumalo, Nonhlanhla 20, 28–9, 43
Khumalo, Sibongile 30, 35, 38, 47, 51,
68, 73, 77, 101, 137
kingship 192
Kisseberth, Charles (Chuck) 22
Klaaste, Aggrey 3–4, 27–8, 63–5
Klaaste, Jerome 75
Klatzow, Peter (1945–2021) 8, 33,
35, 146
Koapeng, Mokale 30, 70, 71
Kresse, Kai 162
Kumalo, Alfred Assegai 80
Kunene, Mazisi 57, 136, 177, 197
"Kwabase Sabulawa nguDingane" 155
"KwaDedangendlale" 89
"Kwadendani" 42
KwaZulu-Natal Philharmonic
Orchestra 31, 35, 136

La Bohème: Noir (Puccini) 150
"Lala sithandwa, lal'uphumule" (Sleep,
dear one; sleep and rest in peace)
88–9
Lamm, Pavel 108
language 28
Lefoka, Dan 34
Lenake, John 57
Leppard, Raymond 108
libretto 36, 136, 137, 140, 150–1, 156–7,
164, 166, 174, 182, 185–6, 193,
196, 200
linguistics 11–14, 22–4, 37–8, 42, 89,
96, 98, 108, 112, 115, 167, 172, 181,
188, 201
"Linoto" (sounds produced by hitting
objects) 81
Lovedale Missionary Institute (1841–
1955) 3
Lucia, Christine 6–7, 77, 87
Lwandle Loyiso (album) 88

Madlopha, Themba 27
Magangane, Ludumo 9, 14, 27, 34, 63,
70, 71, 73, 138, 140, 151
Magogo, Constance 10, 15
Magoqwana, Babalwa 195
Mahlase, Abiah 19, 27
Mali, Ntsikelelo 136
Mandela, Nelson 4, 71, 82, 88, 94, 108,
140, 142, 165–6
"Ma Ngificwa Ukufa" (When death is
upon me) song (Khumalo) 14, 16,
20, 28, 81, 88, 215–23
Mankulumana 117, 160–3, 183–4,
193–4, 203–4
Mann, Peter 64
Mann, Sussens 64–5
Maseko, Pamela 194
Masote, Michael 34
Matshikiza, Todd 81
Maxym, Robert 14, 30–1, 36–7,
70, 105–6
Maxym Music 108
Mazibuko, Jabulani 27, 85
Mbembe, Achille 11
Mcebi, Peter 30–1, 73
Meer, Fatima 57

Mendelssohn, Felix   8
menial tasks   3
Messiah (Handel)   18–19, 135
Mgqwetho, Notsizi   195
Mhlambi, Innocentia   6, 12, 14, 146, 155, 163, 178, 190–1
Mhlongo, Sidwell   52
Mignolo, Walter   10
Mkhize, Edwin   5
Mkhize, Nomthandazo   73
Mkhwani, Themba   30–1
Mkwani, Themba   73
Mngoma, Khabi   26–7, 30, 36, 39, 43–4, 57, 77, 101–2, 135, 137, 139, 177
Mngoma, Linda   68
Mngoma, Sibongile   30, 73
Mnomiya, Phelelani   70
Moerane, Michael Mosoeu (1904–80)   7, 80, 87
Mofolo, Thomas   124
Mogolagae, Joyce   73
Mohapeloa, Joshua   87
Mokgoba, Stanley   19–20
Mokhitli, Vusi   73
monotheism   58
Mony, Walter   30, 100
Mozart, Wolfgang Amadeus   8, 44, 100, 135
Msimang, Themba   12, 28, 31, 36, 43, 89, 99–100, 103, 108–10, 137, 138, 140, 146, 157, 175, 179–80, 190
Mugovhani, Ndwamato George   6–7, 10, 29, 92–3, 146, 148–9, 166
Multi-Party Negotiating Council   57
music education   3
music theater, South Africa   149–50
Mxadana, George   63
Myataza, B. B.   81
Mzobe, Enoch   5

Nandi   124
national anthem, South Africa   13, 57–61, 70–1
National Anthem Committee   13, 57–61, 70–1
  members of   57
  shortened anthem   58–61
  submissions by   60–1

nationalism   2, 5, 10, 148, 179, 190–1, 196, 199, 201–2, 204–5
National Symphony Orchestra   71, 73
Nation Building Massed Choir Festivals   13–14, 63–75
  audience participation   72
  choirs   67–8
  conductors   71
  legacy   74
  logo of   67
  music and notation   69–70
  National Anthem   70–1
  new directions   75
  orchestra   68–9
  soloists   68
  spinoff   72–3
  sponsors   66
Nation Building Orchestra   68–9
"Ndabezitha nansi indaba"   197
"*Ndabezitha!*" (Your Majesty!)   99–110
"Ndikhokhele, bawo!" (traditional song)   94
Ndlovu, Duma   137, 180
Ndlovu-Gatsheni, Sabelo   11
Ndodana-Breen, Bongani   70, 137
network   191
Newcater, Graham (b. 1941)   8
New Music Indaba   33, 167–8
"Ngibambeni, Ngibambeni" (song, Princess Magogo kaDinuzulu)   178
Ngubane, Ben   57
Nguni poetry   96–7
Nkandla District   180
Nkosi, Busi   73
"Nkosi Sikelel' iAfrika" (Sontonga)   6, 57–9, 70–1, 80
Norburn, Charles   26
notation
  dual system   4, 13
  Nation Building Massed Choir Festivals   69–70
  staff   3–4, 6, 13–14, 18, 26, 30, 34, 52, 69, 71, 77–8, 83, 86, 114
  tonic sol-fa   13–14, 30, 52, 77–86
Ntuli, D. B. Z.   22, 24
Nyembezi, Sibusiso   195

ogogo (grandmothers)   195
Oluranti, Ayodamope   10, 92–3, 146, 148–9, 166
Olwage, Grant   6
omama besizwe (women of isizwe)   191
opera   14–15, 34–8, 145–6, 171–8; *see also Princess Magogo KaDinuzulu* (Khumalo)
  adaptations of   150
  Enoch, Prophet of God   150
  Impempe Yomlingo   150
  infrastructure of   172
  La Bohème: Noir   150
  medium of   172
  political power of   146
  in South Africa   150–1
  streams of influence   146–7
  theater   171
  uCarmen eKhayelitsha   150
Opera Africa   135, 175
  African identity for productions   136
  board   137
  Princess Magogo KaDinuzulu (opera)   135–43
  production   135–6
operatic syntax   172
Opera Wonyosi (Soyinka)   142
oral art   92, 111–12, 126
oral history   125, 196, 204
oratorio   112–13, 116–17, 125–6, 128, 130–3, 175
orchestra   68–9
Oslo Opera House   141

Papaya Choir, Norway   68
Parker, Roger   171
Peires, J. B.   191
Performing Arts Council of the Transvaal (PACT)   65
politics of Black nationalism   10
Pooe, Danny   71
Pooley, Thomas   12, 13, 39–55
post-apartheid   2, 4–6, 11–12, 16–17, 37, 145–6, 149–50, 163, 166–8, 173, 179, 182, 188–9
postcolonial   171–2
praise poetry (izibongo)   29–31, 99–100, 109, 162, 166, 175

Princess Magogo KaDinuzulu (Khumalo)   4, 7, 9–10, 14–15, 24–5, 35–7, 48, 77, 88, 172, 190
  African American audiences and   141
  artistic team   137–9
  choral music   147–8
  eponymous   177–8
  Khumalo's original contributions to   158–65
  libretto for   137
  Magogo in   189–205
  music of   145–69, 174–7
  nested contexts in   171–88
  operatic stage   152–5
  orchestration   142
  performances   143
  rainbow nation   145, 165–7
  "Sabulawa KwaZulu"   155–7, 184
  Shembe elements in   141–2
  streams of influence   146–7
  synopsis and music   174–7
  traditional Zulu musical elements   158–65
  unification   163–5
  unique collaboration behind   135–43
  Zulu and *ugubhu* bow music   148–9, 152–5

Queen Silomo   10, 173, 189, 192, 194–8, 201
Qwabe, Mlungisi   73

race   7, 9, 21
racial ideology   2
rainbow nation   15, 145, 165–7
Ramasia, Nehemiah   34
Ravinia Festival, Chicago   141
recitative   162–3
Richards, Jill   35
Roos, Hilde   6
Rosselli, John   171
Rycroft, David   10, 27, 35, 146, 148–9, 155, 178

SABC; *see* South African Broadcasting Corporation (SABC)
"Sabulawa KwaZulu" (traditional anthem)   155–7, 184

Salvation Army   2–3, 17–19, 22, 26, 39–42, 49, 88
SAMRO; *see* Southern African Music Rights Organisation (SAMRO)
Schubert, Franz   8
segregation   6, 19, 64
serious music   9, 13, 16–17, 26, 32–5, 37–8, 112, 150
Serote, Wally   57
Shaka (1787–1828)   99
Shaka Zulu (television series)   180
Shange, Kholeka   15
Shaper, H. D.   61
"Shayan' Ingungu MaZulu" (Khumalo)   160–1
Shembe   141–2
Simelane, Jabulani   73
Sithole, Elkin   20
"Siyakhuleka, amaZulu" (Khumalo)   164
"Sizongena Laph'Emzini!" (We will enter this homestead!) (Khumalo)   85, 96
"S'khala Kini Makhos'ohlanga" song (Khumalo)   82
Slavin, Patti   135
Sobukwe, Robert   21
Soga, Tiyo (1829–1871)   6, 10
soloists   68
Solomon, Nomthandazo   51
Sontonga, Enoch (1873–1905)   6, 10, 71, 78, 80
South Africa   1
  Africanized productions of operas in   135
  art music   9, 87
  Black composers and musicians in   5–6
  Black opera in   2, 6, 14–15, 34–8
  choral music   5–10, 147–8
  decolonial contexts   10–12
  music archives in   87
  music theater in   149–50
  national anthem for   13, 57–61, 70–1
  opera in   150–1
  traditional musics in   17, 26, 32–5, 50–1, 53–4, 66, 149, 166–7, 176–7, 183

South African Broadcasting Corporation (SABC)   8–9
  Choir   63
  TV   66
South Africa Sings (Khumalo, editor)   8, 14, 34, 74, 87–8
Southern African Music Rights Organisation (SAMRO)   4, 32–4, 48–9, 69
Sowetan newspaper   66
Soweto Songsters   65, 73, 88
Soweto String Quartet   137
Soweto Teachers Choir   27
Soyinka, Wole   142
St. Vincent's Choir for the Deaf   68
staff notation   3–4, 6, 13–14, 18, 26, 30, 34, 52, 69, 71, 77–8, 83, 86, 114, 148, 151
  Khumalo's music in   138
  piano using   146
  versus tonic sol-fa notation   78–80
  Western   108
Stockhausen, Karlheinz   8
Sussens, Aubrey   64
"Sylvia Mntakwethu" (Sylvia my beloved) (song, Moerane)   80
symbolism   165–6
Symposium on the Intellectual Legacy of Professor James Steven Mzilikazi Khumalo   12
syncopation   81

Taylor Conda, Christine   141
Temmingh, Roelof   150
Theme Committee One   61
Thiong'o, Ngũgĩ wa   28
Thwala, Joseph   179–80
Tisani, Nomathamsanqa Cynthia   191–2
Tommasini, Anthony   37
Tonic Sol-fa College of Music, Earlham Grove   78
tonic sol-fa notation   13–14, 30, 52, 77–86
  background   77–8
  versus staff notation   78–80
  use by Khumalo, Mzilikazi   80–5
tonology   23, 53
Tracey, Andrew   33
Tracey, Hugh   33

traditional musics in South Africa   17, 26, 32–5, 50–1, 53–4, 66, 149, 166–7, 176–7, 183
transcription   35, 71, 77, 109, 151–3, 182
Transnet   66
Transvaal Chamber Orchestra   64–5, 68
Transvaal Philharmonic Orchestra   101
Transvaal Symphony Orchestra   30
Transvaal United Teachers' Association (TUATA)   20
Tshivenda   69
TUATA; *see* Transvaal United Teachers' Association (TUATA)
Tutu, Desmond   15, 19–20, 145, 165–6

ubukhosi (kingship)   192
uCarmen eKhayelitsha (film)   150
"U ea kae?" (Where are you going to?) song (Mohapeloa)   81
"UGqozi" (Power of Inspiration) (song, Khumalo)   24–5, 42, 54, 81, 89, 250 n.1
ugubhu (Zulu bow) music   10, 28, 35, 142, 148–9, 152–5, 175, 183, 185
ukubonga (to praise)   125
ukuhaya (flowing melodic form of singing)   116–18, 125
"Ukureka" (to sing in Ragtime style)   81
umama wesizwe (a woman of the nation)   191–2
"Umgwagwa Usehlomile" (anthem)   160, 176
"Umntakababa" (My sibling)   81
Umoja (musical)   75
"Umshado" (A wedding)   81
umzansi (dance style)   126
University of South Africa (Unisa)   11–12, 20–4, 28, 30, 46, 100
University of the Witwatersrand (Wits)   4, 11, 19, 21–4, 30, 44–6, 48, 88, 100
University of Zululand   27, 33, 39, 77, 101, 135–7
UShaka KaSenzangakhona (epic by Khumalo)   4, 7, 9–10, 14, 24–5, 28–31, 43, 47, 77, 84, 88
  as artistic work   109–10
  choirs   101–2
  composition   99–101
  evolution of   99–110
  music dancing history and politics in   111–33
  orchestration of   103–7
  piano vocal score   108
  rehearsal   101–2
"Uthingo Lwenkosazana (The Rainbow)"   164–6
uvulandlela   195
"Uyephi Na?" (bow song by Princess Magogo kaDinuzulu)   152–4, 158, 183

van Beethoven, Ludwig   8, 100
van Dijk, Péter Louis   100
van Klemperer, Margaret   189
van Wyk, Arnold (1916–83)   8
van Wyk, Carl (b. 1942)   8, 30, 100
Vela Zulu (choral symphony, Ndodana-Breen)   179
Venturas, Themi   36, 135, 141, 175
Vermaas, Jacky   135
Verster, Andrew   36, 135–9, 141–2, 175
Verwoerd, Hendrik   2–3, 21
vice-chairperson   32, 38
Vilakazi, Benedict Wallet (1906–47)   21, 25, 88
Volans, Kevin (b. 1949)   8, 33
"Vuka Deborah" (Wake up Deborah) (song, Bokwe)   80

"Wangeza Bambatha?" (from *Princess Magogo KaDinuzulu*)   178
Weir, Jennifer   193
"Wena Wendlovu, Bayede"   162–3, 194
Western modernity   10
white supremacy   8
Wikner, Stephen   101
Willemse, Hein   72
Williams, Michael   150
Wilson, Rory   64
Wolf-Ferrari, Ermanno   103
world premiere   35, 103, 138, 140, 143
"Woza, Mmeli Wami!" (song, traditional)   95–8
"Woza S'ambe" (from *Princess Magogo KaDinuzulu*)   158–9
Wright, Roy   66

Xaba, Makhosazana   195
Xitsonga   69
"Xola Hleziphi" (Be forgiving Hleziphi)
    (song, Khumalo)   82–3
Xulu, Musa   57

Zaidel-Rudolph, Jeanne   57, 59
Ziyankomo and the Forbidden Fruit
    (Mnomiya)   179
Zondi, Bhambatha   198
Zulu
    bow music   10, 148–9, 152
    culture   24–5
    identity   48, 189, 193
    indunas   142
    language   89
    monarchy   36
    music   10, 14, 148–9, 165–7
    nationalism   47, 179, 190–2, 196–205
    sovereignty   178
Zulu Ragtime music   81
Zulu Royal House   141
Zungu, Mameyiguda   5